¡VIVA LA HISTORIETA!

UNIVERSITY PRESS OF MISSISSIPPI
JACKSON

BRUCE CAMPBELL

¡VIVA LA HISTORIETA!

Mexican Comics, NAFTA,
and the Politics of Globalization

www.upress.state.ms.us

The University Press of Mississippi is a member of the Association
of American University Presses.

First printing 2009

∞

Library of Congress Cataloging-in-Publication Data

Campbell, Bruce, 1964–
  ¡Viva la historieta! : Mexican comics, NAFTA, and the politics
of globalization / Bruce Campbell.
     p. cm.
  Includes bibliographical references and index.
  ISBN 978-1-60473-125-5 (cloth : alk. paper) —
ISBN 978-1-60473-126-2 (pbk. : alk. paper)   1. Comic books,
strips, etc.—Mexico—History and criticism. 2. Globalization
in literature. 3. Globalization in art. 4. Canada. Treaties, etc.
1992 Oct. 7. I. Title.
  PN6790.M48C36 2009
  809'.933552—dc22   2008026759

British Library Cataloging-in-Publication Data available

CONTENTS

ACKNOWLEDGMENTS   vii

1 INTRODUCTION
Reading the Politics of Globalization in Mexican Comics   1

2 GRAPHIC POLITICS
Political Elites, Globalization, and "*lo Popular*"   22

3 LOST IN THE BLUE EYES OF THE NORTH
El Libro Vaquero Envisions the U.S. Side of the Border   47

4 NEOLIBERALS ALSO CRY
El Libro Semanal and the U.S. Cultural Model   70

5 EMPIRE AT WORK
Comic Books and Working-Class Counterpublics   92

6 MEMORIES OF UNDERDEVELOPMENT
La Familia Burrón and the Politics of Modernization   118

7 CAPITALISM'S HERO
Las aventuras del Dr. Simi   142

8 *OPERACIÓN BOLÍVAR:*
The Work of Art in the Age of Globalization 164

9 EL BULBO VS. THE MACHINE
Graphic Artistry as Superpower 187

CONCLUSION 212

WORKS CITED 221

INDEX 227

ACKNOWLEDGMENTS

This book could not have been written without the support of my wife and best friend, Jessica Cohen. Her loving patience and encouragement sustained me throughout the arduous process of conceiving a book-length argument, and her frequent willingness to shoulder more than her share of our domestic labor afforded me the luxury of stealing time during weekends and vacations to write. I also benefited from friends and colleagues who spent time with all or part of the manuscript. Gladys White was kind enough to read each and every chapter in draft, as they emerged, and urged me on toward completion of the full manuscript. Steve Macek, Corey Shouse Tourino, Sebastián Carrillo, Edgar Clement, and Dan La Botz also read individual chapters and allowed me the kind of objectivity one can only achieve by seeing a project through someone else's eyes. An afternoon-long conversation over coffee with Edgar Clement and José Quintero in Mexico City in May 2007 energized me and confirmed the value of my project from the perspective of two of Mexico's premiere graphic artists. Chip Mitchell generously gave me the kind of painstaking, critical feedback that only a top-notch writer and editor can provide. In addition, I am immensely grateful to Seetha Srinivasan, director of the University Press of Mississippi, for encouraging me to turn my thinking about Mexican comics and globalization into a book, and giving me the opportunity to publish it. Lastly, I am immensely thankful for the support provided by St. John's University and the College of St. Benedict through a research award in fall of 2007.

INTRODUCTION

Reading the Politics of Globalization in Mexican Comics

This book examines the participation of Mexican graphic narrative in the continuing dispute over economic and cultural globalization in Mexico. Eight chapters focus on graphic narratives produced by and for Mexicans in the period following the implementation of the North American Free Trade Agreement (NAFTA) in 1994. NAFTA represents an important historical reference point because the economic accord institutionalized the so-called Washington consensus—that is, the U.S.-led "free-market" vision of globalization, which favors private sector control of economic policy and the rollback of public guarantees for social services, education, health care, and the like—in the relationships between the United States, Mexico, and Canada. NAFTA also firmly established neoliberal doctrine as the official policy of Mexico (Warnock). Analysis of the semiotic, aesthetic, and discursive features of Mexican comic books produced in the years since the implementation of NAFTA reveals a diverse field of ideological positions produced for Mexican popular consumption, ranging from overt, propagandistic celebrations of the neoliberal worldview to incisive critiques of the same, and a variety of perspectives in between. Overall, this national cultural field confirms the dominance of the U.S.-led model of global trade and culture in Mexican popular cultural consumption. At the same time, many of these comics reflect important preoccupations about the consequences for Mexican society and culture of the U.S. model—enduring anxieties about foreign cultural influence and economic control, cultural commodification, moral decay, exploitation or marginalization of the poor, and even racism.

Economic globalization and talk of a neoliberal "New World Order" based on trade liberalization, privatization of public goods and services, and a "postnational" ethos became ascendant among elites in the Americas in the 1990s. The implementation of NAFTA in January 1994 was followed by other U.S.-led regional trade initiatives, beginning with the proposal of a continental Free Trade Area of the Americas (FTAA), announced at the Summit of the Americas hosted by the Clinton administration in Miami in December 1994. Although the FTAA failed to materialize, the George W. Bush administration aggressively sought to expand the NAFTA paradigm throughout the hemisphere through related trade initiatives. Beginning in 2003, the United States sought an Andean Free Trade Agreement (AFTA), including Colombia, Peru, Ecuador, and Bolivia. The extension of the NAFTA model to Central America via the Central American Free Trade Agreement (CAFTA) was narrowly approved by the U.S. Congress in July 2005. But public preoccupation with loss of national sovereignty and popular resistance to economic privatizations and their consequences for working people emerged throughout the hemisphere, right alongside the dominant proglobalization discourse. In fact, regional politics in the early twenty-first century began to shift significantly against the grain of the "Washington consensus" on market liberalization of the 1990s. Popular opposition to AFTA was partly responsible for ousting Ecuadorian president Lucio Gutierrez in 2005, and forced the United States to shift its strategy to seeking separate trade agreements with Peru and Colombia. (Peru subsequently came very close to electing nationalist and anti-neoliberal Ollanta Humala to the presidency.) Bolivia elected the socialist critic of neoliberalism Evo Morales to the presidency in 2005 in a landslide victory, suspending official U.S. hopes of achieving a trade agreement with that country. Argentina, Uruguay, Venezuela, and Ecuador all elected critics of neoliberalism to the presidency during the same period that the George W. Bush administration attempted to expand the NAFTA paradigm on a hemispheric basis.

Conflict over the neoliberal model of globalization was nowhere more in evidence than in Mexico, a country with both a robustly nationalist public culture inherited from the twentieth-century's first social revolution and a shared border with the United States, the world's principal promoter of trade liberalization and capitalist globalization. Just as NAFTA figures as a milestone in official Mexico's transition to a neoliberal state, it represents, in the same measure, a critical touchstone for Mexico's contemporary social movements and counterofficial activism. Simultaneous to the implementation of NAFTA in January

1994, the Zapatista National Liberation Army led an indigenous uprising in the southern state of Chiapas against, among other things, the evisceration of the country's 1917 constitution with regard to the protection of communal land tenure from market speculation. Drawing on the revolutionary legacy of early-twentieth-century campesino insurgent Emiliano Zapata, the Chiapas uprising, and the subsequent spread of the neo-Zapatista indigenous rights agenda to the rest of Mexico, demonstrated that conflict over neoliberal governance was an undeniable fact of Mexico's political landscape.

The years that followed brought the gradual collapse of the one-party system of political rule established by the Partido Revolucionario Institucional (PRI; Institutional Revolutionary Party) and embarrassingly effective local resistance to official policies and projects. To mention just a few well-publicized examples: From late 1994 through the end of the decade, sustained community resistance blocked the government-backed sale of communal lands to the globally financed Kladt Sobrino development company for use in a private golf course construction scheme in the town of Tepoztlán, Morelos. A massive 1999 student strike at the National Autonomous University in Mexico City protested tuition increases and privatization of services at Latin America's largest public university. Outraged campesinos disrupted official plans for a new international airport at San Salvador Atenco in the state of Mexico in 2002, when they refused the government's expropriation of local landholdings, built barricades around the town, and took local government officials hostage, effectively blocking official plans for a globalization-friendly piece of transportation infrastructure.

In the cultural sphere, Mexico's comic books, or *historietas*, are one of the national cultural media in which conflict over the neoliberal model played out for public consumption during this same period. Mexico's cultural nationalism is famously visible in Mexico's modern mural arts, but it can also be frequently seen in a domestic comics industry that saw its hey-day in the 1960s and 1970s. Armando Bartra and Juan Manuel Aurrecoechea trace the origins of Mexico's modern comics industry to the same period that spawned the country's mural movement. "In the 1920s," they write, "there exists a new consumer public with new attitudes with regard to recreation and entertainment possibilities, and the post-revolutionary state is also forging a new cultural politics with a popular and nationalist character" (1988, 182). But whereas the Mexican mural movement was radically nationalist, the modern Mexican comic book industry was somewhat more ambivalent in its cultural profile: "the foundation of our modern comic book [*historieta*] results from the insistent combination of two divergent compulsions: the imitation of North American models and extreme Mexicanism; the new comic arose from the tension between irresistible mimetic will and deeply felt national vocation" (1988, 182).

Despite a decline in readership during the 1980s and 1990s, Mexican comics culture took on an overtly public profile as conflict over Mexico's political economy intensified. In the 2000 presidential election, for example, Vicente Fox's successful campaign boasted an endorsement by "Kalimán, el hombre increíble," a made-in-Mexico comic book superhero from the golden years of the domestic comics industry. In 2003 the conservative Fox administration published a comic book narrative titled "A mitad del camino" (Half Way There) in order to explain and promote its stalled free-market economic and social policies. Meanwhile, the center-left administration of the mayor of Mexico City, Andrés Manuel López Obrador, had earlier begun publication of its own *historieta* series—*Historias de la ciudad* (Stories of the City)—treating life in Mexico's sprawling metropolis. In the context of heightened interparty political conflict preceding the 2006 presidential campaign, López Obrador sparked controversy by turning installment #3 in the *historieta* series, "Las fuerzas oscuras contra Andrés Manuel López Obrador" (The Dark Forces against AMLO), into a polemical defense of his populist social agenda and an exposé of his right-wing ideological enemies. In 2004, faced with Fox administration efforts to privatize the publicly controlled energy sector, the Mexican Electrical Workers Union published its own didactic graphic *folleto*, "Que no nos roben la luz" (Don't Let Them Steal Our Light), and distributed more than four million copies in a mobilization of energy workers and consumers against the neoliberal policy proposal.

Such explicitly political comics are most obviously relevant to debates over economic globalization in Mexico—privatization, neoliberal policy doctrine, U.S. cultural influence, and the like—but their mass appeal comes from the extensive demographic reach and long historical arc of a rich comics culture in the country. Although precise data are difficult to come by, it has been calculated that production levels for the Mexican *historieta* reached more than seventy million per month by the early 1980s (Hinds and Tatum), and despite erosion of circulation provoked by the economic crisis beginning at that time, twenty years later production remained at more than seven million per month (see the *Encuesta Industrial Mensual* published since 1994 by the Mexican government's Instituto Nacional de Estadística, Geografía e Informática). Based on these production figures, *historietas* represent a major portion of the national print diet—a source of considerable concern for book publishers in Mexico

(Alatriste), while at the same time a crucial source of revenue for Mexican enterprises such as Novedades Editores (now NIESA Editores), which until 2005 had subsidized its less lucrative daily newspapers with the *historietas* that it publishes. Even the National Reading Survey conducted by the Consejo Nacional para la Cultura y las Artes (National Council for Culture and the Arts), where respondents are likely to significantly underreport the less prestigious consumption of comic books, found that more than 12 percent of the country's population reads comics.

In this broader symbolic market, *historietas* consumed mainly for their entertainment value also frequently organize their plot, characters, or thematics through representations of the relationship between Mexican national realities and the materials, technologies, and consequences of economic and cultural globalization. In fact, the two most widely distributed print publications in Mexico, the *historieta* series *El Libro Vaquero* and *El Libro Semanal* (both published by NIESA Editores), place their protagonists in direct contact with either U.S. cowboy archetypes of the Wild West (*El Libro Vaquero*) or with characters modeled on a transnational business class and U.S.-style, upper-middle-class consumer lifestyles (*El Libro Semanal*). *La Familia Burrón*, the country's most storied comic book series, and arguably the series most readily associated by Mexican readers with Mexican national cultural identity, tends to immerse contemporary events and political issues in the fantastical adventures of a group of recognizably Mexican social types, with an emphasis on Mexican working-class and popular cultural sensibilities. Recent efforts by a new generation of graphic artists to revive the independence and higher artistic values of the Mexican author's comic—for example, Edgar Clement's *Operación Bolívar* (1999) and Bachan's *El Bulbo* (2001), discussed in chapters 8 and 9, respectively—have combined artistic experimentation with heightened social awareness and insights into the national peculiarities of Mexico's globalized cultural environment.

Graphic narrative is therefore a useful medium in which to study the cultural politics of globalization in Mexico. The narrative character of the comic opens it to an abstract social vision, much as Benedict Anderson and others have observed that the novel form has historically imagined the nation. The interactive combination of narrative and visual image allows the comic book to serve as a unique vehicle for representations of the principal actors and processes of globalization, by literally visualizing national and global realities and the relationships between them. And because of the breadth of its popular readership, the comic book circulates its representations of globalization among social sectors that are typically marginal to official decision making.

The broader global market for comics—including Japanese manga and U.S. superheroes, and the extensive production of graphic novels—is undeniably a significant economic and cultural force in Mexico. For example, the 1998 "Pan-Latin American Kids Survey" conducted by Audits & Surveys Worldwide, Inc. found that 28 percent of Latin American children between the ages of seven and eleven had read one or more of five U.S. superhero and action comics (Batman, Spiderman, the Fantastic Four, X-Men Adventures, and Superman), with the level of consumption in Mexico (34 percent) well above the average (Soong). Nonetheless, the elaboration of storylines and characters for the major transnational comic book companies usually occurs at a geographical and sociocultural remove from the Mexican public sphere, Mexican cultural habits, and Mexican cultural histories. Mexican comics afford a special view onto the national dispute over economic and cultural globalization. Mexican comics culture offers a unique vantage from which one can discern distinct imagined relations at work between, for example, working-class experience and global market forces, or between Mexican national values and U.S. cultural and economic dominance. For this reason, the chapters that follow focus on a selection of individual comics and comic book series produced with Mexican consumers specifically in mind.

Critical analysis of a national experience of globalization as mediated through a popular narrative genre allows us to recognize the extension of U.S. cultural and ideological influence, and also to discern the limits of such influence. It bears noting, however, that the assertion of U.S. cultural hegemony through market-led globalization in recent years has not been documented or analyzed in the media of popular culture in the same manner as the critical dissection of U.S. cultural imperialism a generation ago. During this earlier period, anti-imperialist cultural critique took up a position alongside, or within, discourses of cultural nationalism. These included an influential theory of economic and political dependency, which asserted that Latin American underdevelopment was in fact a direct consequence of the first world's enrichment through resource extraction and political control vis-à-vis the third world. Anti-imperialist cultural critique was thus also linked to national liberation movements, and even official national projects, such as the Popular Unity government in Chile under the presidency of socialist Salvador Allende (1970–73), who was deposed by a U.S.-backed military coup. The most well known example of this kind of critical position-taking in cultural analysis is *How to Read Donald Duck* (Para leer al Pato Donald), coauthored by Ariel Dorfman and Armand Mattelart in 1971, which demonstrated the diffusion of imperialist ideology in Latin America through the mass distribution of the adventures of Disney's comic strip duck. This critical approach, reprised in Dorfman's *The Empire's Old Clothes* (1983), was directed at exposing how the importation by developing nations of U.S. behavioral models and their consumption in popular cultural form "clashed head-on with the immediate needs of their consumers" (4). The nation and the national, grounded in the concept of popular sovereignty, were the stakes of anti-imperialist cultural analysis during this period (see, e.g., Kunzle).

Much subsequent movement away from the Dorfman and Mattelart approach has been marked by a globalist cosmopolitanism. Ilan Stavans, for example, writing in the foreword to his *Latino USA: A Cartoon History* (2000) and with reference to the Dorfman and Mattelart book, dismisses as "nonsense" any link between the comics industry and U.S. imperialism: "Our global culture is not about exclusion and isolation, but about cosmopolitanism, which, etymologically, derives from the Greek terms 'cosmos' and 'polis,' a planetary city" (xi). On this view, globalization and a globalist ecumenism would remain the only legitimate frame of reference for the politics of cultural criticism, for the political meaning of the production, distribution, and consumption of popular culture, despite the still heavy hand of national interests and values in determining the shape of the global in the Americas. In view of the frequent emphasis on globalism in treatments of popular culture, before turning to an examination of Mexican graphic narrative specifically, it is important first to trace—beginning with official U.S. discourse—the continued relevance of nation and empire as points of reference for cultural analysis in the context of globalization.

For cultural analysis, the relationship between cultural text and context is fundamental. The complexity of globalization's cultural dimensions has been summed up usefully, if somewhat statically, by Arjun Appadurai's spatial nomenclature for the overlapping, shifting contours of global cultural production and flows in the realms of mass communication, identity, ideology, technology, and investment: mediascapes, ethnoscapes, ideoscapes, technoscapes, and financescapes. Appadurai's terminology frames global culture flows in the manner of a landscape painting, but more as perspective than as procedure—more as cultural environment than as cultural politics. What is left out of Appadurai's perspective is the manner in which globalization itself is often the *object* of cultural representations, where competing discourses seek to organize the view onto the features of the global landscape, efforts that often respond to and deploy national cultural media and materials, constructing meaning and identities through the intersection of national and other differences in the mediated environment. Extending Appadurai's visual-spatial constructions to comprehend a kind of cultural praxis, one is inclined to call this form of politics "culturescaping."

The "culturescaping" performed by Mexican comics with respect to the global context occurs against the backdrop of the dominant U.S. paradigm on globalization. Without discounting completely the moralizing framework offered up by Samuel Huntington to U.S. policy elites, the ethical guidelines (and hence the cultural parameters) of U.S. policy in Latin America have been neoliberal ones for some time. In order to confirm the predominance of commercial ethics over Huntington's "civilizational" politics, it is sufficient to note that beginning in 1995, one year after NAFTA went into effect and following the FTAA proposal, the U.S. Department of State put into practice an extension of section 2202 of the Omnibus Trade and Competitiveness Act of 1988, requiring that U.S. embassies collaborate in an annual evaluation of the legal, economic, cultural, and political conditions for private foreign investment in all countries with which the United States maintains diplomatic relations. In order to fully appreciate the degree to which this represented a programmatic, ethical priority for projecting U.S. power abroad, it should be noted that these *Country Commercial Guides* were modeled on the annual *Country Human Rights Reports* instituted by the Carter administration in the late 1970s.

If we observe closely the application of commercial criteria in U.S. discourse on Latin America—in this case, a discrete overlapping of what Appadurai calls ideoscapes and financescapes—it is possible to discern the fusion of national interest with neoliberal doctrine in official U.S. "culturescaping." The following selections of text come from the *Country Commercial Guide: Mexico*, for fiscal year 2001:

> [NAFTA] has been a net boost to all three economies and, in its undeniable role in spurring competitiveness, institutional reform, worker rights, and environmental stewardship, has served as a positive force for change in Mexico in areas beyond trade. (2)

> While Mexicans are a diverse and independent people, U.S. standards, business practices, and consumer styles are embraced in Mexico. (3)

The upper middle class represents about 18 percent of the population and is characterized by university educated people, who serve as professionals or company managers, who own homes and cars, have capacity to buy a wide range of household appliances, and occasionally travel internationally. (3)

In two decades, Mexico has been transformed from one of the most protectionist economies, with a large role for government, to one of the most liberalized. (10)

The discourse of the *Commercial Guide* emphasizes the agency of the market, the privatization of public goods, and the extracommercial benefits of trade liberalization—all characteristic ingredients of neoliberal discourse. One can also observe several significant points of contact with the emergent Huntington doctrine—in particular, the importance of shared cultural values and attitudes, and, even more tellingly, the articulation of U.S. norms as the dominant axis of the international relationship. Although unnamed, culture is posited as a strategic element, à la Huntington, despite the fact that, according to analysts of the accord, NAFTA contains very little relative to cultural issues or production (Waisbord). When Huntington wrote prior to the implementation of NAFTA that the trade accord's success depended on "the convergence already underway between Mexican, U.S. and Canadian culture," he did not elaborate on the prime mover of such a convergence (27). Official U.S. discourse in the *Country Commercial Guide* suggests that the primary mechanism is the market itself, serving "as a positive force for change in Mexico in areas beyond trade."

Later issues of the *Country Commercial Guide* for Mexico (that is, those of the George W. Bush administration) eliminated references to the embracing of U.S. norms in Mexico and placed greater emphasis on problematic differences, such as a slower pace of decision making ("the concept of time is flexible in Mexico," the reader is informed) and the Fox administration's stalled pro-business reform agenda. Other significant changes include more detailed and targeted strategic information for investors, all within the same transnational frame of NAFTA ("the most outstanding feature of the bilateral relationship") (U.S. Department of State 2004, 2). The readership of these commercial reports is global, facilitated by the availability of the texts as Portable Document Files (PDFs) on the Internet. (The Canadian government also posts them.) If the sector-by-sector analysis of obstacles and opportunities in the Mexican commercial environment reads like a transnational political agenda for Mexico, that is an effect of the culturescaping implicit to the text's official function. An imperial moment of economic globalization is legible in this organized view onto the nation, a studiously constructed perspective on the insufficiency, and necessity of reform, of Mexico and "Mexicanness" vis-à-vis transnational capital and official U.S. cultural norms.

Despite the evident operation of this perspective on the global cultural and political landscape, many of the discussions that orbited around the concept of "globalization" during the 1990s tended to elide nationalist accenting of cultural politics and critique. This elision of the national marked a range of discursive positions, from globalist triumphalism to calls for a transnational cultural politics responsive to global movements of capital, labor, information, and symbolic goods. Néstor García Canclini's emphasis on cultural hybridization and Arjun Appadurai's "postnational" ethics sought to counterbalance the tendencies toward cultural homogeneity and "Americanization" promoted by capitalist globalization. At the same time, these critical discourses sought leverage against the recrudescence of nationalist fundamentalisms in response to globalizing trends. In an important sense, however, it was the principle of popular sovereignty that faded under the bright lights of globalization. By 2000, Michael Hardt and Antonio Negri would posit "Empire" as a postnational condition, as an ideological and institutional frame-up of the entire globe by a transnational juridical sensibility now unmoored from its historical origins in the national poles of the world system. Hardt and Negri's counterweight to official Empire was to be "the multitude" (2005), an oceanic conception of the popular unbounded by the nation-state. Not surprisingly, the principal resonance for this argument outside the academy could be found among antiglobalization activists whose resistance to "globalization from above" sought an alternative discourse on globalization (see, e.g., Brecher and Costello) capable of uniting and catalyzing an otherwise implausibly fractious aggregate of multi- and transnational grassroots alliances.

The Hardt and Negri argument was challenged initially by a questioning of its scientificity. The positing of such sweeping agency for ideation raised many doubts, most prominently about the relationship between the authors' analysis and basic Marxist insights regarding material conditions (Brennan). But in the final analysis, the greatest challenge to the Hardt and Negri thesis came in the form of the U.S.-authored global "War on Terror," which countermanded most globalist prophecies and shoved antiglobalization activism to the margins of public debate everywhere. The ideological fundamentalism on which U.S. foreign policy doctrine became predicated under the George W. Bush administration (à la Huntington's "clash of civilizations" hypothesis) had the cultural and ideological effect of restoring "nation" to a place of prestige in elite discourse, and of repositioning it as a central category of "empire." Importantly, in Latin America this restoration of the national as a counterbalance to the global coincided with a growing antipathy for neoliberal economic policy and a revalorizing of national identity and popular sovereignty under pressure from broad-based, often extraofficial, social movements. The shift against U.S. neoliberalism was driven in part by elite hostility to the hard-line unilateralism of the Bush administration. But popular movements played an important role in disciplining national elites who followed U.S. direction too closely. In Argentina, Bolivia, and Ecuador, mass mobilizations unseated numerous presidents between 2000 and 2005.

As the bloom went off the rose of U.S.-led globalization in the Americas, one lesson that emerged was that neoliberal cosmopolitanism was not, in fact, nation free. As suggested by the language of the *Country Commercial Guides*, which are only available in English despite their alleged use value, in theory, for a postnational commercial order, it could be observed that neoliberalism posits a nationless subject everywhere except at home. Insofar as the Cold War–era modernization hypothesis (that is, that market-led cultural diffusion generates the U.S.-style individualism, consumer rationality, and capitalist ethos necessary for the one true modernity) continues to be the primary axis of institutionalized globalization, cultural analysis must continue to dissect cultural discourses in order to trace the signs of empire in the management and diffusion of meaning, particularly in the media of popular culture, where the cultural reproduction of the nation remains rooted to a significant degree.

There are, nonetheless, several important criticisms of the Dorfman and Mattelart approach. Chief among these, and the one most relevant to the discussion of Mexican comics, is the authors' binary construction of empire/nation, which assumes a unified and authentic national identity opposed to a coherent and invasive imperial culture. (For a broader critique of Dorfman and Mattelart, see Barker.) The coherence and unity of both categories were complicated by the decentering effects of globalizing processes that accelerated in the last two decades of the twentieth century, resulting in more complex North/South power relations. For example, García Canclini notes that the ongoing global processes of hybridization include not only U.S. cultural influences in Latin America but also a simultaneous and dramatic "Latinization" of U.S. culture and society.

And U.S. regional influence must compete with what García Canclini calls the "Neohispanoamericanization" of Latin America, which is to say "the expanding ownership of publishing houses, airlines, banks and telecommunications by Spanish companies" (2005, xxxvi). Without a doubt, the either/or opposition of nation to empire in *How to Read Donald Duck* became obsolete in the face of historical developments in the region. Nevertheless, the cultural hybridizations theorized by García Canclini are evidence of an intensified politics of meaning. Despite the fading away of national liberation projects in the post–Cold War era, what remains of the earlier conditions to which Dorfman and Mattelart responded is cultural diffusion as a site of ideological contest.

This, after all, is the key insight motivating the Dorfman and Mattelart approach, the historic contribution to cultural analysis made by critiques of modernization theory prior to the emergence of the globalization problematic and "the end of history" in the 1990s: that is, the recognition of the market not as a neutral abstraction but as the arena of distribution of not just wealth but of cultural goods and meaning as well. The much-vaunted market, in other words, remains a locus of North/South power differentials and struggles. The Dorfman and Mattelart approach presumed the application of state power to the problem of a neocolonialist structure to regional cultural diffusion and consumption. In Mexico, the country where domestic comic book production and consumption has been most intense in Latin America, the state mainly has concerned itself with controlling the perceived moral effects of graphic narratives (Rubenstein) but otherwise ignores the implications for national identity of the market for DC Comics, Marvel, and other U.S. companies. The central question for this study is not the imperial influence of U.S. popular culture on Mexican national consciousness, but rather the work of Mexican popular culture in presenting globalization, including the role of the United States and neoliberalism, to ordinary Mexican citizens. Critical analysis of Mexican comics with respect to how graphic narratives organize a view onto the place of Mexico and Mexicans in a transnationalized culture and economy provides evidence of neoliberal hegemony, but also of its limits amid the as yet unsettled tensions between Mexican popular sentiments and U.S.-led globalism.

The analysis presented here occurs with reference to the broad social, political, and cultural context of a Mexico *en vías de globalización*, a globalizing Mexico whose national development is no longer assessed, or even much discussed, by its governing interests independently of transnational interests and market liberalization. This is post-NAFTA Mexico, Mexico after the "Tratado de Libre Comercio" (Free Trade Agreement), a Mexico in the image of the U.S. State Department's *Country Commercial Guide* for Mexico. The benchmark for critical analysis of the cultural work performed by Mexican comics vis-à-vis the problematic of globalization is precisely this "cultural model" implicit to official U.S. discourse on globalization. The notion of a "cultural model" is a contribution of French social theorist Alain Touraine, who defines the cultural model as a given society's self-concept, the system of meaning that establishes a society's knowledge of itself, that allows it to articulate a sense of its own history, development, and purpose. Every society constructs a dominant cultural model, which serves as a blueprint for that society's "self-production." The language of the U.S. *Country Commercial Guide* contains just such a blueprint for the reproduction of Mexican society, a concept of Mexico's history, development, and purpose that is projected from the dominant U.S. cultural model. It is hard to miss, in the assessment of Mexico as an investment environment, a yardstick for measuring progress, improvement, or retrogression in a given society's historical development. This projection outward of the U.S. cultural model—where private self-interest supplants government regulation or civil societal organization as the prime mover of national progress—is what underlies the imperial dimension of U.S.-led globalization.

When in 2003 the Vicente Fox administration turned to graphic narrative to present its vision of the nation to the Mexican public, that same U.S. cultural model became visible in comic book form as the organizing principle for official Mexican discourse. The U.S. cultural model was institutionalized through NAFTA, effectively becoming official Mexican policy, and the processes of globalization made their indelible mark in the political, economic, and cultural fields of endeavor that together constitute Mexican society. In the political field, the post-NAFTA era witnessed the decline, and eventual collapse, of the political hegemony of the PRI, which had governed Mexico largely without rival since the party's founding in 1928. In effect, the corporatist structures of one-party rule by the PRI came unhinged as a result of profound contradictions between "free-market" economic and social policies favoring foreign investment and pursuant to final ratification of NAFTA with the United States, on the one hand, and the implicit social contract subtending PRI rule since the 1920s, on the other.

Political corporatism, a governing arrangement through which a full array of social sectors (campesinos, workers, youth, small business, and so forth) are unified under the central direction of the governing party, was not limited in twentieth-century Latin America to Mexico's ruling party, but as a system of patronage and control the PRI's version was uniquely successful in maintaining political stability in the country for decades, even through periods of violent social upheaval elsewhere in Latin America. The PRI regime used a carrot-and-stick approach to manage its political opposition, co-opting critics on the left and right whenever possible, and imprisoning them or assassinating them whenever the stick was deemed a necessity. But the carrot dimension of this approach relied heavily on state-guaranteed benefits for different social sectors, such as subsidized health care, universal access to education, price supports for basic goods, and even government jobs. The social component of PRI rule was gradually crippled by neoliberal policies.

As the PRI's corporatist machinery corroded, so, too, did its earlier forms of cultural representation, which had emphasized popular sectors as the basis of national identity. The shift to neoliberalism meant a final public abandonment of the kind of cultural work exemplified decades earlier in the revolutionary nationalist mural art of Diego Rivera. Instead of supporting domestic cultural production in the service of the public representation of common people, the Fox administration injected neoliberal ideas into the popular cultural medium of the comic book, attempting to turn a unique feature of Mexico's domestic cultural market to elite political advantage. In contrast, the López Obrador administration's comic book portrayals of life in Mexico City offered a counterpoint to official neoliberalism precisely by emphasizing popular experience and government social programs in the same popular cultural medium. The PRI's departure from monolithic power, in other words, meant that Mexican popular culture, and the *historietas* with it, became an arena of open struggle over the terms of Mexico's globalization.

The effectiveness of the corporatist regime had predictably eroded in the face of repeated concessions to transnational capital, which generally required a weakening of the social guarantees provided by the state. One such concession was the constitutional reform that eliminated government protections of the *ejido*, a communal landholding recognized as national patrimony in Article 27 of Mexico's 1917 constitution. As a direct result of this, in the countryside, where for nearly seventy years the PRI had reliably turned to a campesino base for electoral support and to reference the symbolic legitimation of Mexico's early-twentieth-century campesino-led revolution, indigenist insurgencies in the states of Chiapas, Oaxaca, and Guerrero exploded onto the post-NAFTA scene. The most significant of these insurgencies was that of the Ejército Zapatista de Liberación Nacional (EZLN), which initiated its armed insurrection against the official order on January 1, 1994, the very day NAFTA entered into effect, with a daring takeover of San Cristóbal de las Casas, the capital of the poor southern state of Chiapas. Part of the EZLN's political strategy since then has been to revive the symbolic power of the Mexican Revolution as political leverage against the neoliberalism of latter-day Mexican officialdom. As the Mexican state increasingly abandoned the political economy and coalition constructed in the decades following the 1910 revolution, protest and opposition spread across the full range of popular sectors. Energized by a reborn Zapatismo, an oppositional indigenism found new expression in popular cultural production—including in the graphic narratives of Daniel Manrique and Edgar Clement.

The EZLN is only one example of the political consequences of neoliberalism in Mexico. Importantly, the EZLN opened political space and provided a rallying point for other opposition efforts, such as the militant small-farmers' organization El Barzón, which first emerged in 1993 in protest of the growing debt burden of Mexican farmers. The subsequent rapid expansion of El Barzón (whose name refers to the leather strap that attaches the oxen's yoke to the plow) was explained a year later by its national secretary, José Quirino Salas, in frank reference to Mexico's official neoliberalism:

> Small- and medium-sized businesses whether agricultural, services or manufacturing have suffered a tremendous blow during the last four years as a result of the neo-liberal economic policy of Carlos Salinas. In particular, they have suffered because of the indiscriminate importation of products that enter through dumping, that come in with subsidized prices, and that compete in an unrealistic way with Mexican products. . . . So now we are all united as brothers in the same struggle, both farmers and entrepreneurs. (La Botz 1995, 183)

As recently as 2003, El Barzón continued to advocate an official pullback from neoliberal economic policy, this time mobilizing alongside other independent groups from the Mexican countryside in an attempt to force the Fox administration to revise NAFTA's agricultural chapter.

The nascent independence of social sectors previously absorbed under the PRI's corporatist political management was not limited to the rural areas of Mexican society. The urban working-class cultural milieu alternately celebrated and lampooned for six decades in Gabriel Vargas's *La Familia Burrón* also became an arena of political conflict in post-NAFTA Mexico. Independent urban social movements had earlier emerged from the rubble of the 1985 Mexico City earthquake, responding in part to the perceived inability of the Mexican government to care for victims of the disaster. These urban movements would serve, in the post-NAFTA period, as the political base for the center-left opposition Partido de la Revolución Democrática (PRD; Party of the Democratic Revolution) and its ability to break the PRI's hegemony in Mexico City. Urban university students, who dramatically confronted PRI governance in the volatile 1960s, mobilized throughout the 1990s and into the early twenty-first century against efforts to raise tuition costs and privatize services at the Universidad Nacional Autónoma de México (UNAM) in Mexico City. Indeed, UNAM students led the largest student strike in national history in 1999–2000, opposing the application of neoliberal dictates to Mexico's historical commitment to universal access to education.

As the PRI lost its near monopoly on state power, organized labor also began to exercise increased independence from the government on policy matters. The PRI had long relied on a corrupt and obedient official unionism in maintaining social peace despite official policies damaging to working-class interests. The Mexican labor movement in the post-NAFTA period emerged with a divided profile—most of the unions historically affiliated with the PRI remained in the old Congreso de Trabajo (CT; Congress of Labor), but in 1997 more than 130 unions broke away from the CT to form the Unión Nacional de Trabajadores (UNT; National Union of Workers) (Burgess). The powerful public sector union Sindicato Mexicano de Electricistas (SME; Mexican Electrical Workers Union) withdrew from the CT in 1999 in order to organize public resistance to President Ernesto Zedillo's proposal for privatization of the energy sector. The SME also heads the Frente Sindical Mexicano (FSM; Mexican Labor Front), a radical alternative to the UNT formed in 1998. The Frente Auténtico de Trabajo (FAT; Authentic Labor Front) is yet another independent labor federation, and a vocal opponent of neoliberal policies in the post-NAFTA period. In 2007 the FSM, FAT, and other independent unions joined with the national civil societal group Red Mexicana de Acción Frente al Neoliberalismo (Mexican Network of Action Against Neoliberalism, formed in 1991 in opposition to the NAFTA negotiations) in an open call for resistance to neoliberal policies in Mexico ("Unions").

This context of struggle to construct an independent labor movement, and to create new alliances with Mexican civil society, is what resulted in the SME's experiment with graphic narrative as a medium of public discourse. In effect, neoliberal policies, and the globalizing processes they promote, are not simply contested in Mexico; they have generated new forms of social organization and resistance. And in the cultural sphere, the "globalization from above" paradigm has occasioned a range of preoccupations, unintended consequences, and alternative visions, many of which are legible in Mexican comics in the post-NAFTA period. One unintended consequence is that the implementation of NAFTA coincided with dramatic increases in Mexico-to-U.S. labor migration, creating a massive informal foreign revenue stream for the Mexican economy through Mexican migrants' remittances from the United States, estimated at 8 to 10 billion U.S. dollars per year. Meanwhile, the hybrid character of the U.S.-Mexico border region expanded far beyond the international line through the proliferation of transnational communities, as migrants headed north to send dollars home to aid the economic survival of traditional agrarian communities unable to compete with U.S. agribusiness interests in the Mexican countryside. "Economic and cultural umbilical cords now permanently connect hundreds of Latin American and Caribbean localities with counterpart urban neighborhoods in the United States" (Davis, 80).

The Fox administration's *historieta*-like *Guía del migrante mexicano* (*Guide for the Mexican Migrant*, 2004) was published in response to this post-NAFTA reality. Meanwhile, the distribution of the cheap pocket *historietas El Libro Semanal* and *El Libro Vaquero*, published by NIESA Editores, developed a markedly transnational profile as they followed patterns of labor migration northward. Preoccupation with the consequences of globalization and U.S. (or Japanese) influence in Mexico came to be reflected in both the work of newly emergent graphic talents like Edgar Clement and Sebastián Carrillo and in the work of Mexican comics legend Gabriel Vargas.

From the unique perspective afforded a social scientist located in Mexico City, García Canclini observed that free trade accords such as NAFTA, in their reshaping of cultural consumption and its environments, held implications for the character and agency of national citizenship. "Cultural free trade agreements should not effect an indiscriminate opening of markets, but instead should take into consideration the unequal development of national systems, as well as the protection of production, communication and consumption rights of different ethnic groups and minorities" (García Canclini 1997, 161). Writing in anticipation of the implementation of NAFTA, performance artist and cultural activist Guillermo Gómez-Peña called for a "free art agreement" to parallel the "free trade agreement," and wondered aloud: "Given the exponential increase of American trash and media-culture in Mexico, what will happen to our indigenous traditions, our social and cultural rituals, our language, and national psyche?" (8).

The preoccupation expressed by Gómez-Peña could also be applied to the Mexican comics industry. Although Mexico negotiated some minimum protections against foreign control of mass media (protecting the PRI-friendly Televisa corporation's near monopoly over domestic television programming, for example), other provisions indirectly undermined the market share and financial health of domestic cultural production. With regard to print media, the trade accord required the privatization of the state-owned paper production and distribution company Productora e Importadora de Paper, S.A. (PIPSA; Producer and Importer of Paper, Inc.), and the gradual lifting of tariffs on paper imported from the United States. Since 1938, the state-owned PIPSA had served a dual function under the PRI's state-centered political economy: it had subsidized and strengthened domestic cultural production and consumption by holding paper costs low for Mexican newspapers, magazines, and comic books; and it had operated as a useful mechanism for rewarding or punishing publishers when the one-party state determined it politically necessary. At the same time that trade liberalization released domestic cultural production from a mechanism of state ideological control, the increased cost of paper resulting from PIPSA's privatization in 1998 (purchased by the Mexican enterprise Grupo Industrial Durango, S.A.) is believed by many to be an important factor in the weakening of the Mexican comic book industry.

The economic, political, and cultural circumstances sketched in brief above together comprise the context for the production and consumption of Mexican comics in the post-NAFTA period. Each of the eight chapters comprising this book corresponds to a distinct piece of the complex national context of a globalizing Mexico and how that is reflected in the visual and narrative composition in the comics under study. As regards critical method, the approach to these graphic texts is not a formalist one. Analysis balances attention to the formal elements of a particular text or texts with the task of situating those texts within the relevant ideological contexts of their consumption. In doing so, the critical leverage for analysis necessarily shifts from case to case.

The politics of globalization in post-NAFTA Mexico are discernible in different ways in different comic books. The right-wing Vicente Fox administration and the left-of-center Andrés Manuel López Obrador administration both issued *historietas* as official propaganda vehicles that sought to promote a specific model of public authority and popular legitimacy in the context of disputes over neoliberal policy. Here, the critical approach is a straightforward dissection of visual and narrative rhetoric used to manage "*lo popular*" in relation to governing authority. The narrative and visual aesthetics of NIESA Editores' *El Libro Vaquero* construct a relationship between the Mexican reader, in particular the likely migrant, and social reality on the U.S. side of the international border. Analysis in this case draws on the insights of social semiotics in order to connect the *historieta* to the context of labor migration. NIESA Editores' other popular *historieta* series, *El Libro Semanal*, combines Mexican popular sentiment with the U.S. cultural model, disseminating the latter for popular consumption. Ideological analysis of the comic centers on its soap opera–like narrative elements and supporting melodramatic aesthetics. Didactic comics produced for working-class publics can offer militant oppositional perspectives on the history and present of globalization in Mexico, or a management-friendly view of the workplace. The aesthetic representations of the class-specific body are a distinguishing feature of working-class oppositional comics. The upbeat visuals of the legendary, long-running *La Familia Burrón* of Gabriel Vargas are the key to understanding how the comic presents both nostalgia for the working-class social life of mid-twentieth-century Mexico and an exposé of the politics of national economic development, including a questioning of neoliberal globalism. A globalist discourse and transnational corporate model of authority is propagated by *Las aventuras del Dr. Simi*, the monthly comic book series published by the Mexican-owned generic drugs transnational Farmacias de Similares, S.A. In this case, critical attention turns to the integration of the visual language of mass entertainment culture in a comic book that serves as a marketing vehicle for a corporate brand. In contrast, cultural and ideological critiques of Mexico's cultural and economic globalization are clearly legible in Edgar Clement's groundbreaking graphic novel *Operación Bolívar* and in Sebastián Carrillo's superhero parody *El Bulbo*. These are the most aesthetically complex graphic texts in the selection, and thus require the most detailed treatment of aesthetic composition.

The graphic works and series analyzed in this study were selected not only for their genre representativity and formal distinctiveness vis-à-vis the field of comics production in Mexico but also for their ideological differences vis-à-vis the problematic of globalization. With regard to this latter criterion, the analysis of Mexican comics presented here does not consist of a simple paraphrasing of the ideological "content" of the graphic works selected. Rather, in each case the aim is to carefully examine those formal aesthetic conventions—both visual and narrative—of the comic book form that serve to construct and present to the comic book reader a particular sense of reality, history, and/or social perspective. The use of color, the shape of panel borders and their spatial deployment on the page, and the panel size and sequencing are formal visual elements that interact with the story arc, character development, and thematic focus of the graphic narratives. Attention to visual semiotics—images as units of meaning—is at least as important, if not more so, than a parsing of the contents of the dialogue balloons and narrative script that accompany the images. Aesthetic styles of representation are often as ideologically significant as genre-specific narrative conventions.

The formal distinctiveness of each text required that critical interpretation operate multimodally, drawing upon a range of critical concepts from modern cultural and social theory in order to contextualize the comic and understand its singular work on the reader's relationship to the problem of globalization. Considered as graphic art, the comics selected represent a wide qualitative spectrum. At the upper end of the scale of artistic value, Edgar Clement's and Sebastián Carrillo's works demonstrate the well-honed drafting skills and nuanced sense of graphic tradition of a cohort of younger Mexican artists whose work has not yet enjoyed commercial success but whose graphic abilities are as good or better than anyone in the field. Discussion of these more visually complex works demands far more detailed attention to formal visual elements than the official propaganda vehicles *Historias de la ciudad* and "A mitad del camino," which favor rhetorical strategies and the imparting of policy information over visual artistry. Similarly, while those official political deployments of the comic book offer little in the way of aesthetic innovation or uniqueness, the special talents of political cartoonists Rafael Barajas, José Hernández, and Antonio Helguera make visual form and aesthetic effect compellingly central to any analysis of the political critique launched in the Mexican Electrical Workers Union's oppositional *historieta*, "Que no nos roben la luz." Mural artist Daniel Manrique's experiment with cartooning in "La discriminación en México" is, like most "author's comics," marked by the artist's individual style and autonomy of aesthetic decision. In contrast, formulaic commercial vehicles like *El Libro Semanal* and *El Libro Vaquero* tend to hem in the distinctive styles of the different artists who work on the series in favor of a standardized look. As a result, artistic value is subordinated to the series editor's more functional criteria related to production costs and market appeal. *Las aventuras del Dr. Simi* also evinces this commercial standardization logic, but with the novel twist of combining the photographic image with the hand-drawn figure, celebrity and corporate symbol with the graphic construction of the comic book hero. For its part, Gabriel Vargas's long-running and self-published *La Familia Burrón* is distinguished by formal elements proper to the individual artist's vision for a production sequence developed with commercial viability in mind.

The selection of graphic narratives for analysis is intended to be representative rather than comprehensive. Each text selected represents a distinct kind of graphic narrative, whether due to its formal visual components, narrative genre, audience, or discursive purpose. Anyone familiar with the Mexican comics industry will immediately notice that there are countless Mexican comic book series, graphic novels, didactic comics, and other examples of sequential graphic art not discussed here. Some of these were excluded due to the scope of the study. *Memín Pinguín* (Editorial Vid) and *Kalimán, El Hombre Increíble* (Kaliman, The Incredible Man; Promotora K), for example, enjoy a large reading public and a long history of publication dating to the 1940s and 1960s, respectively, but their current issues are reprints or reedited versions of older issues. José Quintero's mordant *Buba* comic strip, published since 1989 in the daily newspaper *La Jornada*, was reedited and published in comic book form by Editorial Vid in 2007, but as a comic strip, it does not comprise a sustained narrative. Similarly, Oscar González Loyo's outer-space fantasy *Karmatron* (¡Ka-Boom Estudio!), published first in 1986 and then relaunched in 2001, is distanced from any recognizable social or political context. In 2006 Editorial Caligrama began publishing the graphic novels of a younger generation of Mexican artists—including a reprint of Clement's *Operación Bolívar* and a reedited version of Carrillo's *El Bulbo* comic book series—but these published works of Tony Sandoval, Patricio Betteo, and Ricardo García Fuentes are not self-evidently relevant to the scope of this study (nor is Carrillo's own work in *Vinny, El Perro de la Balbuena*). Other graphic texts—*historieta* series like *Lagrimas y Risas* (Tears and Laughter; Editorial Vid), or *Frontera Violenta* (Violent Border; NIESA), or the seemingly countless other romance, adventure, "true crime," and soft-porn comics that circulate in Mexico—were set aside in favor of the two series (*El Libro Semanal* and *El Libro Vaquero*) with the broadest distribution, including a wide circulation within the United States.

GRAPHIC POLITICS

Political Elites, Globalization, and "*lo Popular*"

The end of more than seventy years of uninterrupted rule by Mexico's Partido Revolucionario Institucional (PRI) coincided with an enhanced profile for the comic book in the Mexican public arena. For the first time since the establishment of one-party rule in 1928, an opposition party defeated the PRI in the 2000 presidential election. The historic victory went to the candidate of the conservative Partido de Acción Nacional (PAN; National Action Party), Vicente Fox. Fox had campaigned with the public endorsement of "Kalimán, el hombre increíble," a turbaned Mexican superhero with mystical powers who has been a staple of Mexican comics dating to the industry's golden years in the 1960s. The domestically produced and consumed, and morally charged, *Kalimán* series represents an important piece of the nation's popular cultural history: "Gallant with the women, tender with the children, implacable with the wicked, thus is . . . Kalimán."

Only in a comic book could such superior moral status be publicly claimed. PAN electoral strategists sought to mobilize the nation's popular culture as political capital by associating their candidate with the Mexican superhero (created by Cuban dissident Modesto Vázquez in 1962). The PANistas were able to secure the public endorsement of Silvia Flores, who claimed to be heiress to the comic book character's copyright. Speaking to reporters in April 1999, Flores likened the conservative presidential candidate to a turbaned hero whom the Mexican public knew to be endowed with special powers (that is, telekinesis, telepathy, and mind control, as well as the ability to feign death): "they are both important people who fight against injustice, they are on the side of the people" (J. M. Carrillo). The idea was, in effect, to make of Kalimán's oft-repeated comic book philosophy—"serenity and patience"—a kind of subliminal mantra for Fox's bid to finally undo one-party rule in Mexico. The PRI's candidate, Francisco Labastida, evidently failed to capture the popular imagination with his autobiographical forty-eight-page *historieta*, "Una vida ejemplar" (An Exemplary Life, 2000), distributed on the streets of Mexico City.

At the other end of the spectrum of partisan opposition to the PRI, the leftist Partido de la Revolución Democrática (PRD) had taken political control of the country's largest urban center, Mexico City, also known as the Federal District. In 1997 the central megacity, constituting as much as one-quarter of the national population, chose Cuauhtémoc Cárdenas of the PRD as the first democratically elected mayor of the Federal District in Mexican history. The city remains firmly in the control of the PRD, and serves as the epicenter of the nation's center-left electoral politics. Successive PRD administrations appear to have made graphic narrative part of a strategy designed to secure a popular base for a party that did not form until 1989 (following an apparently fraudulent presidential election that Cuauhtémoc Cárdenas almost certainly won but which was awarded by a PRI government to the PRI's Carlos Salinas de Gortari). The government of the Federal District financed the publication of *Sensacional de Chilangos*, a collection of short graphic narratives of urban life published in October 2000 and distributed free to 25,000 Mexico City residents. This project featured the work of the megacity's most talented graphic artists, and recalled on a small scale the official support for public art that became government policy following the Mexican Revolution. *Sensacional* would be followed by the *historieta* series *Historias de la ciudad* (Stories of the City), which also offered the public tales of life in Mexico's capital in graphic format, albeit in less experimental and fanciful forms, and now as evidence of successful PRD governance. Notably, as a consequence of its Internet diffusion, the series reached a national audience.

Intriguingly, then, as the Mexican presidency and its largest urban population came under the administration of opposition parties almost completely excluded from government power for most of the twentieth century, the comic book and its popular readership moved conspicuously into the political arena. A relationship between comics and politics in Mexico is certainly nothing new. As Anne Rubenstein argues in her political history of Mexican comics, comic books emerged in the 1940s as a focal point for negotiating the hegemonic rule of the PRI (which had formed as the Partido Revolucionario Nacional in 1928). In the "moral panics" stirred periodically by the development of mass media in Mexico through the 1970s, the state-led modernization project of the PRI, left-wing nationalist sentiment, and the antimodern discourse of Mexico's conservative opposition could find common cause: that is, state control of representations of modernity and of "Mexicanness" available for popular consumption. "The interactions of the Mexican government with the popular entertainment industry, and with the industry's fiercest critics, worked to maintain a political and economic status quo: Gramscian hegemony made visible" (Rubenstein 109). In service of this status quo, however, the comic book operated under the PRI as a pretext for negotiating political "consensus" instead of as a textual medium for exercising political power. Governing authority negotiated its legitimacy not by publishing comics but by constructing, in alliance with the opposition, controls over the publishing industry, regulating content through the fines meted out by an official morals commission, through access to preferred postal rates, and through the state's monopoly over the paper supply.

What appears different in the early twenty-first century is that despite a relative decline in comics readership for the Mexican industry during the 1980s and 1990s (see Bartra 2000), the comic book medium has been used to project official interests and organized political positions in Mexico. This expressly political profile for Mexican graphic narrative (as well as the weakened readership for Mexican-made comic books generally) arises in part from market liberalization. The terms of NAFTA required the privatization of the state-owned newsprint supplier Productora e Importadora de Papel (PIPSA; Paper Producer and Importer), carried out in 1998. And although it represents a small fraction of Mexican comic book production overall, this new profile—comic book narrative as vehicle of explicit moral suasion and propagandistic mass appeal—has expanded as organized conflict over the nation's political economy has deepened. Mexican conservatives and the nationalist Left no longer have their differences mediated by a paternalistic and corporatist political structure. The decline of the PRI thus meant greater competition to shape the character of both national economic development and national cultural identity. The more polarized political arena of post-PRI Mexico (or more accurately—given that the PRI remains a factor in Mexican politics—post-one-party rule) coincides also with a heightened dissatisfaction with PRI-initiated government economic policies driven primarily by market considerations.

The *historieta* format, with its readerly (that is, as Roland Barthes uses the term, authoritative and stable in meaning) visual constructs and social imaginary, and its parsimonious and easily assimilable written discourse, is a key popular cultural "language" of this political conjuncture. The Vicente Fox administration set a national precedent when, in 2002, it published a version of its constitutionally mandated annual status report in the form of a thirty-two-page comic book narrative, "Acciones" (Actions), two million copies of which were distributed in Mexico City. In July 2002 the Fox administration had published a similar *historieta*—"El cambio en México ya nadie lo para" (Change in Mexico Can No Longer Be Stopped)—commemorating the second anniversary of the PAN candidate's electoral victory over the PRI. Later, beleaguered by political setbacks on several fronts for its neoliberal policy agenda, the administration would publish two more annual reports in *historieta* form: "A mitad del camino" (Half Way There, 2003) and "Construyendo un México fuerte" (Building a Strong Mexico, 2005).

Meanwhile, a similar process was under way on the political left. In response to conservative efforts to derail Mexico City mayor Andrés Manuel López Obrador's left-of-center candidacy for the presidency, the mayor's administration published in 2004 "Las fuerzas oscuras contra Andrés Manuel López Obrador" (The Dark Forces against AMLO)—issue #3 in the *Historias de la ciudad* series— which gave the Mexican public a Manichaean frame of reference for understanding recent political maneuvers by López Obrador's right-wing opponents. Other episodes in the *Historias* series promoted social programs of his administration, which also had published a million copies of a graphic narrative celebrating in populist terms the 250th anniversary of nineteenth-century independence fighter Miguel Hidalgo, titled "La Bola del padre Hidalgo" (Father Hidalgo's Rabble, 2005). The Xochimilco precinct of the Federal District even published a *historieta*, "¡No compres problemas!" (Don't Buy Trouble, 2005), instructing residents on the official urban development plan for the precinct. PRD activists published two brief comic book series for the 2006 presidential campaign: one of them, *Super Marcelo* (2006), featured López Obrador's successor as mayor of the Federal District, Marcelo Ebrard, as a defender of the truth endowed with special eyeglasses capable of seeing through the lies of the PRI and the PAN candidates; the second also was a superhero comic, *PGMan*, starring the candidate as a powerful agent of popular sovereignty engaged in combat with conservative enemies of democracy and the popular will.

Other political players got into the act, too. Large trade unions had been political clients of the PRI, but became increasingly independent of the post-PRI central government. Unions made their own retorts to neoliberal policy initiatives through the comics medium. In 2004, faced with Fox administration efforts to privatize the publicly controlled energy sector, the Sindicato Mexicano de Electricistas (SME) published its own didactic graphic *folleto*, "Que no nos roben la luz" (Don't Let Them Steal Our Light), and distributed some five million copies as part of a mobilization of energy workers and consumers against Fox's policies (see chapter 5). Mexico's public sector health workers union of the Instituto Mexicano de Seguro Social (IMSS; Mexican Social Security Institute) also produced in 2004 a *historieta*—titled "Alicia en el pais de la inseguridad social" (Alice in Social Insecurity Land)—in order to publicly criticize Mexican legislators who had voted to weaken Mexico's social security law. In 2004 several taxi driver groups issued 5,000 copies of a comic book parody of López Obrador's "Fuerzas oscuras"—a public retort to an administration these cabbies perceived to support freelance taxis (Flores).

The visual aesthetics and narrative discourse of the comics issued by the conservative Vicente Fox administration (2000–2006) and the left-of-center Mexico City mayor Andrés Manuel López Obrador, Fox's most prominent political detractor in a governmental position, reveal competing constructions of Mexican national identity. These cultural texts can be situated within the tensions between two poles of orientation for public discourse about Mexican identity and national progress. The currently dominant, postrevolutionary official paradigm of nationhood emphasizes mobility, private interests and investment, and U.S.-style middle-class lifestyles instead of the indigenous culture, campesino lifeways, emphatic nationalism, and revolutionary histories emphasized by official discourse during most of the long period of PRI rule. The latter, revolutionary nationalist paradigm of national identity dates to the period from the aftermath of the military phase of the Mexican Revolution (1910–20) through to the implementation of the policy demands of radicalized popular sectors—for example, agrarian reform and nationalization of the petroleum industry—under Lázaro Cárdenas (1934–40). This older concept of nationhood (a variant of which is visible in "La Bola del padre Hidalgo") represented the cultural and ideological dimension of state-directed import-substitution strategies—public support for domestic industrialization—which required an alliance between popular social sectors and technocratic elite governance. The currently dominant, effectively neoliberal construct of nationhood is consistent with the economic liberalization policies begun in earnest by president Miguel de la Madrid (1982–88), accelerated by Carlos Salinas de Gortari (1988–94), and advanced by the collapse of PRI rule into the conservative government of Vicente Fox.

Change in the ingredients of official representations of the nation, as well as the recipe for combining these ingredients in support for specific policy objectives, corresponds to changes in and conflicts over Mexico's national political economy. The present configuration of dominant and subordinate economic interests and their relationship to governing decisions about who gets what, when, where, and how flows from half a century of political struggle over the direction of the country's economic development. A recitation of successive presidencies and dates of administration obscures an ongoing history of mass political mobilization in opposition to the privatization of public goods, funding cuts to social programs, a growing breach between rich and poor, and declining real wages that characterize the neoliberal model everywhere it is implemented. The reshaping of Mexico's political economy occurred under pressure from the processes of globalization—that is, propagation of neoliberal doctrine regarding national economic controls; expansion of the reach, efficacy, and speed of communications and transportation technologies; and segmentation and transnationalization of networks of production, publicity, and distribution of goods. The Mexican state abandoned most vestiges of the import-substitution policies that subtended, through the 1960s, the national-popular linkage in official discourse and cultural production.

The revolutionary era's concern for popular sovereignty and popular economic interests has been mostly superseded by a neoliberalism that achieved its national apotheosis in many ways in the government of Vicente Fox (continued under his successor, PANista Rafael Calderón). In the new national scenario, what remains of the PRI's corporatist political model (patron-client relationship between state and civil society, use of public resources to reward and punish political actors, and so forth) has been retooled in order to contain, direct, or marginalize opposition to the transferal of wealth from the public to the private sector. Yet despite its dominance in the Mexican public arena, neoliberal discourse has not settled into hegemony, into a consensual model of moral and political leadership. Far from enjoying social and political consensus, Mexico's official neoliberalism continues to be shadowed by the struggle over the symbolic and cultural materials of nationhood, and by the emergence of social and political organizations aimed at challenging neoliberal technocracy. The most famous instance of this phenomenon is, of course, the neo-Zapatista movement.

One can also discern in official political predications on the *historieta* form the as yet unrealized dream of neoliberal hegemony. Fox's "A mitad del camino" and López Obrador's *Historias de la ciudad* series are useful in this regard, as distinct representations of the nation in the context of globalization and as contrasting models for governing authority in that context. Moreover, these comic book narrations are evidence of elite recognition of the need to rhetorically pitch neoliberal globalization, or deviation from it, directly to the popular sectors of Mexican society. Exemplars of the recent deployment of the *historieta* as a mass communications strategy for organized politics, these cultural documents suggest, in their contrasts, the as yet unsettled dominance of neoliberal discourse in Mexico, even among the policy-making elite. Their conflicting appeals to the nation's working majority contain distinct conceptions of *"lo popular"*—of the working class and the poor as subjects of official power. For a government-issued comic book, there are two kinds of popular subjects: those represented in the comic book, and those who consume that representation. Thus the comic book is a vehicle for the symbolic legitimation of state power by what Guillermo O'Donnell described as a "we" that is "a carrier of demands for substantive justice which form the basis of the obligations of the state toward the less favored segments of the population" (278). These graphic texts each wed public authority with *"lo popular"* through distinct, tendentious visions of the global.

The Fox administration's "A mitad del camino," published in September 2003, is a comic book presentation of the Federal Executive's third annual report to the national Congress. The Executive's annual report on the general state of the nation and its public administration is required under Article 69 of the Mexican Constitution, but before Fox took office these reports had never before been made available for public perusal in comic book form. Circulation of two million copies of the comic book was designed to reach "popular sectors in the entire country" by using as distribution outlets Liconsa stores, a state-owned enterprise that supplies milk to the low-income population, as well as the health clinics of the IMSS. Although the first two comic books published by the Fox government (both in 2002) were created by graphic artists at Oscar González Loyo's ¡Ka-Boom! Estudios, a Mexican company with production credits that include work on Matt Groening's *The Simpsons* and Warner Bros. and Disney projects, "A mitad del camino" was developed by the General Office of Public Opinion and Image, where Guadalupe Bribiesca Azuara authored the storyline and Nicanor Peña Cabrena and José Luis Peña Cabrera created the graphics (Ruiz).

The political conjuncture for the unprecedented document is important. The PAN's sweeping agenda of neoliberal "reforms" to labor law, the state-owned telecommunications company Teléfonos de México, and the energy sector had stalled in the Mexican legislature. High-profile controversies had erupted over privatization of public goods, like mass citizen opposition to the government's 2001 sale of the Casino de la Selva in Cuernavaca to U.S.-based Costco, a transfer of public wealth that also resulted in the destruction of national cultural patrimony—hundreds of square feet of mural art irreparably damaged by the transnational company's commercial designs on the space. In addition, the refusal of the rebel Zapatista army in Chiapas to disarm, a high-profile Zapatista tour of the country and recriminations over a betrayal by Fox's allies of rights legislation demanded by the indigenous rights movement in 2002, and the ruling U.S. Republican Party's dismissal, in the wake of the 9/11 attacks, of Fox's proposals for liberalized U.S.-Mexico border controls, all weakened the government politically. The graphic text was published in order to explain and promote the PAN administration's stymied free-market economic and social policies to a Mexican public that in the July 2003 midterm elections delivered only 30 percent of the national vote to PAN, down from the 40 percent it received in 2000.

The narrative structure of the text coordinates the broad sweep of Fox's "state of the Republic" message with the itinerant dialogue of two young working-class Mexican families whose long bus ride, from the border city of Nuevo Laredo to Mexico City, carries them to a celebration with extended family on September 16, the anniversary of the Mexican struggle for independence from Spain, begun on that date in 1810. The comic is text-heavy; Fox's message fills speech balloons, inset didactic boxes, and the "gutters," or spaces between panel frames. The visuals—scenes of the landscape, character dialogue, economic decision making, construction, and productivity rendered with naturalism and bright color schemes—provide an aesthetic "ground" for the sweeping abstractions of official discourse.

The authoritative discourse of governance, an impersonal script narrating the economic resources and productivity of the nation and the expenditure of public wealth in shaping details of the economy, is displayed on each page as a banner across the top, bottom, or center margins of the image panels, and/or frequently in speech balloons attributed to Mexican citizens from different walks of life. As the young families wend their way across the national landscape, their more personal discourse (about family decisions and economic opportunities) accompanies that of the Fox administration, a kind of popular escort assuring that economic abstraction meets with a lived reality.

Thus one reads of the abstract nation that "the total transfer of resources toward federative entities and municipalities has been increased considerably during the current administration, and in 2003 they reached 275 billion pesos," while on the same page the families discuss how both had relocated to the border city of Nuevo Laredo as a result of new job opportunities. "There was an opportunity to come to work at the factory . . . and we didn't have to think twice!" says Isaac to his workmate Fernando (3). The *historieta*'s visuals seek to close the gap between official discourse and lived experience, encouraging the reader to link official policy (decentralization, in this case) with the happy personal circumstances of the workers and their families (that is, new jobs in the provinces). The imagery of the comic book narrative is strategic in carrying out this ideological strategy, from the very first pages: the full-page cover image—two young couples with their small children stand together smiling at the reader in front of a bus whose destination is prominently marked "Mexico"—turns back to reveal a visually parallel single-panel title page inside—a mariachi band plays at the base of a flagpole in the *zócalo*, the public plaza in front of the National Palace, as a massive Mexican tricolor flutters above.

The precise visual symmetry of these two pages, repeated one after the other, offers up the personal and familiar narrative (deploying the second-person familiar "*tú*" of the subtitle) as a subordinate corollary to the abstraction of the official nation. Both images occupy the full page, but split it in two. On the cover, the families beam back from the lower half of the page, where the comic's subtitle (Building for Your Future) traces the lower margin of the image. The square front end of the modern luxury-travel bus shapes the upper half of the page under the bold letters of the title (Half Way There). Inside, the first page is bifurcated at an exact parallel to the cover page, top and bottom half separated by the firm horizontal line of the National Palace cutting across the image. At bottom, the mariachis are foregrounded against an indistinct sea of celebrants that surges with musical notes toward the sharp upward limit of the palace; at top, the national flag shares space with the bold-face title and an inset narrative box explaining the significance of the celebration below. The families (and by extension, the reader) are an instance of a nation managed austerely and handed down from the upper reaches of Mexico, from the top half of the page, as it were.

The narrative thread woven throughout the vague techno-speak of the government report (for example, "Mexico has had a favorable performance and at the same time strengthened its position in the financial markets" [5]) is sustained by the panel-sequencing equivalent of camera work: alternating panels generate a perspectival "cutting" between different scenes—urban and rural landscapes, interior and exterior settings, schools and public parks are displayed in an otherwise conventionally sequential arrangement of comic book panels.

Most of the image panels (rarely more than four to a page) are, in themselves, little more than visual props that support the assertions of the Fox administration's discourse on the nation's well-being. A mention of educational quality, for example, is backed by a scene of diligent children studying at their desks (9); mention of health care "reform" is staged against the backdrop of surgeons at work in the operating room (10). But the "filmic" manner in which the comic book's visual discourse coordinates the reader's perspective with the premise of the storyline allows the images to operate as more than simple illustrations. Thus some panels construct "wide-angle" views of the bus from Nuevo Laredo in motion across the countryside, and these panel frames then transfer the reader's narrative expectations to other panels, suggestive in turn of a passing view from inside the bus. Although many of the scenes presented are impossible to conceive as visible to the bus's passengers, these too are framed, by frequent "cutting" back to the bus or its passengers (which occurs on nineteen separate pages of the comic book), as part of a concurrent national reality that unfolds alongside the travelers' passage from the northern border town south to the capital. By linking official discourse to a variety of social milieus and landscapes, the bus ride provides the narrative pretext for a quasi-omniscient visualizing of the nation.

This same visual coordination of the nation with official power reveals the key elements of the PAN administration's discourse on globalization. On page 12 of "A mitad del camino," the reader encounters one instance of the neoliberal vision of Mexico on the path to globalization (see figure 2.1). Mobility and the technological infrastructure for commerce are presented here as components of a strategy for promoting "equality," but the concept of equality visible in the coordination of the image panels is abstract to the point of being metaphysical. In other words, equality is imagined not as a concrete, social condition but as a rarefied Platonic form—wherein the smiling campesinos in the frame at lower left and the government or business functionaries at lower right can be viewed as inhabiting Mexican national reality at a strict parallel (reinforced by the perfect visual symmetry of their respective image panels), despite the obviously disproportionate financial wealth, social status, and political power enjoyed by the decision makers in the conference room. While the public expenditures on highway infrastructure celebrated in the didactic banner at top are most obviously of interest to those in the business class, who require improved transportation and communication networks in order to operate transnationally in the context of NAFTA, the dialogue between bus passengers asks the reader to

Figure 2.1. "Promoting equality between men and women in all spheres of public and private life is an indispensable condition for development," reads the text at center left. Indigenous campesinos call for the elimination at lower left, while at a visual parallel elite policy makers talk about "defending respect for human dignity" at lower right. From "A mitad del camino," third annual report of the government of President Vincente Fox.

view infrastructural spending as an indigenous rights and rural development program: with highway infrastructure, "One can avoid isolation, which is one of the causes of inequality," comments one of the young mothers.

The emphasis on mobility and technology is repeated in image after image throughout the comic—computers, road construction, manufacturing assembly lines, installation of drainage systems, electrification projects, agricultural machinery, and, of course, transportation technology appear on nearly every page as signifiers of Mexico's modernization. Words like "change," "different," and "transform" are commonplace. Modernity is depicted through this semiotics as in place or in the process of implementation throughout the national territory. But this infrastructural modernity is depicted as the housing for an otherwise staid national subject, oriented obediently around the family and the nation, and geared to strictly economic pursuits. Modernity, in other words, is not embodied in a democratic subject—in a citizen—but in an economic one. And strikingly, with few exceptions, the people portrayed in the comic are whiter and more middle class than the Mexico in which Mexican readers of the comic book in fact live.

It is difficult not to interpret this portrayal as part of an ideological vision of a "properly" globalized Mexico. Much like the classic parameters of modernization theory (see, e.g., Lipset), the Fox administration's vision of the transformation of Mexico imagines not only the nation's adoption of advanced technology and capitalism but also the reinvention of the national subject as the ideal user of that technology and social system—which is to say, as a middle-class consumer and worker in the U.S. style. The U.S. cultural model, the system of meaning through which the nation's development is evaluated, weighs so heavily on this official vision of modernity that the comic book appears to have replaced Mexicans with a more European-looking populace (the demographic profile is frankly more Chilean than Mexican). The visual semiotics of race deployed in the comic can be read as mirroring, on this point, the infamous assertion by a major proponent of the modernization hypothesis: "If country X in Central America, say, were emptied of its inhabitants, and a similar number of Swedes substituted for them, there can be no doubt that in a very short time country X would be fundamentally changed—and obviously in the direction of greater modernization" (Silvert 80).

Adoption of the U.S. cultural model in the form of a middle-class subject of indistinct ethnic heritage allows the comic book narrative to connect the national to the global in strategic ways. When the workers' wives converse about family members' travel to Europe, they are simultaneously linking their personal, familiar experience to global realities, and performing the rational economic decision making theorized as central to capitalist modernity by modernization theorists and globalists alike: "How long were your in-laws in Europe?" asks one woman. "Almost two months. It was a trip for which they saved for years, and they planned it perfectly," responds the other, admiring the rationality of the undertaking more than the trip itself (27). The exchange also invites the visual discourse of the comic to shift beyond Mexico's national borders, as the voice of officialdom announces in the following panel, against the backdrop of Mexico's Ministry of Foreign Relations, that "Mexicans, who travel abroad for a variety of reasons, are pleasantly surprised to find that Mexico today occupies an important place in the world community" (27).

Subsequently, after a mug shot of the NAFTA countries' heads of state in which a speech balloon attributes to Fox an affirmation that "we have sought to deepen strategically our relationship with the United State of America and Canada" (27), the very next page focuses on the most concrete nexus between Mexico and the global order—that is, the U.S.-Mexico border. But the orderly and optimistic border imagined here discloses none of the violence, struggle, political confrontation, illegality, and cultural contradictions that in fact shadow the entire stretch of the binational frontier. A worker at the top of the page, speaking from the U.S. side of the border, reassures the Mexican reader that "the government continues to demonstrate its concern for us Mexicans who live [in the United States]" (28). At the bottom of the page, visually counterbalancing this faint workerism, two young Mexican women stroll through a U.S. shopping mall, dialoguing about the importance of the Institute for Mexicans Abroad (Instituto de los Mexicanos en el Exterior). Their youth, gender, and exposed midriffs (the only hint of sexuality in the entire comic) indicate that a promise of personal liberation—change, difference, transformation, all key tropes of modernity—lies on the other side of the border, and that this liberation is linked to U.S.-style consumerism.

Perhaps most revealing in "A mitad del camino" is the neoliberal conception of governance legible in the comic book. Although the discourse of officialdom and the experience of the working class are represented as cohabiting the same national space, they are nowhere presented in dialogue. Even though the *historieta* itself represents an ideological strategy for closing the breach between elite decision making and the working-class lifeworld, it does not bother to visually represent democracy or a democratic ethos (that is, a model of government designed to resolve that very same breach between the official and the popular). On page 4, the official narrative asserts that "today, Mexico is different, advancing constantly toward consolidating a true democracy." The small image panel to the right of this text depicts the workers' bus slowly climbing a mountain road, an apparent metaphor for the alleged advance toward "true democracy." Here, as throughout the text, the measure of Mexico's circumstances is taken with a technician's metrics. The assertion with respect to democracy, the only point of visual reference for which being two working-class families talking among themselves on a bus ride, shares the page with two large vertical panels in which businessmen chart the economy on a graph in the boardroom, and follow its fluctuations on computer screens in Mexico's Stock Exchange. No other visual support for "democracy" is provided, unless one measures democratic progress by a lower rate of inflation, increased "international reserves," or low interest rates.

The gap between elites and *"lo popular"* is "closed" in effect only by presenting these two as equally Mexican, by joining them in a coeval but not co-equal relationship. As a consequence, "A mitad del camino" reveals at its core a technocratic vision of the nation and its relationship to the global order: elites (public and private authorities mostly indistinguishable in the visual discourse of the comic book) decide how to best organize the infrastructure, productive resources, and wealth of the nation; the Mexican working class lives these decisions, in a manner ethically and politically indistinct from the relationship between scientist and laboratory subject. *"Lo popular"* is certainly present as an ethical claim on this relationship as represented in the comic; but its presence has more of a theocratic or paternalistic quality than a deliberative one. Governing authorities, in both the public and private sectors, can be trusted to meet the needs of the "less favored segments of the population" as a consequence of their technical adherence to neoliberal doctrine, and not because they are responsive to the demands of the popular sectors through any democratic mechanism. The comic concludes with a single, full-page panel depicting the working-class families in the middle-class Mexico City home of Isaac's elderly parents, three generations of Mexicans waving miniature flags and celebrating Mexico's independence in front of a large television screen: a spectator nation removed from the public sphere.

One feels compelled to return to the first page of the comic book, to reexamine the vision of the nation painted there. The perfect symmetry and hierarchy of that initial image is not casual. The official nation is organized against any vestigial threat of the national-popular, of the implicit promise of popular sovereignty that had subtended the legitimacy of PRI rule. The powerful and the "less favored segments of the population" are instead each put in their proper place. Officialdom above and "*lo popular*" below, the institutional order appears as a severe line of demarcation between the national and the popular. But the symmetry, underscored by fireworks and musical notes mirroring each other above and below the horizon of government, also binds together the official order and popular experience. The nature of that relationship as it unfolds in the comic book tells the whole story. "What we all hope for is a government that functions and offers quality public services," observes one of the workers (29). "The federal government is building for the future," asserts the other. "Building for YOUR future," his father emphatically adds (31). In the Mexico of "A mitad del camino," the workers speak on behalf of the powerful, not the other way around.

López Obrador's *Historias* series configures the relationship between official power and "*lo popular*" differently. The first issue of the *Historias* series was published and distributed free on June 7, 2002, under the direction of the Federal District's Office of Citizen Participation, at an approximate cost to the public purse of two million pesos, or roughly one peso per copy of the comic book. The expense was justified, according to Mexico City mayor López Obrador, because of the much higher price of advertising via electronic and print media (Grajeda). In addition to free distribution to two million households in the Federal District, this and subsequent issues in the series would be published online at the government Web site for the district. Although the topical orientation varied with each episode, the basic formula remained the same throughout: the social programs and political prospects of López Obrador are experienced and celebrated in the everyday lives of a cast of Mexico City residents—a young working-class couple, Bertha and Juan; the elderly Tinita; Marisol, a schoolgirl from a poor family, and her stepfather, Luis; an educated middle-age professional named Don Joaquín; Lupita, who owns and runs a restaurant; the wealthy, retired General Dominguez Lizardi and his pampered granddaughter; Susi, a schoolteacher, and her school's principal, Cristina; and Rui, a working-class youth who aspires to be a musician.

In contrast to the Fox administration's happy and problem-free representatives of Mexican society, in *Historias de la ciudad* Mexicans encounter a host of problems, including crime, poverty, broken or dysfunctional relationships, alcoholism, and unemployment. The somewhat sketchy, at times blurred and indistinct visual details of the characters' portraits and the bright but restricted color palette tend to deflect the reader's attention more to the characters' relationships and behavior than to the visual artistry of their rendering, or to their internal, psychic reality. Indeed, the aesthetic center of gravity of the series complements the experience of the everyday presented in the *historietas*, organizing the characters into a soap-operaesque storyline worthy of Mexico's vaunted *telenovelas*. Unlike in the Fox administration's comic book, the dialogue in *Historias* is generally uninterrupted by self-evidently official discourse, despite occasional deployment of statistical charts, letters from the mayor directed to the citizens of the Federal District, or didactic discourse describing official programs or policies.

Instead, what prevails aesthetically is an interpersonal, even gossipy feel to the discourse of the comic. The narrative aesthetic is also an effect of the comic's visual dimension. The cover art of the first issue presents portraits of the central players, a smiling, personalized pantheon framed in a cloud of exhaust from Juan's Volkswagen Beetle, with the modern architectural details of Mexico City's skyline (its colonial features are not visible) looming monumentally overhead. The setting for the series is thus framed not only by the urban built-environment but by the world of individual personalities, biographies, and relationships as well. The greater emphasis on interpersonal dialogue in *Historias* relative to Fox's "A mitad del camino" is reflected in the greater number of image panels per page: typically eight to ten, and sometimes more, in order to accommodate the larger number of characters and their discursive interaction. In addition to this richer dialogue, character and plot development hew closely to the private-sphere preoccupations and interpersonal conflicts of the soap opera genre—and includes the social class–specific details of the Mexican *telenovela* tradition. In representing an enclosed, morally freighted, private-sphere universe of interpersonal experience, the comic book narrative bears a close formal resemblance to Mexico's *telenovela* melodrama (see Estill).

The reader first meets Juan and Bertha—and their infant son—as Juan arrives home eager to show off his Volkswagen *"bocho,"* after he has spent the couple's meager savings to have the car reupholstered in pink and black tiger–striped faux fur. Bertha's frustration with Juan's poor judgment is a consistent theme of the *Historias* series, and Juan supplies throughout a proletarian exemplar of impulsivity, bad planning, class resentment, and flawed financial management. Moreover, Juan's bad taste and judgment serve, from this very first encounter, as a deliberate pretext for thematizing core political values. The middle-class Don Joaquín, who happens upon Juan and Bertha outside arguing about the car's new upholstery, upbraids Juan in clear moral terms: "Nobody has the right to anything unnecessary as long as anyone lacks what is necessary." Juan dismisses this ethical precept on the grounds that it is outmoded, asserting that "nobody thinks that way anymore"—to which Don Joaquín responds in an image panel tightly focused on his demeanor, his gaze firm and reprimanding: "The head of government [i.e., López Obrador] thinks that way" (*Historias* #1, 2).

The primary didactic function of the series, of course, is to explain and defend López Obrador's policies, promoting a broad menu of city government programs—including pensions for the elderly, scholarships for poor school-age children, economic supports for people with disabilities, microlending for small businesses and the self-employed, programs for the expansion of transit and public transportation, as well as health care supports for city residents. On one level, the soap opera format and feel of the series lends itself to exactly this purpose because each character enjoys the benefits of a distinct social program, allowing them to gain control over some element of their personal circumstances. Lupita draws microcredit from the city in order to become a business owner; Marisol's mother receives monthly payments from the city in order to keep the girl in school and out of the informal economy; Tinita has access to affordable public transportation and her pension money; Cristina's permanent physical disability resonates with official supports for people with disabilities; and everyone is relieved by an expanded police presence in the city, which incidentally also provides a job for Marisol's unemployed stepfather, Luis. But the generic narrative conventions of the *telenovela* and its emphasis on interpersonal relationships (instead of on an individual protagonist, for example) also lend themselves to the construction of a determinate ideological perspective, and of a model of governing authority centered on personal morality.

Alongside the troubles of Juan and Bertha, a parallel plot line follows the melodramatic reunion (consummated in issue #2) of Don Joaquín with his lifelong love, the school principal Cristina. Having lost her leg in a terrible accident in her youth, Cristina had abandoned Joaquín in order to relieve him of the burden of his commitment to her. Juan meanwhile plays matchmaker, scheming to arrange a marriage between the financially well-established Don Joaquín and Juan's cousin Susi, which would allow Juan to benefit from a well-off relative's resources. Yet another subplot tracks the amorous interest that develops between the upper-class general's granddaughter, Clara, and the working-class aspiring musician, Rui. These relationships and the components they borrow from the soap opera genre (the melodrama of frustrated desire, fate, personal tragedy, and the boundaries of social class) manage class differences, social desire, and public authority in particular ways. Don Joaquín's middle-class economic philosophy of self-abnegation finds an emotional homology in the fulfillment of a lifelong love deferred but never abandoned. Juan's "low-class" machinations, which evince a get-rich-quick logic, necessarily fail in the face of destiny's reward for the two professionals' abstinence. In the case of the youthful Clara and Rui, love insinuates itself against the grain of social convention and promises upward mobility for the aspiring Rui. In keeping with the moral dimension of the Mexican *telenovela* genre, fate predictably rewards perseverance and good character. Estill's description of the *telenovela* genre fits *Historias* perfectly: "The audience can follow the conventions (I have yet to watch a Mexican *telenovela* in which the evil people do not suffer) and expect certain endings. . . . [L]ove and marriage are the highest reward" (175).

And this is precisely how López Obrador's social programs are legitimated. Consider the manner in which *"lo popular"* is thus structured into the series. The reader's attention is steeped in popular experience: Juan's *"bocho"* is emblematic of working-class life in urban Mexico, as is Lupita's *pozolería*, or popular restaurant serving hominy soup. Similarly representative is Marisol's former subjection to economic necessity as a street vendor of *chicles* (surviving as one of what popular Mexico's black humor refers to biblically as "the children of Adam's," after the chewing gum company whose product they peddle). Bertha's veneration of the recently beatified Juan Diego, the indigenous man to whom, according to legend, the Virgin of Guadalupe miraculously appeared at Tepeyac in 1531, also serves this end. Bertha's relationship to Juan Diego is an especially prominent trace of the national-popular imaginary in the discourse of the *historieta* series. The explicit indigenism of Bertha's private altar to Juan Diego is an important symbolic note struck by the narrative, and her appeals to him to assist her in setting Juan straight (*Historias* #1, 15, #2, 11) are indicative of demands for justice arising from a "less favored segment of the population."

And yet because the drama of the series unfolds almost exclusively within the personal realm of individual desire and interpersonal relations, the indigenist touch never reaches beyond private sentiment into the public sphere, and the issue of economic justice for Bertha (and for Juan) remains a matter of personal choice and individual decision making. Juan Diego, like any *telenovela* character, speaks to the fate of the individual, not of the nation. Similarly, the desires of the series' characters explicitly reference social class, but are contained within the sphere of self-improvement and personal fulfillment.

This privatization of "*lo popular*" is not complete, however. The demand for social justice remains a private concern only for the working class, presumably because a working-class voicing of "*lo popular*" would challenge the central governing authority implicit to a comic book series distributed by the Mexico City mayor's office. Meanwhile, the wealthier and more powerful the interlocutors in the comic, the more public and collective becomes the claim on popular justice voiced by them. Whereas Bertha appeals privately to Juan Diego for personal assistance, and Don Joaquín frames a middle-class financial ethic of personal austerity in language suggestive of a redistributive social justice (and locates the moral authority of the claim in the mayor's office), it is the general who imagines a "different national project," "concerned more with the people and less with money and power" (*Historias* #4, 2). There is a clearly delineated hierarchy, in other words, among the multiple social classes represented by the comic book characters. Governing is a paternal endeavor, and the self-enclosed community of the soap opera–style narrative represents the moral order upheld by the political "father."

One can detect here the presence of political corporatism in the peculiar manner in which *Historias* conjugates public discourse with *telenovela* conventions: the same multiclass cohort of citizens typical of the Mexican soap opera becomes strongly suggestive of the PRI's centralized, multisectoral paternalism: the general—a member of the economic and political elite (signified by his smoking jacket and pipe)—also enjoys a well-deserved, even patriotic status that distinguishes him from the idle rich or the corporate executive. His military background and proposed "national project" appear to be deliberately reminiscent of General Lázaro Cárdenas, father of Cuauhtémoc Cárdenas and populist president from 1934 to 1940, whose administration consolidated many of the social demands of the Mexican Revolution. Don Joaquín is a middle-class professional, educated and gainfully employed, who moves easily between upper- and lower-class strata. Juan and Bertha are lower middle class (the "*bocho*" is an unequivocal class signifier), and Marisol is working poor. Not only do these central characters' ages increase as they move up the class hierarchy, with the general representing a kind of paterfamilias, their moral status in the narrative is self-evidently childlike in the lower strata—as Marisol and Juan both evoke the necessity of some governing supervision.

Not surprisingly, therefore, the *Historias* series holds a dim view of civil society, despite the fact that social life is more detailed and variegated than what appears in Fox's "A mitad del camino." While the first two issues of the *Historias* series had passed mostly unnoticed by the national conversation in

Mexico, issue #3 was quickly elevated to national prominence for this very reason. Arguing that "The Dark Forces" comic revealed a paranoid and authoritarian personality and an abuse of public sector resources, the Mexican right-wing eagerly noted the similarity between López Obrador's *historieta* and a comic book series distributed by Venezuela's controversial populist president Hugo Chávez, *El Patriota*, in which "an indestructible superhero confronts the 'dark forces' of the oligarchy with nothing but a baseball bat" (Sánchez). Mexican cultural critic Carlos Monsiváis's publicized concern about the discourse of the third episode echoed from the Left this concern about the relationship between the comic book series, as official speech, and Mexican civil society. For Monsiváis, "the Manachaeanism of the comic" did not lend itself to "political explanations" (Cancino). Presumably, the simplistic binary political morality of "Dark Forces"—complemented visually by crude black-and-white doodles of López Obrador's enemies as hooded executioner figures—was not conducive to the more reasoned and analytical approach to politics required for citizens' participation in a democratic form of government.

The fourth issue of the series, in which characters discussed the problem of crime and commented on the June 27, 2004, "March of Silence" organized to protest kidnappings and murder in Mexico City, stirred controversy precisely because of its representation of civil society. The headline of a report on the comic in *El Universal* summed up this criticism: "March is ridiculed in comic." The interpretation motivating this criticism centered on the policeman Luis's disrespect for his neighbor, who attended the march, and the attitude of the general's privileged granddaughter, who admits that she attended the march in order to "be seen" (*estrenar*) and to have a photograph of herself taken at the event as a personal souvenir. Most telling, however, was the manner in which the comic book organized the reader's view of the civic protest through the dialogue between the general and his granddaughter.

The comic book format allows the interpersonal and visual dimension of the narrative to corrode the public significance of the march. As her grandfather expresses concern about how the march will distort public perception of the city, the obviously privileged and narcissistic Clara, who appears to be text-messaging on her cell phone, interrupts and comments: "And I wasn't the only one who went to be seen," and, "Being seen is part of my background, remember that I am studying fashion design" (*Historias* #4, 12). Clara's personality, privilege, and self-interestedness supplant the mass demonstration as public discourse. Reinforcing this point, Clara shows the general a photograph of herself with her fashionable friends ("I look good, no?") in the final panel of page 13. The rectangular form of this photo is turned out of alignment with the rectangular form of the panel in which it is displayed, so much so that its upper left corner intrudes into, and is superimposed upon, the large horizontal panel above, in which the reader beholds an aerial view of the massive gathering around the nationally symbolic Angel de la Independencia monument on Reforma Avenue in Mexico City. In governing, it turns out, perspective is everything.

Perspective, in fact, is an ideologically strategic visual element in the representation of Mexican civil societal concerns (see figure 2.2). Of the nine image panels that visually structure the dialogue between the general and Clara on page 12, three use the large picture window of the general's residence as a frame for the characters' speech. At the top of the page, two panels of equal size depict side-by-side the view from inside and outside the general's window, while in the final panel Clara faces the reader with the window behind her, through which an airplane can be seen flying overhead. The perspectives arranged around that window identify relations of power: at upper left, a street-side view from below of the wealthy general's property, on the outside looking in, past the barbed wire of the general's security wall; at upper right, the general's own commanding view of the city, the wealthy and powerful insider looking out, preoccupied with public perception; and at lower right, a third view, referenced by the airplane flyover and by Clara's own discourse ("I would have liked to see the demonstration from the helicopter flying over us"). This third perspective is the view of governing authority as protector. Civil society is not only lampooned in the interpersonal space of Clara's idiosyncratic and petty concerns; Mexican society is also visibly riven by social class, and therefore legitimately subordinated to the "higher" public interest of security. The implicit threat of the "view from below" is visually counterbalanced by the guarantor of public order—surveillance and the "view from above."

Indeed, in *Historias* more advanced modes of transport, like helicopters and airplanes, are not associated with globalization or mobility but with security and governance, as with the helicopter flyover to survey the progress of the Gran Canal water processing project, and to view the future site of the Benito Juárez civic plaza (*Historias* #2, 22–23). Unlike in "A mitad del camino," in *Historias* the localized, interpersonal vantage afforded by the *telenovela*-style narrative never expands to a larger, imagined community à la Benedict Anderson's concept of the nation. An enlarged frame of vision only occurs in flyovers, maps, and sudden shifts to an aerial view of the action or its urban space. Image

Figure 2.2. The general and his granddaughter discuss security and a mass demonstration against crime in Mexico City. "I would have loved to see the demonstration from the helicopter that was flying above us," says the granddaughter in the panel at lower right, reminding the reader of López Obrador's attention to security measures while suggesting that the demonstration was a mere lark for wealthy youth (*Historias* no. 4, 12).

panels framing aerial perspectives punctuate the narrative throughout the series, reminding the reader that the characters' lives are always accompanied by a view from above, a godlike governing perspective, surveying their reality in numerous image panels: Tinita and Don Joaquín walking and conversing on the street (*Historias* #1, 17); Juan's "*bocho*" in traffic (*Historias* #2, 2, 18); expanded, modern thoroughfares around the city (*Historias* #4, 13); the March of Silence at the Angel de la Independencia (*Historias* #4, 13); traffic and pedestrians circulating around the Angel de la Independencia (*Historias #5*, 6); and traffic circulating on major thoroughfares around the city (*Historias #5*, 10). Instead of the space of a national collective project, an imagined community extended beyond face-to-face encounters (Anderson), the comic book imagines the characters within a theater of official operations—a self-contained city-state.

None of the *historieta* characters travel beyond the cityscape; transportation technologies like helicopters and airplanes are not conduits to a global network of social, cultural, economic, and political realities, but are instead signifiers of modernity connected to governance and supervision of the space of the city. Whereas personal mobility in the Fox administration's comic is expansive, transnational, and even presented incredibly as a vehicle for equality, in *Historias* mobility is limited to public transportation between urban sites, pedestrian traffic, the occasional bicycle, and the intraurban travel of Juan's "*bocho*," the movement of which serves as a pretext for a citizen's view of public works projects financed by the Federal District. The global moment is referenced obliquely, in the main, such as with the general's "different kind of national project," which the reader is most likely to assume distinguishes itself from the national project pursued by the Fox administration's neoliberal, proglobalization agenda; or in issue #5, when the entire cast of characters dines with Pierre, the French journalist who is researching the López Obrador administration and who reports that while "some businessmen told me they wanted to remove [López Obrador], . . . the people love him so much" (*Historias #5*, 5).

But globalization per se is never thematized in *Historias*, and in fact its most obvious representative elements—information and transportation technology, foreign nationals, and non-Mexican culture—are present but carefully contained within the boundaries of Mexico City, urban modernization, and matters of public security. The foreign journalist is French, conjuring historical cultural affinities with Mexico City that date to the nineteenth century, instead of the hemispheric political conflicts that would have been conjured by selecting a U.S. journalist for the storyline. And then there is the one eerie moment in which global culture flashes into view: while sitting at a stoplight in Mexico City traffic, Juan suddenly beholds in the crosswalk the British rock band the Beatles. In a long horizontal panel at the top of the page, the Fab Four stride confidently across the broad white hash marks as if they were crossing Abby Road. This image is followed underneath by two tight vertical panels depicting Juan's incredulity, and then another horizontal frame revealing Mexican pedestrians in the same crosswalk. "I think I hallucinated," reflects Juan in this last frame. The visual disruption of everyday Mexican life is never integrated into the narrative, never explained, never discussed. What is most noteworthy in *Historias* is not only that globalization is relegated to the illusory realm of fantasy but that all of the conflicts and debates associated with globalization are made to disappear as well.

The recent emergence of graphic narrative in the Mexican public sphere coincides with the privatization of print media infrastructure with the 1998 sale of the state-owned paper production and distribution company, PIPSA, which had underwritten Mexican print media since the 1930s, including the golden era of the Mexican comic books industry. One likely factor behind the recent public profile for comics in Mexico is that, as one-time opposition parties that now have a claim on government power, both the PAN and the PRD share a strategic interest in communicating with popular sectors that historically had been the corporatist PRI's clientele. Due to the instabilities of post-one-party Mexico, governing interests evidently view the popular cultural medium of the comic book as a strategic public communication tool. The privatization of PIPSA undoubtedly loosened indirect state controls over print media, facilitating the overt political use of the comic book. At the same time, because the very same neoliberal policy directions that resulted in PIPSA's privatization have been widely perceived as contravening nationalist tenets and working-class interests, the problem for governance of legitimacy, of securing the "consent" of the governed, has been exacerbated.

On both counts—political competition for popular loyalties and the necessity of legitimating governance—the comic book offers an important cultural "language" of the Mexican working and middle classes. Within this "language," political actors represent official policy, the nation, and social reality for mass consumption. Understanding the official use of graphic narrative requires placing the phenomenon within the unique context of the sprawling megacity that serves as the federal capital of the republic of Mexico, notably the primary distribution target of the comics examined in this chapter. The mediation of official public authority and leadership is intensely politicized in an urban center that houses simultaneously Mexico's largest concentration of working-class citizens and its largest mass media market, making it central to the cultural politics of globalization. The Fox and López Obrador administrations' *historietas* involve the construction for popular consumption of competing models of political leadership, of the relationship to public authority of popular experience. There are clear formal differences in the use of the *historieta* to impart official discourse to popular Mexico. While Fox and López Obrador both use the popular "language" of the comic book, only *Historias* makes effective use of popular aesthetic "vocabulary" like the *telenovela*'s emphasis on melodrama and the interpersonal dimension of the social world. For its part, the Fox *historieta* contains characters who represent the nation's popular sectors, but their conversations sound like official ventriloquism, and the cultural practices referenced map closely onto a tourist's experience (mariachis, travel, the mall).

The immediate prehistory of these dueling comic books, and of López Obrador's propagandistic use of the superhero *historieta* in the three-issue *PGMan* series, includes an important civil societal precedent: the emergence following the 1985 Mexico City earthquake of an independent working-class social movement, based in the city's barrios, which effectively destroyed the PRI's political hegemony among the working class. In many respects, the Mexico City barrio activists of the 1980s and 1990s pioneered the use of popular entertainment culture as a vehicle for political communication, as seen famously in the "superhero" professional-wrestler mascot of the citywide Asamblea de Barrios, Super Barrio Gómez (Schwarz). Despite the political importance of the independent social movement (or perhaps because of it), civil society in any substantive sense is absent from López Obrador's comics. In López Obrador's *PGMan* series, this absence can be ascribed to the electoral function of the comic—an unmitigatedly personalized conception of power and politics perfectly consistent with an election campaign. The *Historias* series, however, also displays a vision of civil society subordinated to vertical decision making and subsumed by a corporatist ethos.

Unlike the Fox administration's *historieta* (where there is no glimpse of an outside to the neoliberal utopia-in-progress of the globalized nation), *Historias* includes images of opposition to official public authority. But these are presented only in order to manage them as objects in the visual field (the field of public perception, of surveillance, of "being seen") and not as social subjects or agents worthy of acknowledgment or dialogue. Unsurprisingly, neither of the two official comics gives voice to a critique of neoliberal globalization. *Historias* wears the aura of such a critique in the general's vaguely posited "different national project," but the national view from below is so effectively silenced that the global order is never questioned or resisted. The symbolic "we" visible to the reader either carries water for the globalist position or remains mute regarding how the working-class reader might be implicated in the workings of globalization.

LOST IN THE BLUE EYES
OF THE NORTH

El Libro Vaquero Envisions the U.S. Side of the Border

The *historieta* form is consumed predominantly by popular social classes whose cultural representation in official public discourse in post-NAFTA Mexico is used to emphasize an upper-middle-class experience and values in a manner consistent with the U.S. cultural model discussed in the introduction. Despite important conflict among political elites, official discourse generally is cut more to the measure of upper-middle-class sensibilities, even when the comic book is used to give that discourse mass appeal. This explains why the Fox comic book's representation of Mexican workers is immersed in technical economic details and tourism, and why López Obrador's comic book version of the working class is not unionized or politically combative, but supervised by a paternal middle-class and elite hierarchy. Meanwhile, the working-class reader (that flesh-and-blood worker who carries the *historieta* in a hip pocket) most avidly consumes comics whose principal goal is not political propaganda but fantasy and entertainment, and whose narrative and aesthetic dimensions appeal to popular experience and the popular social imagination, even when they do not represent the Mexican worker directly.

The weekly *Libro Vaquero*, published by Nueva Impresora y Editora (NIESA, formerly Novedades Editores), is one such comic book. Whereas official comic books present for popular consumption a tendentious version of national reality and the reader's place in it, *El Libro Vaquero* is a profit-driven, formulaic treatment of the U.S. "Wild West," pitting broad-chested, square-jawed gunslingers

and buxom women against corrupt and menacing villains in the western frontier states of the late-nineteenth-century United States. One could easily conclude that the Mexican reader encounters here nothing more than a fantastical
departure from Mexican national reality, a cultural object designed for escape
from the real, and hence more a flight from the difficulties of the globalized
economy than a commentary on those realities. And yet *El Libro Vaquero* (along
with *El Libro Semanal*, also published by NIESA—see chapter 4) was selected
by the Fox administration's Secretaría de Relaciones Exteriores (SRE; Ministry
of Foreign Relations) as a strategic vehicle for diffusion of an official appeal
precisely to Mexican migrants' sense of transnational reality.

El Libro Vaquero, it turns out, is one of several comic books of choice for
Mexico's transnational labor force, and the comic book's distribution has tracked
the binational geography of this important segment of the Mexican working
class—as available for purchase in New Jersey, Los Angeles, and Chicago as it
is in Oaxaca, Mexico City, and Guadalajara. NIESA's own published data on
Libro Vaquero readership identify 40 percent of its readers as "workers and artisans," and indicate that 22 percent of its readers earn the minimum wage or less
(NIESA.com). The SRE's strategy for communicating with Mexican migrants
underscores the relevance of *El Libro Vaquero* to the politics of globalization. In
2004 the SRE published a didactic *folleto*, or pamphlet, titled *Guía del migrante
mexicano* (*Guide for the Mexican Migrant*), combining *historieta*-style graphics
with explanatory text in a survival guide for Mexican migrants who seek to cross
Mexico's northern border into the United States. The SRE distributed 1.5 million copies of the thirty-two-page *Guide* in both the United States and Mexico.
The text was circulated as a supplement/insert in NIESA's *Libro Semanal* and
Libro Vaquero. These two series are NIESA's most widely circulated publications, and in fact have enjoyed a wider readership than any other magazine published in Mexico (Medios Publicitarios).

The strategy for distribution of the *Guide* centered on two related markets:
the transnational market for cheap labor in the United States, which draws disproportionately from a handful of Mexican states (Oaxaca, Jalisco, Michoacán,
Zacatecas, and Puebla); and the transnational market for cultural goods like *El
Libro Vaquero* and *El Libro Semanal*, which can be found as far north as Minnesota. The target market meant that two-thirds of the first print run circulated
in the states of origin for most Mexican migrants, and additional copies were
distributed to Mexicans living on the U.S. side in New Jersey, Atlanta, and Dal-
las. Distribution of the *Guide* was designed to extend well beyond retail sales

of the *historietas*, since the comics are typically passed along to multiple read-ers beyond the point of purchase. (The *Guide* was also made available via the Internet.) The cultural market corresponding to Mexican wage-laborers' trans-national diaspora also determined the visual aesthetics of the SRE text, which closely mirrors that of the NIESA publications.

The visual dimension of the *Guide* and its relationship to *El Libro Vaquero* construct an informational resource for the Mexican worker who seeks employ-ment in the U.S. labor market. But the contact of the *Guide* with *El Libro Vaquero* is nonetheless politically significant in several ways. First, the *Guide* is evidence of official recognition that public policy operates in a national cultural environment shaped as much by informal, popular experience (and practice) of globalization as by the formal dimensions of the global economy (that is, corporations, capital markets, trade agreements, and so forth). Despite the Fox administration's posi-tive gloss of post-NAFTA Mexico, many Mexicans evidently find it necessary to leave the national territory to find gainful employment. (Former president Carlos Salinas de Gortari in fact promised that NAFTA's implementation in 1994 would so positively benefit Mexicans' standard of living that immigration to the United States would decrease. The opposite appears to be the case.)

Increased migration from Mexico to the United States comes as no surprise to critics of regional free trade policies, who noted worsened conditions for the Mexican working class in the aftermath of NAFTA: a significant decrease in real manufacturing wages between 1994 and 2001, a sharp increase in Mexico's poverty level (from 51 to 58 percent) between 1994 and 1998, and a continu-ously expanding gap between Mexico's rich and poor since free trade became an official shibboleth in the 1980s (Cavanagh and Anderson). And the increased migration northward is a central component of Mexico's political economy: Mexican migrants sent home a reported 3.34 billion U.S. dollars in remittances in the first quarter of 2004 alone, the year in which the *Guide* was published (Authers). The *Guide*'s message and its reliance on graphic narrative as a com-municative channel are symptomatic of these circumstances. Second, the *Guide* operates on a particular object of the Mexican popular imagination—a com-ponent of Mexican national reality that, not coincidently, also appears in *El Libro Vaquero*: namely, the U.S. border region. What could be more politically significant than the *Guide*'s articulation of a Mexican government claim on this central structure and space of the migrants' lifeworld?

The *Guide*'s relevance to the politics of globalization was not overlooked by readers on either side of the U.S.-Mexico border. The *Guide* provoked outrage among certain nationalist sectors of U.S. society, drawing denunciations especially from right-wing activists and politicians of the U.S. border region amid claims that the *Guide* represented an "act of war" on the part of the Mexican government, and encouraged violation of the U.S. legal order (*Washington Times*). Mexican readers encountered in their national newspapers descriptions of the *Guide* as responsibly offering practical advice to migrants—Mexican citizens—regarding the treacherous overland border crossing, tips on avoiding unwanted attention from authorities on the U.S. side, information about their rights, and how to contact the nearest Mexican consulate. Understandably, Mexicans seemed more likely to view the SRE text as an affirmation of Mexican rights (Aguayo Quezada). Although its function is technical and descriptive instead of narratological, the *Guide*'s text is supplemented with comic book–style depictions of migrants, the border, and the institutions that manage the international line. The visual discourse of the *Guide* is indicative of a bureaucratic effort to intervene in the economic informality that haunts institutionalized globalization. And there is perhaps nowhere on the planet where the contradictions between official globalism and unofficial popular practice are more profound than at the U.S.-Mexico border.

How the *Guide* negotiates these contradictions offers a useful benchmark against which to read the politics of *El Libro Vaquero*. As noted, the *Guide*'s graphics bear a strong resemblance to the representational aesthetics of *El Libro Vaquero*. The male migrants depicted wading across the Rio Bravo possess the same muscled physique as many of the male protagonists of the *Vaquero* series (see figure 3.1). Like their *Vaquero* counterparts, female migrants' bodies boast sexualized physical features, such as ample, rounded buttocks and accentuated cleavage. But this *historieta* standard for the rendering of the human form has more than just an aesthetic effect on the representation of the migrant. Skin color is blanched out, leaving no recognizable racial characteristics of the *mestizaje* or the indigenous heritage common to Mexico other than dark hair and eyes. Only the migrants' physical relationship to the border-as-obstacle clearly marks their socioeconomic class position in Mexico (or in the United States), or acknowledges the unofficial realities of globalization.

The migrant of the *Guide* is an abstraction, devoid of any visual anecdote or texture suggestive of specific regional origin, stripped of any discernible motivation for making the crossing in the first place. The *Guide* addresses itself on the first page to the "*connacional*" (conational) who has made the "difficult decision to seek new labor opportunities outside your country." These migrants are not

PELIGROS POR CRUZAR EN ZONAS DE ALTO RIESGO

Cruzar por el río puede ser muy riesgoso, sobre todo si cruzas solo y de noche.

La ropa gruesa aumenta su peso al mojarse y esto dificulta nadar o flotar.

Figure 3.1. "Americanized" migrants cross the Rio Bravo in the Mexican government's *Guía del migrante mexicano* (*Guide for the Mexican Migrant*), published by the Ministry of Foreign Relations, Mexico. The heroic musculature of the migrants mimics that of the frontier characters of the *Libro Vaquero* series. The accompanying text warns of the dangers of crossing the river.

identifiable as indigenous Mexicans making the trek into the U.S. economy from as far south as Chiapas because the poorly capitalized agricultural niche into which they were born in Mexico can no longer sustain a community. Nor are they urban working-class Mexicans who move back and forth across the U.S.-Mexico border as required by the ebb and flow of the labor market, and steady downward pressure on real wages in Mexico. In fact, *lo popular*, and hence in any significant sense *lo mexicano*, has been artfully expunged from the bodies and belongings of these Mexicans, except for the transnational signifiers of the backward baseball cap, tennis shoes, and blue jeans. National identity is thereby reduced to the moment of mutual recognition between citizen and consulate, a moment presented in the front-page graphics under the symbolic authority of the Mexican tricolor. The only moment in the text where an unambiguous identification of the Mexican migrant with national popular culture and experience might be perceived is precisely at the moment of its suppression: the migrant is informed that it is unwise to draw attention on the U.S. side of the border by playing loud music or participating in parties.

The abstract character of the migrant in this text marks clearly again the political distance between the neoliberal state and the national-popular discourse that characterized the revolutionary nationalist state during much of the era of dominance of the Partido Revolucionario Institucional (PRI). The visual language of the *historieta* form possesses little more than a phatic discursive function, opening a communicative channel between the state and popular sectors regarding the experience and practice of the latter in the context of neoliberal globalization. Equally on display, in the communicative content of the *Guide*, is the extremely attenuated agency of the state with respect to shaping, directing, or responding to popular experiences of globalization. The premise of the *Guide* is that Mexicans are crossing the border, and will continue to do so. (Cynically, one might observe that the unstated premise of the SRE text is that this migrancy is the closest thing to a national jobs program available under the neoliberal model.) Working-class response to the globalization of the national economy—flight from the declining wages and employment prospects at the periphery toward better wages and virtually guaranteed employment in the metropolis—is acknowledged, but unexplained, and national contrasts (political, economic, cultural, social) are nearly erased from view. This version of the border, as a zone of physical risk to be traversed in order "to seek new labor opportunities outside your country," presents the "inside" and the "outside" of Mexico as virtually indistinguishable. It is only the geographical boundary in between that is problematic; the Mexican migrant is already Americanized, at least as far as appearances go, and his or her propulsion across the border has no Mexico-specific profile.

So, in what sense is *El Libro Vaquero* relevant to the politics of globalization? Inasmuch as *El Libro Vaquero* entertains the same Mexican audience to which the *Guide* speaks, one may observe that the series conveys an image of the U.S. border region that competes for popular attention with the Mexican government's version of the border. Against the *Guide*'s sanitized presentation of the border as a mere physical obstacle that lies between laborers and a transnational labor market, the Wild West series presents the U.S. side of the border as a violent social space through which individuals move, and are transformed, in pursuit of a better life. In this sense, *El Libro Vaquero* also envisions the U.S. border region as a site in the global economy (and, paradoxically, in the Mexican national economy), but it does so with reference to the nineteenth century and U.S. history and social typology. Drawing upon the popular social imagination and a U.S. national historical frame of reference, the series fashions a view of the U.S. side of the border as a semi-unregulated space of dramatic contest between distinct positions in the social order: masculine and feminine, white and nonwhite, wealthy and poor, political authority and subordination. While the *Guide* either empties the border of such boundaries or recommends their avoidance, *El Libro Vaquero* centers its dramatic fantasies on transgressions against these same social frontiers. This latter observation, however, requires analytical attention to the visual, narrative, and aesthetic discourse of the *Libro Vaquero* series, and the ways in which it develops a relationship between the imagined space of the U.S. side of the border and the social categories and objectives of the Mexican migrant.

The question of what is politically meaningful about a comic book such as *El Libro Vaquero* must be answered, at least in part, by an examination of the text as a system of representation—as an organized arrangement of signs that together are constitutive of a version of reality and a relationship to that reality. This is what was demonstrated at work in the official comics discussed in chapter 2. But, one might argue, the political meaning of those texts was clear because official representations necessarily relate to politics. Nevertheless, that same linkage can be seen on practical display in the representational logic of cultural media generally, wherein entire social groups or conditions may be portrayed in the surrogate figures of narrative, character, and/or visual image. Cultural representation entails the construction or reinforcement of an imagined relationship to the social order, rather than an attempt to "copy" an independent, objective reality in the manner of empirical proposition. Insofar as a particular representation organizes a sense of the social world and a relationship to that world, it tends to have real social effects, and hence a "reality" of its own (see Hall). The politics of this resides in the conflict between a given representation and alternative social perspectives and sensibilities.

The disputable dimension of the "real" connects cultural representation to politics and ideology because, as communication theorists Hodge and Kress observe, the ultimate function of ideology is to secure acceptance of "categorizations of social persons, places, and sets of relations" as true or real (122). A text's ideology (its assertion as universal "truths," ideas, or values that serve particular social interests) is thus operationally linked to what Hodge and Kress refer to as the text's "modality," its appeal to the reader's acceptance of the claims of the message as more or less "real" or "true." When linguists speak of "modality" and "modal markers," they are mainly concerned with elements of speechlike intonation, forms of interpersonal address, verbal modifiers like "may" or "might" or "should"—which raise or lower the audience's social affinity for the speaker and/or the authority of the message communicated. Thus a speaker might "talk down" to an individual or group, employing "modal markers" that reinforce both the authority of the message and the social distance between speaker and audience. Similarly, a speaker might employ other forms of modality (common jargon, for example, or informal means of personal address) in order to construct a high degree of social parity between speaker and audience, as a strategy for authorizing his or her claims. Or the modal quality of a message—say, a questioning intonation, or the use of adverbs like "maybe," or the conditional tense— might subordinate the speaker to the audience while hedging the propositional content of the message.

Although they draw their insight from linguistics, Hodge and Kress develop "modality" as a component of visual discourse as well. As we shall see, the path to the ideological meaning of the *Libro Vaquero* series runs through its "modal cues"—semiotic markers that serve as the basis for the reader's evaluation of how "real" the visual and narrative representation is, and of the social relationships that structure the text. Such cues, in other words, allow the reader to assess both the mimetic value of the text and the social relations it implies (Hodge and Kress, 128). Even though fictional, the *Vaquero* series shapes a view of the U.S. side of the border that is grounded in appeals to a Mexican working-class and *machista* sensibility vis-à-vis social reality. In the process of constructing this appeal, the series does more than simply offer an entertaining, fictional account of the U.S. side of the border to Mexican migrants. It stakes a claim to a set of social categories and relationships that characterize this otherwise foreign space of the U.S. side as a recognizable social reality for Mexican migrants. These categories and relationships put the U.S. side of the border on the ideological map in peculiar ways.

The formal characteristics of the *Libro Vaquero* series contrast sharply with the official comics discussed in chapter 2. The *Vaquero* stories, averaging roughly 100 pages in length, seldom employ more than two panels per page, usually rectangular and horizontal in orientation, in order to establish the sequential axis of the action. Although the presence of more than two panels is rare in the series, the narrative flow is frequently punctuated by single-panel landscape or portrait images, either situating a character within an expansive view of regional geography, foregrounding a character heroically against a natural backdrop, or presenting the character face-to-face with the reader in the manner of a film-style "close-up." Like the official comics examined earlier, the *Vaquero* series employs a varied color palette, but in this case the use of color is more nuanced and combines shading and nonprimary colors to depict a more earthy and rugged, less civilized, environment. Each episode is a self-contained narrative, and most of these involve an itinerant lone cowboy gunman, a female love interest, a town in a U.S. frontier state of the nineteenth century, and dramatic conflict arising from greed, corruption, and/or a will to dominate on the part of one or more characters, or from some personal experience of injustice (rape, robbery, murder, manipulation or deceit, and so forth) on the part of the protagonist.

The series' installments lean on several interlocking modal cues. The representational style of the series emphasizes a high degree of realism, hinging on detailed attention to three-dimensionality. Volume and relative position in space are represented through shadow, vanishing point, foreshortening, and modulation of visual detail to represent distance from the viewer. As noted, the color palette conjures an imagery that is "gritty," thereby indicative of a more "natural" or "objective" treatment of the representation. These elements of visual realism are complemented by the periodic use of full-page splash panels to contextualize the storyline with panoramic views of the landscape. Although modal cues cannot be assumed to be universal standards for evaluation, landscape is a visual genre conventionally accorded a high modal value of "objectivity" cross-culturally because nature and geography are the primary subjects of representation.

Similarly, the portraitlike close-up underscores the subjective "truth" of the stories' characters, the human face signifying conventionally the seat of emotional reality. This latter element is an especially emphatic modal cue when the figure of the person extends outside the margins of the panel frame, a technique often employed in the series to break with the potential visual monotony of the otherwise predictable repetition of uniform frames. Subjective states of emotion, particularly in moments of interpersonal conflict, are conveyed with inorganic background colors, such as pink or purple or black, in which human figures appear to float outside the realm of physical objects. All of these visual elements communicate a close mimetic relationship between the visual representation and a corresponding reality (see figure 3.2).

The combined figures of personhood and geography are especially important as appeals to the reader's sense of reality. Landscape imagery, a feature of every installment of the series, is further secured as "real" due to the setting of the fictional action within a known, nationally specific geography. In one recent episode, "Como buitres hambrientos" (Like Hungry Vultures, 2006), the story opens at "the 'Socorro' prison in the state of New Mexico"; in another, "Sobre cadáveres" (Over Dead Bodies, 2006), the first page is a full-page image of a street scene, including a sombrero- and poncho-wearing Mexican vaquero, and is accompanied by a narrative text: "In 1879, San Antonio, in Texas, was no longer a simple town, but still developing small city, where law and progress were being imposed" (1). Episodes do not always name so explicitly the U.S. state in which the action transpires, but towns usually carry a name (Pine

Figure 3.2. Leena, aka Blues Eyes, defends her Cheyenne husband, denouncing white people's theft of ancestral indigenous lands. "You have brought light to my life, Blue Eyes," says Angry Bear in the top panel. "You speak like a real Indian," observes her Anglo interlocutor in the bottom panel. From *El Libro Vaquero* #1359, 65.

Creek, Cheyenne Junction, and the like) that sharply delimits the setting as Anglophone, and the occasional appearance on the scene of the U.S. flag offers an additional unambiguous territorial marker. All of these textual details combine to invite the reader to accept the fictions as "truthful," while at the same time carefully distancing the reality portrayed from the social world with which the Mexican migrant is most likely familiar.

The historical setting for the series is important in this regard, as it is not uncommon for specific dates to be cited to contextualize the action. The series turns repeatedly to a U.S.-centered historicity as the crux of its realism, embedding the exploits of its heroic cowboys in the overtly referenced post–Civil War context of a nation in development. Here we find a first inkling of the way the modality of the series—such as its grounding of fictional narrative in the received historical record—lends itself to an ideological orientation. Whereas the magnetic north for the revolutionary nationalist model of cultural production consonant with the rule of the PRI had been, for three generations, the Mexican Revolution (1910–20), *El Libro Vaquero* locates its action not only north of the national territory but in the prerevolutionary period as well. The heroes and heroines and villains of the series are all social subjects with no knowledge or awareness of an assertive Mexicanness, not only because they are generally cowboys and gunslingers of the American "Wild West" but also because the Mexican Revolution has not yet happened. The U.S.-Mexico War, on the other hand, has already taken place, making these "Wild Westerners" the social subjects of a manifest destiny working its way toward completion, occupying the border zone as defined in the 1848 Treaty of Guadalupe Hidalgo, which ceded the northern third of Mexico's territory to the United States.

This historical setting simultaneously elevates the profile of a fractious individualism as the foundational ethos of the U.S. side of the border and renders inert the collective Mexican imaginary that would be engaged if a group of Pancho Villa's revolutionary pistoleros were to ride in to the peripheral vision of *El Libro Vaquero* storyline (or if General Santa Ana's assault on the Alamo in San Antonio were referenced). The historicity of the series, a key modal element, is thus managed in such a way as to minimize potential conflict between the Mexican reader's social and political sensibilities (and national allegiance) and the social world depicted in the series. One can easily imagine the political volatility for a Mexican migrant audience of U.S. cowboy stories that directly referenced the violent usurping by U.S. citizens of Mexican land and property in the period following the signing of the Treaty of Guadalupe Hidalgo. And this is no far-fetched counterfactual; Mexican and Mexican American popular culture traditionally encodes precisely these historical experiences in the combative *corrido* musical tradition (see, e.g., Paredes). The ideological necessity of managing the Mexican reader's relationship to the action of the series requires a certain degree of ambivalence in the modality of the texts. Aesthetic realism and historical discourse are charily avoidant of Mexican national history, perspective, and reality. Indeed, many of the elements of realism in the visual plane are also reminiscent of the Hollywood western film genre—the photographic standard of representation thereby simultaneously highly mimetic and highly mythological.

And yet the ideological meaning of the series is not exhausted by this simple transposition of the reader's attention to a foundational political mythology of the United States. If this were the case, there would be no place in the texts for a relationship between the Mexican migrant and the "reality" depicted in the *Libro Vaquero* series. The Mexican reader is, in fact, integrated to the text via additional modal cues that organize the likely degree of affinity felt by the reader for different characters in the stories, cues that also afford a recognition of one's relative position within the social order represented. Upon closer inspection, one can discern amid the relatively realistic visual codes a constellation of more exaggerated, even fantastical, representational strategies that mark the narratives and their characters. Against the backdrop of the modal markers described above, it would be difficult to overlook a system of social classification that includes exaggerated markers of race, class, and sex—in effect, selectively applying popular cultural codes to an extranational social space in order to open up a relationship to the Mexican reader.

Consider the modal dimension of gender in the *Libro Vaquero* series. Larger-than-life sexual characteristics of the female characters—impossibly ample breasts and buttocks on strikingly hourglass-shaped women, who appear at least partly nude in nearly every episode—tend to de-emphasize the "real," at least as referenced by everyday experience. And these hypersexualized female characters contrast noticeably with the mostly male primary and secondary characters that populate the series, males whose physiques are at times Hollywoodesque to be sure, but remain consistent with the broader visual realism of the series. Although male protagonists are square-shouldered and triangularly torsoed, and frequently depicted stripped to the waist, their musculature remains nonetheless within the world of possibility, and in fact presents itself as an instrument (of violence or of labor) for acting upon that world. Male characters are thus more easily related to the ordinary object world and to the historical plane of reality, whereas the women correspond more to a realm of (male) fantasy and desire. One might say that women are "unrealized" in the discourse of the *Vaquero* series, their visual representation placing them out of reach of an empirical sense of reality. At the same time, that same fantastical image of the feminine conjures up a contrast that encourages the reader to "realize," and identify with, the masculine.

Similarly, visual attention to racial characteristics tends toward a more theatrical modality with respect to certain markers of "whiteness": blue eyes and/or blond hair take center stage in most episodes in the series, marking the countenance of hero, villain, or female love interest in virtually every episode. These two racial signifiers appear with a frequency far exceeding any reasonable or realistic expectation with regard to their normal occurrence in the U.S. population. Notably, the bright blue and yellow employed to represent the unambiguously non-Mexican characters are the only primary colors consistently present in the visual plane. These details also figure into a distinction in *El Libro Vaquero*'s visual discourse between objective and subjective realities. Whereas "organic" nonprimary colors, like brown and gray and green, predominate in the series' realistic treatments of the object world, pink, purple, red, and blue are commonly used as ambient background colors in the portrayal of interpersonal conflict and emotional states—that is, the subject world. Blue eyes and blond hair are representational strategies for foregrounding this latter world. Against the otherwise "earthy" and realistic tones of the series' generally nonprimary color palette, the blue eyes and blond hair become glaringly significant—a hyperbolic "otherness" projected out against the Mexican reader's own (national) frame of reference for assessing reality and his or her relationship to it. (In Mexican popular culture, light-colored eyes and hair are viewed as "*güero*," or white, even when accompanied by a predominance of nonwhite phenotypal characteristics.)

These highlighted phenotypal details, underscored further by the frequent use of portrait panels that feature the faces of the characters, therefore express a kind of dual modality in the *Libro Vaquero* series. On the one hand, they represent spectacular embellishment that runs counter to standards of realistic visual discourse followed in other details of the comic book. The strikingly racialized features of the main characters cue a sense of unreality or foreignness in the subject world one encounters in the comic book. On the other hand, the clearly demarcated racial typology of the comic book stridently evokes racial difference as a component of the reader's relationship to the narrative's characters. There is nothing more real than this intersubjective, social distinction for a nonwhite immigrant to the United States. Thus the social relation into which the reader is invited by the series is one where the women are classified as objects of desire, a social categorization that proposes a closer affinity with the masculine agency of the storyline, while at the same time the male heroism (and villainy) is not only racially marked but in such a spectacular fashion that any possible social solidarity felt by the reader must result from some circumspection. Just as the fantastical representation of the feminine serves to instantiate the reality of the masculine, the acute signifiers of whiteness serve to open a position of discernment for the nonwhite reader, "realizing" race as a component of the social world. One is invited to be both masculine and racially self-aware in relating to the social world portrayed in the comic book.

The aggregate of modal cues positions the reader in a relationship of high affinity with the masculinity of the male hero, while inserting a racialized separation between Mexican reader and U.S. protagonist. Blue eyes are a crucial modal marker: they signal a subjective reality and experience that stands outside the lived experience of the typical Mexican reader. The moral struggle that occurs in the space north of the U.S.-Mexico border, its terms and stakes, are thereby to be recognized as arising categorically from that Other nation, where a certain kind of individual faces certain kinds of conflicts with certain other kinds of individuals. Although the Mexican reader is invited by one set of modal cues to identify with this masculine model of moral agency, the usually blue-eyed distinction of the heroic U.S. subject (and of his villainous antagonists) also summons a subjective sense of national difference through the racialized aesthetics of color. One can almost feel the scene of reading, where the Mexican migrant looks into the comic book hero's eyes and is reminded that the gaze is cast across the international border. Through the magnified semiotics of race, the reader is asked to recall that his or her own social position is indirectly at stake whenever he or she witnesses this Other nation struggling with racial differences in the interpersonal drama of the *historieta*.

An analysis of a *Libro Vaquero* episode, paying careful attention to the modal dimension, is the best way to demonstrate how the ideological operations of the comic book series tend to invite the reader to enter into a particular relationship with the social reality depicted. The imaginary deed of entering into a relationship with the cultural representations of the *Libro Vaquero* series corresponds closely to a sociocultural phenomenon of the U.S.-Mexico border, a border ethnographer Pablo Vila describes thusly: "[P]eople changing countries are not only crossing from one country to another, but are also moving from one national system of classification to another—both systems in which they have a place. In changing their country of residence, immigrants expose themselves to a new set of expectations about their attitudes and behaviors, expectations to which they must respond by constructing a social identity that has meaning in this new social context" (81). The visual and narrative discourse of the *Vaquero* series invites the migrant to construct that social identity within a particular ideological frame.

"Viejos rencores" (Old Grudges, 2006) is an especially useful episode because it is rich in modal cues, due to the presentation within the storyline of different characters' own narrations. In the opening pages, the reader is introduced to Titus Granger, an opportunistic civilian ally of Captain Bolland, a U.S. Army officer in charge of the local campaign to capture the Cheyenne rebel Angry Bear. As Bolland and Granger discuss over drinks their efforts to capture the Cheyenne warrior, a stranger walks in and confronts Granger. As it turns out, Angry Bear has taken the stranger's fiancée, and the stranger now competes with Granger to track down the Indian. A fistfight ensues, during which the reader discovers that Granger and this second man, a self-described "simple cowboy" named Gus Campbell, have also competed for the affections of the fiancée, Leena Sullivan, who was taken by the marauding Cheyenne under Angry Bear. The conflict between these two (blue-eyed) men is the axis around which the story develops. The honest and forthright Campbell and the underhanded and self-serving Granger compete to eliminate the Cheyenne rebel from the local landscape, Granger motivated by money and Campbell by a more pure interest in love and honor.

The story of the subsequent hunt and capture of Angry Bear is collated with a series of three personal flashbacks, visually demarcated as subjective reminiscence by the use of rounded, cloudlike corners for the panel frames, and by a color fade in the images, modal cues suggestive of additional distance between the visual representation and the reality of the comic book's historical present. First, Campbell explains himself to Captain Bolland by narrating his long-standing, class-based rivalry with Granger ("We grew up near each other, but we were never friends because he was rich and I was not"); his romance with Leena, a wealthy rancher's daughter who had been promised to Granger but loved Campbell; and then the Cheyenne assault on the Sullivan ranch that resulted in Leena's kidnapping. Finally, as Campbell explains, his pursuit of Angry Bear had been interrupted by the Civil War, which deepened the antagonism between Campbell and Granger, because Campbell fought on the side of the Union against the Confederacy, while Granger—"because he was rich"—became an officer in the Confederate army (11–22).

Immediately following Campbell's testimony, Granger recounts his own story to the prostitute with whom he left the bar. (Campbell's narrative is accompanied by an idealized Leena in a Cinderella-like pink gown; Granger's female companion is a nude whose sexual assets are wildly disproportionate to human physical norms.) From Granger's point of view, the same period of history is immersed in rank bitterness and angry personal entitlement. He does not retell the loss of Leena to the Cheyenne, only his competitor's efforts "to take her from me." While Campbell only reluctantly participated in the Civil War, Granger's commitment to the Confederacy is presented as strong. Instead of the Cheyenne assault on the Sullivan ranch, he recalls his surrender to Union troops, and with obvious rancor. "[Campbell] was among my enemies," recounts Granger in a panel that foregrounds several African American Union soldiers who gaze upon Granger's surrender, "mocking me when I had to lay down my arms at the end of the war" (24).

The class-based antagonism between the two men is here linked to race and racism, a link cemented by the prostitute's defense of the impoverished Campbell's allegiance to the Union side: "I was from that social class," she relates in a panel filled by her face, eyes looking down and away from the reader, "and I remember that we poor people were viewed by the rich as barely better than the Blacks" (25). This is the first of two occasions in which Granger's narrative is contradicted, the second occurring when Granger presents his current wealth as a consequence of his hard work. It seems the defeat of the Confederacy reduced even Granger to poverty, which he overcame by "making my own way in life and coming to have all that I have now." His personal story is interrupted here by the comic book's narrative voice, presented above a vertical half-page panel showing Granger robbing a bank. "Of course," the reader is told, "the man did not mention his first steps in getting easy money" (28).

Truth-telling and the truth are key moral values embedded in these narratives, as the moral character of the person is the driving force behind the conflict on display. It is noteworthy that the visual representation of the characters' storytelling does not hedge or significantly distort the claims made by these characters. They are, in a word, believable, but their veracity can be called into question, as it is in the case of Granger. In fact, in virtually every episode of the *Libro Vaquero* series there are untrustworthy, and hence questionable, characters whose dubious morality is typically the trigger for conflict in the storyline. The manner in which these characters are presented marks them as dubious for the reader by significantly lowering the reader's affinity for them, as with Granger. The reader is "saved" from believing Granger's mendacity by the intervention of the narrator, and by other characters with whom the reader enjoys greater solidarity. Here again, a connection is drawn between modal cues and ideology.

The least trustworthy characters pose the greatest threat to the moral order; the most believable characters are the most likely agents for a reassertion of the threatened moral order.

In keeping with this schema, in the end Angry Bear surrenders and leads his people to life on the reservation, but not before Granger attempts to murder both Angry Bear and Captain Bolland, planning to make it appear that the Indian attacked Bolland and then was killed by Granger, who would thus be the sole recipient of the $10,000 reward for Angry Bear's capture. Only the unplanned-for presence of Campbell—the trustworthy "poor cowboy" who has never been interested in the reward money—thwarts Granger's latest scheme for "getting easy money." This denouement is framed, however, against the backdrop of a third personal testimony: that of the shared object of desire, Leena, who has become Angry Bear's wife. Her narrative overlaps Campbell's, but augments his by filling in a personal experience to which he did not have access. His earlier story of the savage, marauding Cheyenne is supported in the main, and only modified by her tale of Angry Bear's heroic defense of her honor when men from his tribe attempted to rape her. Notably, she does not contradict Campbell's testimony, only humanizes Angry Bear, who, she reports, offered to return her to her own people. Granger retorts, "What!? And why didn't you accept that damned Indian's proposal!?" (62)

Leena responds in a two-panel sequence (see figure 3.2) that first recalls her decision to stay with the Cheyenne, emphasizing her own traditional role as wife and mother, and then criticizes the white spoliation of indigenous lands. The juncture of the two panels underscores the truthfulness of Leena's speech. The memory panel, with her voice narrating in the upper left text box, emphasizes a close correspondence to the realism of the comic book's overarching storyline. The comparatively faded image represents the mimesis of memory, at one additional remove from the comic book's depicted reality, but there is no other suggestion of distortion. The rectangular frame is intact, without the rounded, cloudlike borders of the other characters' narratives in the episode, and there is no other narrative voice to contradict her story. Leena is evidently a truth-teller here. The contrast between this panel and the one at the bottom of the page is sharp, and emphatically affirms Leena's response to Granger's racist question. In the lower half of the page, her countenance breaks through the frame, as if leaning out into the three-dimensional space of the reader, and the physical reality around her is replaced by a hot violet radiance, signifying her ardent, emotionally charged, personal defense of her husband: "I have respected my husband and his struggle to live in his way on the lands of his elders, which the white people have taken from him unjustly" (65).

Yet this latter comment on U.S. history and society is distinguished from the truth of Leena's narration of her personal history. Her more "factual" assertions at the top of the page (that she has had three children with Angry Bear) contrast with her passionate speech at the bottom of the page, speech marked as strongly subjective, even idiosyncratic, by a collection of modal cues. The background color, which is similarly employed on several occasions throughout the story to frame verbal or physical attacks, codes Leena's speech as personalized and redolent with emotion and militancy. At the same time that her dramatically blue-eyed and blond-haired Anglo visage foregrounds the personal commitment of her testimony, her obvious "whiteness" combines with the man's exclamatory retort (we don't know which one) in the upper right corner of the frame to create a discursive ambivalence, the truth-value of her speech both supported and undermined: "You speak like a true Indian woman!" (65).

Thus a critique of U.S. power and territorial claims is partitioned and contained, modulating this view of political reality in such a way as to partially neutralize the racial, and national, parameters of Leena's assertions. The Mexican reader is encouraged to sympathize with the plight of the Cheyenne, but not to identify with it. (By way of contrast, imagine how incendiary Leena's declamation might be for a Mexican reader if her features could be interpreted as Mexican, and thus seen to reference a shared subjective reality cementing the reader's solidarity with her denunciation of U.S. power and domination.) The personal advocacy of indigenous rights is much safer, because far more "other," coming from Leena—or Blue Eyes, as Angry Bear calls her in the upper panel at right: "You have brought light to my life, Blue Eyes" (65).

Blue eyes emerge through the narrative as an ambivalent sign of intersubjective struggle. The blue-eyed Campbell, the hero of the story, is in conflict with the blue-eyed Granger, the villain, over the blue-eyed Leena, who has sided with the Cheyenne. The national subject world conjured in this blue-eyed image of the North is riven with moral discord: greed and personal enrichment face off with love and honor, deception runs headlong into righteous testimony. Although such conflict is fundamentally personal, removed in a sense from the public sphere or collective concerns, the blue eyes focus the reader's attention on the social dimensions of the moral clash, and its racial aspect especially. The humble, hard-working cowboy's (blue-eyed) embodiment of the United States collides with that of the wealthy, criminal racist. Their blue eyes mark them as the same (that is, in national identity) despite their moral and social differences. The narrative's references to social class, and the appearance of the African American Union soldiers in the foreground in the image of Granger's surrender, remind the reader of the social (and racial) stakes of the battle between the two.

Meanwhile, although Campbell's code of personal honor wins out over Granger's greed in the end, the cowboy nonetheless loses his one-time fiancée to the defeated Angry Bear. The decision of "Blue Eyes" to remain with the Cheyenne even as the tribe is escorted to a subjugated life on the reservation is also a matter of love and honor, an evidently selfless act of loyalty that cannot possibly benefit Leena personally. As moral order is restored through the resolution of the narrative, an image of the northern nation takes shape. On one level, this is a conservative, status quo image of racial and sexual hierarchy. The white woman accepts her place as a subordinate to her man; her indigenous man accepts his place as subordinate to the white man; the subversion of the ex-Confederate officer is exposed and destroyed; and the U.S. Army reasserts its authority. Ultimately, only Gus Campbell emerges as a dominant sign in the subject world: "I will return to my work, which is the only thing I have in life" (89). As Campbell rides away in a final full-page single-panel image, a U.S. Army officer comments, "It's not every day that one meets a man truly worthy of respect" (91). The Mexican reader finds an opportunity to identify with the moral order of the North through Campbell's (moral) character. Amid the ethical and social schisms of the U.S. side of the border, Campbell is the blue-eyed embodiment of what is morally right.

In the final analysis, moral crisis is revealed and resolved at the level of the individual subject. Leena's blue-eyed defense of native peoples is distanced from a national and/or racial politics because of the degree to which it is subordinated to an interpersonal sexual politics. But the fact that Leena's primary allegiance is to her man rather than to her race or nation also serves as an invitation for the Mexican reader to perceive in her, both despite and because of her pronounced racial otherness, evidence of a certain plasticity in the system of racial classification reigning beyond Mexico's northern border. (Her earlier love for the working-class Campbell signifies a parallel transgression against social class boundaries.) At the same time that her character enables the "realization" of masculinity discussed above, her blue-eyed loyalty to her racially and economically subordinated man, fiercely held over and against dominant national/racial norms, opens up a legitimate place in the northern social world for a nonwhite, "second-class" masculinity. The story is thus a story of triumph for a work-oriented, male-dominated, multiracial morality available deep in the blue-eyed reality of the North, all the while preserving the moral legitimacy and social hierarchy of that Other nation. The class-specific, racially conscious, and masculinist elements of heroism and villainy, of disruption of the moral order and its reaffirmation, offer numerous points of entry into U.S. reality for the Mexican reader.

Leena's conspicuous transgression against the social order, crossing otherwise firmly established, even rigid, social boundaries, is not a rare occurrence in the series either. In fact, story lines involving white women falling in love with Native Americans have constituted a significant subgenre in the *Libro Vaquero* series for some time. In "Extraños Enemigos" (Strange Enemies, 1999), for example, a white woman kidnapped by the Comanche later helps her Comanche captor and suitor escape after he is subdued by the U.S. Army. The woman's violently possessive white boyfriend is killed by her Comanche lover in a final confrontation. "Venganza Natural" (Natural Vengeance, 2000) tells of a Sioux chief who kidnaps a white woman as part of his plan for tribal survival via assimilation to "white customs." Through the heroic actions of a white U.S. Army officer, the competing bellicose plans of other Sioux are defeated, and the noble Sioux chief and his white bride consummate *mestizaje* as social progress in the end. "Hermandad Sagrada" (Sacred Brotherhood, 2001) ends with a former U.S. Army officer, now unemployed cowboy, riding into the sunset in search of his newfound love Light of Dawn, a Sioux woman he had rescued from racist white would-be rapists.

This kind of social boundary transgression frequently extends also to other social categories. To offer a few recent examples: "El Color del Mal" (The Color of Evil, 2006) tells the tale of a black cowboy who becomes sheriff of a racist western town, and then discovers that he is doing the bidding of a manipulative (blue-eyed) white mayor whose apparently progressive racial attitudes disguise an abuse of official power. "La Mano de la Venganza" (The Hand of Vengeance, 2006) offers a story in which a young ranch hand is nearly murdered by his boss for sleeping with the rancher's daughter, and then takes justice into his own hands when the rancher continues to flout the law. "La Mujer del Bandido" (The Bandit's Woman, 2007) features a woman who becomes a pistolero to be reckoned with, besting her male enemy in a gunfight in a closing scene (leaving him on his back with legs splayed wide like a "feminized" sexual conquest). In these few examples, one can see the two faces of the *Libro Vaquero* series—a moralizing orientation to the social status quo, joined to a transgressive dramatic sensibility, explicitly violating hierarchies of the same social order it presents as context for the action. In other words, social boundaries and hierarchies of all kinds—racial, sexual, moral, class—are sharply drawn and carefully conserved in the visual aesthetics and narrative arc of the series. And yet within this semiotic structure—that is, as an aggregate of binary oppositions paraded through the reader's visual field and coordinated in the story arc—the drama of *El Libro Vaquero*'s narratives frequently flows from symbolic border transgressions. The failures and successes of these social border crossings most entertain the reader's imagination.

That all of this transpires on the U.S. side of the U.S.-Mexico border is suggestive of a textual mediation of the Mexican migrant's imagined relationship to the border crossing. Transgression is presented as a fact of life in the northern nation, one that carries clear dangers, but also represents real opportunity. The themes and plot structure of "Viejos rencores" are consistent with a formula legible across the broad range of *Libro Vaquero* episodes. The working-class heroes who triumph in some way in most episodes are one ingredient of the formula. Another ingredient is the pronounced and violent quality of moral danger. Still another is the manner in which deception is the public face of moral threat. All of these narrative elements are consistent with what sociologist of culture Herbert Gans has described as "low culture"—that is, cultural production serving the symbolic wants of lesser educated, working-class subjects. "Low culture content thus depicts how traditional working-class values win out over the temptation to give in to conflicting impulses and behavior patterns," and "is often melodramatic, and its world is more clearly divided into heroes and villains" (Gans, 116). Although Gans's observations were developed for the U.S. popular cultural environment, they closely match the *Vaquero* series' aesthetic characteristics and readership.

Emblematic of this social class–specific aesthetic, *Libro Vaquero* episodes typically end with a full-page splash panel that refers the story's resolution to a future moment of personal fulfillment. The protagonist, having passed through the tribulations and risks of the morally vexed social world of the United States, contemplates the possibilities of a better life. Generally, this entails, in the words of one cowboy hero, "to be able to start over in another place" ("Como Buitres Hambrientos," 90). Intriguingly, these final projections of the good life frequently involve fantasies of biracial love and family, as when the black ex-sheriff of the racist town of Pine Creek imagines himself as the lover of Susan, a white teacher who leaves town in frustration over local racism: "Perhaps one of these days we might come together in beautiful babies the color of coffee with cream. . . . After everything that has happened, something good might result from coming to Pine Creek!" ("El Color del Mal," 91). Narrative resolution, in other words, proposes something more than just the Manichaean triumph of good over evil and the elevation to moral prominence of a modest, persevering subject. Beyond the conflict and danger of the narrative, the protagonist moves forward like the cowboy hero in "Sobre Cadáveres"—"with some hope in the future" (89).

In this way, the *Libro Vaquero* series also positions its representation of the border in a relationship to the migrant's pragmatic objectives, which include passage through a dangerous foreign space toward economic and social opportunity. *El Libro Vaquero* operates differently from the official comic books discussed in chapter 2. In the overt content of the comic book, Mexican national reality is abandoned both geographically and historically, and there is no representative of a proletarian contemporary for the Mexican reader. In *El Libro Vaquero*, the working-class reader finds not himself or herself represented, but a monumental structure of Mexican working-class experience after NAFTA: namely, the U.S. side of the U.S.-Mexico border. What semiotic analysis refers to as the modality of the comic book—the text's implicit appeals for the reader to consider its characters and scenery and drama more or less "truthful" or "realistic"—is key to understanding how the *Vaquero* series, no matter how apparently fictional and contrary to present-day realities, enjoys an organic relationship to Mexican popular experience and social imagination.

Whereas the government's *Guide for the Mexican Migrant* underscores the physical dangers of the border crossing, and the legal dangers of seeking work on the northern side of the U.S.-Mexico border, *El Libro Vaquero* emphasizes the moral dangers, and promise, of that same social territory. In the *Vaquero* series, the Mexican side of the border is generally absent; action typically occurs within the United States. The international border itself, in fact, is simply not a factor in the plot. At the same time, borders figure prominently in the narrative structure of the series formula. Importantly for the politics of globalization, an implicit assumption of U.S. moral and cultural leadership is structured into the blue-eyed morality on display, where regular folk are always setting things right before the law, confronting predatory behavior, and contradicting social norms when morally required. When the subjugated Angry Bear declares, "You have brought light to my life Blue Eyes," one need not be a Gramscian theorist of hegemony to notice the substitution of historical domination with an image of moral consent. At the same time, anyone familiar with the Italian Marxist

Antonio Gramsci's concept of ideological dominance as moral and political leadership can see how this clearly applies to the morally freighted portrayal of the United States in *El Libro Vaquero*. Unlike the SRE's guide, which warns the reader about the physical dangers of the border crossing, and largely avoids representations of U.S. society and culture, the *Vaquero* series trains the reader's eye on the moral dangers, and social promise, of the nation to the north.

NEOLIBERALS ALSO CRY

El Libro Semanal and the U.S. Cultural Model

Two young Mexicans, Marco Antonio and Adriana, sit aboard an airplane en route from Canada to Mexico City. She left Mexico after her father died, and completed a university degree in Canada. He was her childhood friend, and bought her father's business shortly before the elder man's death. They have issues. (She doesn't trust his motives.) The scene of their dialogue is displayed in a series of horizontal panels, two per page, the characters and their environment rendered in detail, if somewhat stiffly, in a brownish ink. The perspective alternates from panel to panel between views of the interior and exterior of the plane. This visual sequence generates a sense of movement by breaking away repeatedly from the static surrounds of the first-class cabin ("Adriana and Marco Antonio were traveling in Executive Class," the narrative text helpfully points out). Alternating views of the plane track the flight of Marco Antonio and Adriana through the ether, reminding the reader that they inhabit the pure global space of international transport. Meanwhile, the characters' dialogue floats curiously between the interpersonal concerns of a budding romance and the pecuniary interests of a transnational business class:

> **ADRIANA**: The company continues the same as always, right?
> **MARCO ANTONIO**: It has grown, I now have sawmills in Durango and Sonora. Adriana, I have expanded thanks to our strong currency. I have a well-paid and efficient staff, that's why I want you to work together with me.
> **ADRIANA**: I owe you the money you lent me for my university expenses.

MARCO ANTONIO: You don't owe me anything. That's how things are, they are never done without reason, there is always a purpose, and there are powerful motives that force situations that don't always have a clear explanation.

ADRIANA: Are you referring to you and my father?

MARCO ANTONIO: I am referring to everything. I would like you to understand it without my having to state it so clearly. Feelings push you to do things that you might not have wanted to do. It was easier to forget everything and run away, seek out a new life, seek out new horizons. ("El Interesado," 133–36)

Marco Antonio is a beneficiary of NAFTA: his northern Mexico sawmills are well positioned to compete for the U.S. market for lumber, and his cognizance of this fact is reflected in his comment on the strength of the peso (undoubtedly making technological "inputs" more affordable). His admittedly vague discourse on fate seems to do double duty as business philosophy and guide to matters of the heart. "Feelings" indeed. Adriana, who came to distrust the young businessman upon learning of his purchase of her father's legacy (in effect disinheriting her), is eventually persuaded that "if [Marco Antonio] did not buy what my father was selling, my inheritance [*patrimonio*] would have ended up in strange hands" (137). In the end, the "powerful motive" of self-interest develops a double countenance—revealing itself as both amorous desire and the profit motive, family values and market values—and then falls in love with itself all over again. A Mexican family legacy is salvaged by a successful Mexican business, and a new family is begun.

These characters' reflections on the role of "feelings" in business calculus—including trace elements of Mexicanidad and anxieties over lost "*patrimonio*," which is also the term Mexicans use for national heritage—precede the romantic climax of yet another episode in NIESA Editores' popular weekly *historieta El Libro Semanal* (The Weekly Book) series. The *Semanal* series provides a weekly book-length storyline (typically in excess of 100 pages) organized around a specific lesson in personal morality. Storylines are usually set in contemporary Mexico, and commonly follow the romantic desires and personal ambitions of Mexican characters, whose failure to abide by gendered codes of honor and sexual morality exposes the protagonist to the risk of failure in love, business, and/or professional advancement. In the words of *Libro Semanal* editor Rubén Monsalvo Carreola, "[W]e advise the reader against falling into those errors.

That is how most of our stories are handled. We always give the wrongdoer their punishment. In contrast to the serial novel, which narrates a story chapter by chapter, the *historieta* presents stories with a beginning, development and ending in each issue, and it is centered on the family and the couple" (López Parra, 44). The commercial success of this formula dates to 1952, when the series began publication in monthly installments under the title *El Libro Mensual* (The Monthly Book). The success of the monthly magazine allowed it to become a weekly soon after, in 1956.

The long-term success of the *historieta* series undoubtedly had something to do with the political ties of its publishers, the O'Farrill family, PRIista loyalists through the latter half of the twentieth century. The O'Farrills owned NIESA's predecessor, Novedades Editores, which for more than half a century had published the daily newspaper *Novedades* and Mexico City's the *News*, the most widely distributed English-language newspaper in Latin America, until both ceased publication in 2002. (Indeed, the revenues generated by its *historieta* publications allowed Novedades Editores to continue publishing its newspapers, even though these were not profitable.) Due to state supports for domestic cultural production through the 1980s, a politically connected enterprise such as Novedades Editores was able to benefit from privileged access to subsidized newsprint, and even favored promotion from other PRIista media, like the monopolistic Mexican television company Televisa. On the eve of the historic 2000 elections, it was revealed that the O'Farrills had prohibited the *News* from reporting on the campaign of Vicente Fox, who by then represented a clear threat to the longtime political control of the Partido Revolucionario Institucional (PRI). Josh Tuynman, the American editor of the *News* who resigned in protest over the O'Farrills' restrictive editorial policy, later explained to a U.S. journalist that the publisher's censorship of its news staff extended to "stories about gays, anything that can be interpreted as pro-abortion," and "there was a ban on reporting on the Zapatista rebels . . . and no attacks on the Catholic Church" (Morgan).

The O'Farrills, in other words, represented a case study in conservative inclusion in the PRI's political hegemony. NIESA's *Libro Semanal* and *Libro Vaquero* series have for many years been the two most widely distributed magazine publications in Mexico, each individually representing a significantly larger readership than the influential magazine of Mexican news and politics, *El Proceso*. In recent years, the annual distribution of each of the two *historietas* has been calculated at 41.6 million copies per year, more than five times the annual distribution of *TV Guide* in Mexico (Gutiérrez). In both of these widely read NIESA series, the social reality depicted in the comic book is replete with moral conflict, and the resolution of that conflict positions the reader in an imagined social world frequently alien to his or her own immediate life experience—at least as regards the profile of a *historieta* reader, which, according to the recent national survey of Mexican readers conducted by the Mexican government's Consejo Nacional para la Cultura y las Artes (National Advisory for Culture and the Arts), is most likely to be very poor to middle class (Consejo Nacional, 25–26). NIESA's own published data identify 52 percent of *Libro Semanal* readers as "housewives," and an additional 11 percent as "workers and artisans." For both of the series, 62 percent of the readership reported income of four times the minimum wage (about $25 per day) or less (NIESA.com). While the *Libro Vaquero* series presents the nineteenth-century U.S. frontier region as a staging ground for a wary but accepting relationship between the Mexican migrant (or potential migrant) and U.S. social reality, the *Libro Semanal* series turns the reader's gaze and fantasies toward the upper strata of modern Mexican society.

Both comic books enjoy a large transnational migrant readership, which is the most concrete connection between these *historietas* and the problematic of globalization in Mexico. But each series also lends itself for consumption as a distinctive culturescape—that is, a unique way of organizing a perspective on the relative position within the global order of different kinds of people, nations, and cultures—in this case by brokering a relationship between Mexican popular sectors and specific discourses of globalization. With *El Libro Vaquero*, we saw how U.S. power and moral promise are projected through fantasies of the nineteenth-century frontier region constructed around hierarchical categories of race, class, and sex. With *El Libro Semanal*, the principal social axes are class and sex, but the most salient connection to globalizing forces is the comic book's celebration of an upper-middle-class *habitus*—Pierre Bourdieu's term for the set of attitudes and predilections embodied by a social class—that is central to U.S. commercial culture and its global diffusion. In addition to these clear thematic differences, there are important aesthetic differences between the two NIESA series, formal contrasts that correspond to a divergent readership: according to the publisher, 90 percent of *Libro Semanal* readers are women, housewives in particular (López Parra, 43). If *El Libro Vaquero* demonstrates an affinity for the Hollywood western, *El Libro Semanal* bears a close aesthetic kinship to the Mexican *telenovela*.

The discursive and ideological niche occupied by *El Libro Semanal* is delimited by the manner in which the comic book brings together a Mexican popular cultural aesthetic with a representation of the individualism, leisure, and accumulation of wealth that are the core principles and promise of capitalist development, and of U.S.-led economic globalization. These latter elements are, of course, identifiable in official U.S. discourse on globalization, as when the U.S. *Country Commercial Guide* for Mexico (2007) observes: "Mexicans are drawn to the United States because of its destination diversity, infrastructure and excellent travel and tourism services. In particular, Mexicans enjoy destinations that offer shopping, gambling, entertainment, amusement parks and a cosmopolitan environment" (50). This broad generalization about Mexicans and their desires applies most accurately to those Mexicans with the leisure time and disposable income necessary to travel outside their country to go shopping. (Massive undocumented labor immigration suggests that most Mexicans who travel to the U.S. are doing so for reasons other than its "destination diversity.") In other words, the official U.S. image of Mexico and Mexican desire is a tenuous construct, arising more from neoliberal ideology than from Mexican national reality. But this way of talking about Mexican reality organizes a specific view of the country, and something of this view is present in *El Libro Semanal.*

The same U.S. report unveils the other component of its commercial optic (and one catches a glimpse of contradiction with the earlier celebration of cosmopolitanism as the main attraction drawing Mexicans to the United States) in its euphemistic comments on the high rate of unemployment in Mexico: "There is a large surplus of labor in the formal economy, largely composed of low-skilled or unskilled workers" (U.S. Department of State 2007, 88). One can safely assume that these Mexicans are more likely to be readers of *El Libro Semanal* than of the U.S. State Department reports. But although the U.S. *Country Commercial Guide* for Mexico directs information about middle- and upper-class Mexican consumption (and cheap Mexican labor) to a U.S. investor class, *El Libro Semanal* operates at a kind of inverse parallel—offering up a vision of middle- and upper-class Mexican society for consumption by working-class Mexicans. Despite their many obvious differences, both *El Libro Semanal* and the *Country Commercial Guide* place private wealth and consumption at the center of their conception of the properly organized society. The distinct manner in which the *historieta* series accomplishes this remains significant, however, and offers some insight into how conservative discourse in Mexico attempts to "nationalize" neoliberal doctrine.

The core principles of U.S.-led globalization are articulated not only through the explicit declarations of U.S. power but also implicitly in other cultural media. Whereas *El Libro Vaquero* closely relates to the participation of working-class Mexicans in the transnational labor market consolidated through the implementation of NAFTA, *El Libro Semanal* bears a close family resemblance to the Fox administration's neoliberal narrative of Mexican progress discussed in chapter 2. At the same time, however, *El Libro Semanal*'s moralizing discourse of personal fate ("we always give the wrongdoer their punishment") constitutes a kind of promise of justice that appeals to popular cultural sensibilities in order to negotiate for a Mexican audience the stories' embrace of an upper-middle-class consumerism and individualist ideology consistent with official U.S. neoliberal discourse. Careful examination of the details of protagonists' transgressions and the nature of the punishments meted out to them by fate in a variety of episodes provides evidence of a conservative Mexican vision of economic and cultural globalization, and an appropriation of the U.S. model for that vision.

French social theorist Alain Touraine's concept of the "cultural model" is a useful way of thinking about the shared symbolic DNA of ideological and cultural discourses that are otherwise divergent in form and content. As noted in the introduction, for Touraine, the cultural model is a given society's self-concept, the system of meaning that allows a society to have knowledge of itself and to see itself as having a history, a development, of its own. Every society generates a cultural model, which serves as a template for that society's continued development. Because of its strategic importance in societal reproduction, in the ongoing regeneration of a given social order, the cultural model is also a potential object of dispute. Challenges to the status quo offer up an alternative cultural model (think of how the youth movement of the 1960s famously attempted to upend the "Establishment" with radical principles of freedom, community, and imagination), because otherwise social and political demands must always be negotiated within the settled terms of the accepted system of meaning.

One of the useful things about Touraine's concept is that it facilitates the recognition of a shared cultural logic in phenomena as varied as U.S. State Department discourse on regional commerce and, say, the U.S. television "reality show" format: both construe reality as a circumstance in which private self-interest and competition make things happen, where competitive advantage and aggressive self-promotion are rewarded by investment and thereby success. (The television programs *American Idol, American Inventor, The Apprentice,* and *Survivor* and the U.S. State Department's *Country Commercial Guides* are all "reality shows" in this sense.) For Touraine, the affinity between the two different kinds of cultural texts is no accident, since they are elaborated from the same cultural model, the same manner for U.S. society to see itself, to know itself. Recognition of the imprimatur of a particular cultural model also allows critical attention to how the broader social principles of that model interact with varied formal or aesthetic components of a particular cultural medium. *American Idol,* for example, literally performs the U.S. cultural model by brokering a relationship between individual citizen competitors, the popular musical tastes of the general public, and the "expert" aesthetic judgment of the music industry.

Following Touraine, the dominant cultural model in the United States might best be described as entrepreneurial; the creativity and forward historical motion of U.S. society are viewed as arising from private investment and innovation, led by the vanguard (as it were) capitalist class. Adriana and Marco Antonio enact this cultural model in some obvious ways in "El Interesado" (The Interested One, 2007). But the drama of the *Libro Semanal* series does not present entrepreneurial spirit and success exclusively, nor does it simply reproduce the self-interested protagonist as the prime mover of progress and the resolution of social problems. The imprecise fit between the U.S. cultural model and the *historieta* series is, in part, a function of contradictions between that model and the more traditionalist cultural norms promoted by Mexican conservatives. The paradigm for Mexican "self-knowledge" is framed, in a sense, by the dominant self-concept of U.S. society, but the conservatism and (albeit faded) nationalism of the O'Farrill family can be read in the presence of an alternative Mexican cultural model that places patriarchal family mores at the heart of national economic development.

In large part, the thematic discrepancies with the U.S. cultural model result from the fact that many of the cultural principles celebrated in the dominant, capitalist development-centered model for neoliberal globalization are, on closer inspection, amoral, defining, as Touraine puts it, "situations more than behavior": "Science, technical progress, overcoming distance by mass information, speed, or jets, performances achieved by instruments, machines, or the human body are all cultural themes organized around notions of progress, domination, and control of natural conditions that involve no rule of social conduct" (Touraine, 209–10). What *El Libro Semanal* reproduces most faithfully from the U.S. cultural model are these "situations" of globalization. Marco Antonio's improved market position, Adriana's education at a Canadian university (presumably she could not receive a comparable education in Mexico), a transcontinental flight back to Mexico in the Executive Class cabin, are all situations resonant with progress and the overcoming of barriers to personal desires. What the *historieta* attempts to inject into these situations from "outside" the U.S. model is a moral code of conduct, and an often recognizably national one at that.

In the case of *El Libro Semanal*, it is important to recognize the extent to which the *historieta* borrows for the print medium many of the ingredients of Mexico's *telenovela* form. This adaptation to print of televisual aesthetics has a rich history in Mexico, where graphic narrative has included hybrid genres such as the *fotonovela*, or photo-novels, in which photography replaces draftsmanship in rendering a sequential representation of narrative action. The cross-fertilization of visual forms in the Mexican mass cultural market of the twentieth century can be seen, for example, in the mass circulation of images of the famous wrestler-hero El Santo, who appeared on television, in film, and in *fotonovelas* in the 1950s and 1960s. One could even argue that the large market share enjoyed by *El Libro Semanal* is a residual consequence of its early cultural synergy with Mexico's quasi-monopolistic television broadcasting company, Telesistema Mexicano, later Televisa, which aired the country's first *telenovela* in 1951–52 (Matelski, 64), shortly before the inaugural episodes of *El Libro Mensual* were published. In addition to the politico-economic synergy between the PRI-friendly Televisa and the PRIista O'Farrill family, who were early shareholders in the television company (López Parra, 44), the market success of the *telenovela* formula placed melodramatic and upper-class-conscious aesthetics at the center of Mexican culture industry vitality. By the 1990s, the *telenovela* had become Mexico's leading cultural export.

The centerpiece of the *telenovela* aesthetic is fate. An implicit notion of fate or destiny for the characters is supported, in part, by the fact that the Mexican *telenovela* is designed for a limited run. (The U.S. soap opera, in contrast, is theoretically endless and therefore does not stress narrative finality.) *El Libro Semanal* mirrors the Mexican *telenovela*'s finite narrative form in that it is a self-contained story, with characters whose lives unfold within the story arc of the single episode, and who thus arrive at a definitive existential terminus on the final page. Furthermore, relations of social class are negotiated by the way that the moral comportment of a character leads inexorably to a seemingly predetermined narrative resolution. In this respect, the popular *Libro Semanal* operates in the same vein as Mexico's globally successful *telenovelas*, such as *Los ricos también lloran* (The Rich Also Cry), *El Premio Mayor* (The Big Prize), or *María la del barrio*

(María from the Barrio), in which upper-class life provides the context for emotional and moral travail and social mobility. As noted in chapter 2, the López Obrador administration's *Historias de la ciudad* series made use of the *telenovela's* fated, morally predictable narrative outcomes in order to construct a multiclass political subject—ostensibly corresponding to the political coalition of the Partido de la Revolución Democrática (PRD)—cemented by a public morality. In *El Libro Semanal*, social mobility may be dramatically downward, depending upon the moral fiber and behavior of the character.

The reader can often see this coming, the proverbial accident waiting to happen, as in the storyline of "Insatisfechos" (Unsatisfied, 2007), which tells the woeful tale of a middle-class family that moves to Mexico City from the small town in which they were all born and raised, so that the father can follow a big job opportunity. The father, Porfirio Rodríguez, was a fifty-something lawyer who "had practiced as the town's judge, where he was esteemed and respected" (9). "But it was impossible to refuse the request of my compadre Rafael; he got this job for me in the Attorney General's Office," reflects Porfirio during the family's bus ride to Mexico City (10). The family wakes up the next morning in a modern high-rise apartment, filled with dreams of education and economic opportunity: the teenage son Rubén will study and become a professional; the teenage daughter Beatriz will learn new artisanal skills and go into business. But their old-fashioned small-town ethos ("Study and honest work build character," the mother tells her children) clashes with big-city modernity. The reader will be reminded of this tension throughout the comic book with panels that repeatedly display the cold, abstract geometrical forms of modern urban architecture as the setting for the characters' moral and emotional anguish.

Predictably, one thing leads to another, and before too long the family's embrace of the urban lifestyle leads to moral (and economic) ruin. Porfirio begins an affair with a beautiful young insurance agent, and the costs of maintaining the illicit relationship lead him into financial debt. Beatriz learns to smoke and drink from her new friend Yolis, whose sexualized attitude and loose morals are brought to bear through peer pressure on the impressionable teenager. Rubén falls in with a group of upper-class scofflaws, and descends into a life of drugs and petty crime, leading eventually to betting away his sister's honor in a poker game. The climax of the story—and moral nadir for the family—is reached when a wealthy client of Porfirio throws a party at which prostitutes are made available to the male guests. The father decides to avail himself of the pleasurable opportunity and discovers his daughter, Beatriz, is one of the women on offer. Soon after, Porfirio is fired for receiving bribes, and Rubén, who has been imprisoned for attempting to steal drugs from a medical office, kills himself in despair.

Fate is present in the slippery-slope construction of the storyline, with each bad decision leading inexorably to ruin. But it is also present in the visual dimension of the *historieta*, in the use of urban architectural forms presented from skewed angles within individual image panels to presage the encroachment of a kind of threatening modernity. Fate is also present in the strategic use of unconventional panel frames to indicate moral danger arising from modern, urban situations. In "Insatisfechos," this latter effect is achieved through sharply jagged panel borders bent out of standard rectilinear shape, employed to represent, for example, an "innocent" offer of a motorcycle ride by the rich young sociopath Javier Alcántara, who ultimately seduces Beatriz and becomes her pimp (30). A similar frame is used to present to the reader Porfirio's discovery that Beatriz is a prostitute (114), and Rubén's profound anguish in his prison cell, in this case with a panel frame shaped like an irregular buzz saw, focusing the reader's gaze on an extreme close-up of the teenager's weeping face (135). The moral dangers of Mexico City are thereby consistently visually linked to their inevitable personal, emotionally wrought consequences.

The visual dimension is also where the *telenovela*-like melodrama is anchored aesthetically. We observed in chapter 3 that the modality of comic book discourse, the particular ways the text appeals to the reader's assessment of reality, is located often in its visual semiotics. In *El Libro Semanal*, one can appreciate this aesthetic and discursive element at work, both in the kinds of visual strategies noted above and in the repeated use of full-panel close-ups on characters' facial expressions, literally bringing the reader face-to-face with the seat of subjective—personal and emotional—reality in the storyline. In "Insatisfechos," the reader senses early in the story that there will be an unavoidable head-on collision between the small-town, middle-class moral subject represented by the Rodríguez family and the megacity's immense and relentless corrosiveness (amid the misbehaviors of upper-class Mexicans). When Porfirio lies to his wife the first time to cover for his philandering ways (see figure 4.1), he explains in an upper panel that his boss asked him to entertain a group of visiting functionaries—"and I had to do them the honors, I took them out to eat and there was no way to let you know, since we still don't have a telephone"—while in the lower panel his pained visage presses in upon that lie. His tilted head and the hand that supports it comprise a kind of arrow directing the reader's attention back to the first panel, and the

Figure 4.1. Porifirio's anguish is made visible alongside his dishonesty. The text of the bottom panel narrates: "That was the first time that he sincerely regretted having left the small town." From *El Libro Vaquero* #2636, 47.

lie. The narration in the upper-left-hand corner of the lower panel provides the reader access to Porfirio's subjective experience: "That was the first time that he sincerely regretted having abandoned the town" (47).

In the end, the broken family returns to their small-town origins, financially and emotionally destroyed. The final melodramatic scene is rendered in a full-page panel image of father, mother, and daughter holding hands in the cemetery; the phantasmal countenance of the dead Rubén floats above them, hanging over their heads like a conscience. This cautionary tale pits a middle-class family against not just the moral threat of urban life, but the decadence of a certain upper-class life of leisure as well. Tragedy results from entering into modern "situations" without the necessary rule of social conduct. Instead of fire and brimstone, the consequences of moral error are decidedly economic. Porfirio winds up unemployed and deeply in debt, and Beatriz discovers that while she was infatuated with Mexico City's urbanity, her lifelong love back home married the woman who works at the town pharmacy. In addition to the death of Rubén, the "wrongdoers" are punished with demotion in social status and with economic devastation.

Other episodes in the series also demonstrate how moral error results in a diminished class position. A major subgenre of the *Libro Semanal* series portrays the inevitable social descent of the abusive spouse or father. These bad patriarchs are doomed to failure not only in their violent efforts to control the women in their lives; their flawed moral character carries with it a preordained solitude and financial wreckage. "Con la Cruz a Cuestas" (With the Cross on Her Back, 2007) tells the tale of the long-suffering Ofelia, who endures the oppressive tyranny of her father, Ramón, whose Hitler-style mustache, physical assaults on his wife and daughter, and exploitation of an orphan as cheap labor for his laundry business all belie his public reputation as a man of faith and tradition. When her working-class paramour Salvador asks for her hand in marriage, Ramón and his thuggish sons attempt to beat the boyfriend, and later plan his murder. Ofelia and Salvador elope to the southern state of Chiapas, where Salvador finds work at a sawmill owned by his uncle. Their idyllic romance is cut short by Salvador's accidental death, and Ofelia must return to her parents' home in the city. Ofelia and her mother finally flee with the baby to Chiapas in search of a better life (to be provided by Salvador's uncle) after Ramón attempts to trade Ofelia's charms to a wealthy bar owner in exchange for cash needed to maintain Ramón's concubine. Within the baroque details of the narrative is lodged a dramatic contrast between the hard-working, respectful, and protective model of masculinity (Salvador and his uncle) and the abusive and selfish model (Ramón, his sons, and the wealthy bar owner). The final, full-page image of the *historieta* shows Ramón lying in bed alone, surrounded by liquor bottles and deeply in debt, "perhaps with the only hope of finding relief in death" (154).

The symbolism employed in delivering the moral to this story is nothing if not heavy-handed. "Salvador," of course, is Spanish for "Savior," and the working-class hero is portrayed repeatedly as larger-than-life, his majestic torso and biceps either holding Ofelia protectively or laboring mightily at some manual task—"like the legendary Greek god in his chariot of fire," the narrator describes breathlessly (17). This godlike status of the savior turns his death into a kind of Christ-like, predestined sacrifice on behalf of Ofelia, whose economic security and well-being are then finally afforded not by the honorable working man but by his good capitalist uncle. The Christian reference in the episode's title thus becomes clear, the metaphorical linchpin of a tale that connects a gendered code of moral conduct to a social class framework. Salvador's death is not the death

of a "wrongdoer," but of Ofelia's savior, facilitating the narrative's ability to simultaneously morally elevate a working-class figure and sacrifice the proletarian
Salvador in order to preserve the "proper" social hierarchy. The good, business-
class patriarch provides economic security to the women in the end.

In "Un Ayer Escabroso" (A Rough Yesterday, 2004), the protagonist, Isabel,
successfully completes her *licenciatura* (an advanced professional degree), but instead of being able to pursue a professional career, she is stifled and beaten by her
husband, Vidal. When it becomes clear that Vidal is after her large inheritance
(Isabel's sickly father dies at the beginning of the story), she divorces him and
remarries, this time leaving the city to settle down with a wealthy widower and
businessman from a "*pueblecito*" in the state of Veracruz. At the outset of the narrative, Vidal appears to be an upper-middle-class Mexican professional, with his
own luxury car and a large and modern apartment, a man accustomed to wearing
a suit and tie during the day, and relaxing in a smoking jacket and ascot in the
evenings. (One is frequently reminded that the artists who interpret the *Libro
Semanal* storylines are constructing fantasies of a class position not their own.) In
the end, a bartender ejects Vidal from the local cantina—"Get out of here! You
don't even have enough money to pay for your drinks!"—as the narrator informs
the reader of the moral lesson: "As for Vidal, life charged him dearly for his vanity
and arrogance" (146). Poverty takes on the appearance of tragic punishment.

Amid these many details, one begins to discern an image of Mexico's national economic development, and of the preferred cultural model for its continuation. Stable, traditional values orbit around a patriarchal family structure,
and it is pathology within this structure that produces moral decay and, ultimately, frustration or regression in the individual's economic advancement.
The protagonist of this potential advance is the family (or, in its nascent form,
the couple), and the individual benefits or suffers according to the fate of that
collective moral subject. The recompense, and moral leadership, for living "the
good life" is the propertied, national patriarch. But there is another detail to
this picture that merits exploration: the etiology of the moral decay that grips
El Libro Semanal's "wrongdoers." One notices, across multiple episodes of *El
Libro Semanal*, that the moral pathology that threatens righteous patriarchy
seems to have a specific geography, a particular layout in the national landscape
of Mexico. In many episodes it operates with the consistent logic of a Global
Positioning System: movement toward Mexico City tends to provoke disaster
in the characters' lives; movement away from Mexico City toward the provinces
tends to alleviate the tribulations of the same characters. While this is certainly

not a hard-and-fast rule in *El Libro Semanal,* one finds this moral cartography extensively repeated throughout the series.

The consistent association of Mexico City with moral peril in *El Libro Semanal* most likely responds to the real political and economic centrality of Mexico City to national life, and its centrality to Mexico's more visible integration to the global economy and media networks. The urbanization trend in Latin America, what is sometimes called "savage urbanization" because of its informality, speed, and troubling, unintended social consequences, has generated massively expanded urban cores in once rurally oriented national cultures. In 1930 the entire urban population of Latin America was less than 20 million, a total that climbed to 300 million by the early 1990s. Urban population as a percentage of national population increased in Mexico from 35 percent in 1940 to 73 percent in 1990 (Gilbert, 25–26). Urbanization is a cultural and social reality in many respects coterminous with modernization in Latin America. The trend has resulted in Mexico City's status as one of the three largest urban centers in the world, and has made the Federal District a strategically important cultural and political base for the opposition PRD. This latter datum tinges the moral predilections of the *Libro Semanal* series with a political sensibility, coloring the PRD-governed megacity as corrupt in a *historieta* series published by the longtime PRIista O'Farrills.

Strikingly, crisis is located in Mexico City in *El Libro Semanal* episodes such as "Un Ayer Escabroso" and "Insatisfechos," and salvation in the Mexican countryside, despite the fact that in reality it is in the countryside where small landholders and indigenous campesinos feel compelled to migrate to the cities (or to the United States) out of economic necessity. Chiapas, the southern state where Ofelia finds asylum from the abuse of her father, is in point of fact the poorest state in the Mexican Republic, and home to the indigenous neo-Zapatista rebellion against NAFTA, against neoliberal rule, and against the state's abject economic conditions—"[lagging] behind the rest of Mexico in almost every way measurable: household income, education, and basic standard of living fall far behind the national average, and infant mortality is much higher" (Collier, 16). The wealthy uncle's sawmill is part of a circumstance in which "[t]oday, Chiapas is almost an internal colony for the rest of Mexico, providing oil, electricity, timber, cattle, corn, sugar, coffee, and beans, but receiving very little in return" (Collier, 16). Ofelia and her infant son may find succor and a secure place for their personal development under the roof of the business class there, but it is evident that most Chiapanecos will not.

El Libro Semanal's narrative ploy faithfully represents provincial sentiment about Mexico City's predominance rather than national economic reality. Seeking a resolution of Ofelia's urban crisis through the interventions of a Chiapas-based businessman represents a moral inversion of the historical dominance of urban modernity over rural tradition, of the megacity over the provinces. And this inversion resonates both with peripheral resentment of Mexico City's centrality to the nation's political economy and with the PRI's longtime reliance on rural support to counterbalance growing opposition in the urban centers. As urban geographer Peter Ward observed as early as 1990: "[T]he resentment traditionally felt in the provinces about Mexico City's preferential treatment is nothing compared with the tension and anger expressed today against many *chilangos* [slang for Mexico City residents] who are perceived to be taking housing and jobs which ought, by rights, to be destined for local people. They are also accused of driving up land and housing prices, and generally acting with arrogance and a lack of sensitivity" (26–27). The old provincial slogan "*Haz patria, mata a un chilango*" (Be patriotic, kill a *chilango*) haunts *El Libro Semanal*'s narrative punishment of urban evil.

In organizing the reader's view of the national map in this way, and in the related culturescaping that morally elevates, and conflates, the good patriarch and the economically successful individual, *El Libro Semanal* reshapes the U.S. cultural model. If in the cultural model exported by the United States private self-interest and competition make things happen—competitive advantage and aggressive self-promotion are rewarded by investment and thereby success—in *El Libro Semanal* economic success and security are the rewards of moral investment. What might be called the moral entrepreneur figures most prominently in these comic book stories, serving as a positive or negative model for how to avoid the predictable tragedy of a modernity devoid of a proper code of conduct. Personal wealth and security, class position, and by extension economic development are, for the *Libro Semanal* series, first and foremost a moral problematic; the economic dimension follows as a reward or punishment for the morality of the individual.

Unsurprisingly for conservative discourse, the ethical measure of the individual is taken within the context of a traditional family hierarchy. This particular moral metric tends to de-politicize the "situations" of globalization, because it removes conflict over their implications from the public arena and into the private sphere. But importantly, "proper" conduct within this framework is often subtly tinged with a sense of the "national." Marco Antonio's motives make sense, in the end, because he replaces Adriana's dear departed father as head of household, and averts the sale of his business to a stranger. Porfirio is a moral failure because he is a failed father, but also a failed public official in the bargain, and the entire family suffers as a result. The sad fate of Salvador, however, demonstrates that there is, to paraphrase a key ethical tenet from Latin America's moribund liberation theology, a preferential option for the wealthy that remains consistent with the U.S. cultural model. Salvador's sin, it appears, was to be déclassé. The savior represented no improvement over the class position afforded by Ramón's petit bourgeois family life.

El Libro Semanal's formulaic, gendered morality is, in fact, its distinctive "brand" in the Mexican comics industry. Laura Bolaños Cadena, creator of the series and author of many of its storylines, defended the ideological honor of the publication in a 2003 letter to the editors of the national daily newspaper *La Jornada*, which had published a brief study of the Mexican *historieta* phenomenon and the degrading attitudes toward women presented there. Bolaños wrote: "The *Libro Semanal* does not deal with violent themes, and certainly does not degrade women. Most of its audience is female and its success is based on the defense of women and the criticism of machismo." This "defense of women" is most revealing, vis-à-vis the series' vision of the global order, in those episodes where the woman in question is being defended not from the horrors of spousal abuse, but from market forces, including those "powerful motives" with which Marco Antonio and Adriana struggle in "El Interesado." In such episodes, the "proper" gendered hierarchy of the Mexican family finds itself caught up in or threatened by situations that typify the oft-celebrated advances of economic globalization: in particular, the mobility, independence, and economic progress of women. The "defense of women" in this context sometimes associates machismo with transnational business interests, all the while seeking to "advise the reader against falling into errors," to recall the words of *El Libro Semanal*'s editor Monsalvo.

"Maldita Ambición" (Damned Ambition), published in June 2001, is typical of the *Libro Semanal* series in most respects. It combines the print format of the *historieta* with the melodramatic narrative arc of a television soap opera, offering the reader frequent close-up portrayals of the facial expressions of the characters, in a range of exaggerated emotional states that punctuate the storyline. It employs standardized frames—most of these rectangular, horizontal, half-page panels— and schematically realist line drawings with a minimum of monochrome shading. And it narrates in 146 pages the story of Alba Rojas, a young Mexican woman with ambitions of overcoming her poor, working-class origins. As with the entire *Libro Semanal* series, the narrative aims to reinforce a moral, in this case against selfishness and self-promotion. Nevertheless, in the end the object of moral criticism turns out not to be self-interest as a market value, but female ambition as a threat to traditional gender roles. And, as is the norm for *El Libro Semanal*, the drama unfolds in the context of upper-middle- and upper-class social relations and interactions that test the mettle of the main character.

At the beginning of the narrative, Alba receives her executive secretary's degree and is recognized as "the best student of the group." But when her mother congratulates her for now being able to earn a salary, get married, and have children, Alba responds saying, "I'm not going to do what other women do." This conflict, between Alba's individualist—even feminist—ambition and the family values of her working-class cultural environment, structures the entire plot. Eventually, she does marry, to Efrén, a young man of upper-class birth who manages a small garment factory in the neighborhood. However, Alba grows frustrated with Efrén because, despite his financial success, he is satisfied with an upper-middle-class life. Alba wants more, and so she leaves Efrén to travel to New York with a famous Mexican financier, thinking she will marry him and thus realize her evidently limitless ambitions. At the end of the story, however, she has failed to attain her goal of becoming a wife and business partner of a global capitalist. Instead, when the couple returns to Mexico, the financier leaves her in the airport after offering her some money for her time—effectively marking her as a prostitute. The image of Alba's face—horrified with recognition that her ambition had turned her into a concubine, a useable commodity—is set against the backdrop of the airport, a reminder to the reader of Alba's sudden loss of mobility and social status. She has been ejected from the space of the global, and finds herself a "mere" Mexican again.

There can be no doubt from either the storyline or the visual dimension of the comic book that the frame of reference for this portrait of ambition-gone-awry is the neoliberal model of globalization. Individualist self-interest is presented as the motor for the generation of wealth and modernization. These latter values are prominently represented in the visual scenery for the story, several panels depicting through household interiors the working-class Alba's access to an elite lifestyle. As with most other episodes of *El Libro Semanal*, the external signs of modernization appear in "Maldita Ambición" as mobility, technology, and an expanded luxury in the private sphere. Repeatedly, the action of the *historieta* is framed in image panels portraying transit, either in an automobile or airplane,

Figure 4.2. Alba's ambition appears as an adjunct of globalization. The narrative text above the image of the airplane's departure leaves little doubt about this: "Alba believed she was going after what she deserved . . . , the importance of having money and being beautiful." From *El Libro Semanal*, #2436, 90.

culminating in a round-trip voyage between Mexico City and New York, with extended dialogue about Alba's ambitions occurring in transnational suspension between two globally important megacities. (Inspection of dozens of *El Libro Semanal* episodes across numerous years reveals that transportation and mobility are constantly referenced in the visual facet of the series, and, like Alba, the protagonists of many episodes travel for vacation to resorts like Acapulco and Cancún within the national territory.) Alba's desires are clearly framed by the modernity and power of the airplane: in figure 4.2, the upper panel narrates Alba's thinking as the airplane ascends—"Alba believed she was going after what she deserved, after what had been her goal for many years of her life, after the importance of having money and being attractive." In the lower panel, Alba displays contempt for her husband's choice of family over business success: "That's why he sold the workshop, to have time and dedicate himself to being a nanny" (90).

Although ambition is the central theme, this psychological force (one of Marco Antonio's "powerful motives") is only treated critically with reference to the actions of Alba; neither Efrén nor the famous businessman receive critical attention (or karmic comeuppance) for their own efforts to enrich themselves. Ambition, as it turns out, fits quite well within the logic of the market—it only merits critique when it complicates traditional family roles and gender relations. In "Maldita Ambición," as in official U.S. "free-market" discourse, globalization—present in the comic book through the repeatedly visualized transnational mobility of the business elite and the centrality of commerce for the "good life"—is a logical extension of local entrepreneurial activity. If the reigning image of globalization presented in U.S. culturescaping is structured around a promise of cultural transformations (one should recall the celebration in the U.S. *Country Commercial Guide* for Mexico of the societal change allegedly spawned by NAFTA), in "Maldita Ambición" such promises are contained within the private sphere instead of the public sphere. Within the scenery of private interests and easy movement of people and capital, commerce eclipses labor. With the exception of a lone image of smiling garment workers in Efrén's factory, the human body appears almost exclusively as consumer, whether this be in the *tianguis* (open air market), the bar, the hotel, or the airplane.

Although historically Western capitalist modernization competed publicly with socialist and nationalist development models that posited a practical relationship between popular social sectors and the progress of the nation, in this *historieta* modernization is privatized, carried out as an individual project for which the explicit collective context is the family, not the nation or social class. Official U.S. discourse on globalization is reproduced in this sense in "Maldita Ambición," reinforcing the classic modernizing values of a fictionally expansive middle class that includes both the working-class barrio of the *tianguis* and the wealthy upper-middle-class suburbs of Ciudad Satélite, Alba's poor family, and the transnational entrepreneur. The conflicts that emerge are always and exclusively interpersonal ones, not political ones in a national sense. (As would be, say, conflicts over the wages and benefits of those happy, smiling factory workers in Efrén's employment, or the question of whether the transnational capitalist is investing his profits in Mexico or rerouting them elsewhere.)

And yet the contextualizing operations of the comic book impose certain limits on the unstated utopianism of neoliberal discourse, its implicit notion of a world completely and perfectly absorbed in the fiscal logic of the "free market." In effect, neoliberalism is brought down to earth and "Mexicanized" by the combination of national cultural elements exhibited in the plot and the visual semiotics of the comic—that is, its use of panels that offer panoramic views of Mexico City and its suburbs, closer "background" perspectives of the open air market and barrio life, or images of the factory interior. The actions and moral evaluation of the characters are situated amid recognizable national sites and spaces that conjure specific cleavages of social class, such as the wealthy Ciudad Satélite suburb (referenced visually by its "gateway" public art project, the monumental geometrist towers designed by Mathias Goeritz), luxury tourist hotels and the central urban *tianguis* (which, though unnamed, has all the markings of the legendary working-class barrio of Tepito). Circulating among and between these social spaces is the central antagonism of the tale: a traditionalist concept of the Mexican woman versus an ambitious, self-promoting woman focused on upward mobility.

The latter of these two is the "wrongdoer," and Alba's fate becomes an object lesson in how certain aspects of the social world are not to be metabolized by the appetites of the market. The storyline carefully avoids politicization of the story's moral, however. The transnational financier is himself Mexican, a detail that allows the story's outcome to avoid provoking antiglobalist nationalism in the reader, and the fault lies not with capitalism per se but with Alba's misguided motives. In "Maldita Ambición," the expansive promises of the neoliberal model of globalization are counterbalanced by a traditionalist popular sentiment that has been denatured of national value. The noncommercial values that afford a criticism of the "situations" (à la Touraine) of the global order are private sphere values—embodied in the family and its sexual code of conduct—not public interest values. The potential for a critical social evaluation of self-interest and social exploitation attendant to the neoliberal model of globalization is deflected by censure of individual female ambition, on the one hand, and contained by the alibi of machismo (the only social sin of the transnational Mexican financier), on the other.

At the same time that in the visual plane a certain national feeling is conjured, positioning the characters and the reader firmly within the "imagined community" of Mexico, the narrative plane of the comic book manages and redirects that sentiment so as to accommodate the globalized neoliberal code of conduct (upper-middle-class desire and self-interestedness) to the nation-specific and typically poor-to-middle-class readership of the series. Alba's fate is a national signpost, albeit on the road of *El Libro Semanal*'s populist conservatism: the Mexicanidad to be held in reserve from global cosmopolitanism, the "powerful motives" that should trump financial interests and personal ambitions, are traditional notions of honor, family, and sexual hierarchy. Alba's "punishment" signifies in this way for readers of *El Libro Semanal* residing on both sides of the U.S.-Mexico border. Not coincidentally, the final pages of every issue of the series present personal ads under the heading "Aves sin nido" (Birds without a Nest). Here, the "imagined community" as organized in *El Libro Semanal* is distilled to that same interpersonal sentimentality, but for a cross-border, transnational Mexican diaspora. "Lady of 47, 1.68 (meters) tall, attractive, homey, no vices, seeks relationship with gentleman of 47 to 55, responsible, hard-working, attractive, tall, serious intentions, write and send photo in first letter," submits someone named Lourdes, who provides a Mexico City address. "I am 25 years old, dark complexion, brown eyes and hair, I would like to begin a friendship through this medium, with a girl who is sincere, tender, loving, physical appearances are not important, because the heart can't see, it only feels," writes one W. R. Mendoza from Texas.

In the final analysis, the *telenovela* aesthetic is instrumental for the management of national feeling in *El Libro Semanal* in exactly this way. Recent analysis of U.S. television suggests that the real-time, serial structure of the soap opera narrative, along with the intimacy of the consumer's relationship to characters and the upper-middle-class setting of the drama, makes it an ideal form for an expansive commodity culture (Wittebols). "The [upper-middle-] class correspondence between the soap opera world and the world of advertising further defines for viewers what is considered 'the good life'" (Wittebols, 39). *El Libro Semanal* certainly promotes a comparable concept of "the good life," presenting for popular consumption images of leisure and travel, of access to consumer goods and mobility, proper to the upper echelons of Mexican society's class hierarchy. In this sense, the series trains the reader to recognize and distinguish the markers of social class and status that represent economic success—the market rewards bestowed upon individuals for their shrewdness and hard work.

At the same time, however, the moral failings of the characters are placed in the foreground, training the reader to recognize and distinguish certain behaviors as errors in judgment and weakness of moral character, and to expect the corresponding demotions of class rank and social status executed by the plotline—the punishments meted out by the invisible hand of fate, working alongside the invisible hand of the market. Here, the aesthetic difference between the fate-centered Mexican *telenovela* and the open-ended U.S. soap opera emerges as a significant discrepancy, useful to the morally conservative optic of *El Libro*

Semanal. Mass communications scholar Jesús Martín-Barbero recognizes in this difference a phenomenon of Latin America's "sentimental integration," a shared feeling of regional identity not reducible by the "Americanization" implied in U.S.-led globalization. In the words of a Venezuelan television executive: "The *telenovela* has been the only Latin American product with which it has been possible to defend our identity in a medium as aggressively powerful as television. If it weren't for the *telenovela* our countries would be totally colonized" (Mato, 249). *El Libro Semanal* leverages that critical aesthetic difference into a conservative appropriation of the U.S. cultural model, and then offers it up to a Mexican reader who peers in on "the good life" as presumed and promised by neoliberal globalism, even if that reader remains mostly outside its material situations.

EMPIRE AT WORK

Comic Books and Working-Class Counterpublics

Reading comic books is generally prohibited on the job—except, that is, when the comic book in question is part of the internal communications strategy of the employer. The Mexican auto parts enterprise Rassini, for example, distributes to its 4,550 employees *Contacto Comix*, thematic stories featuring fictional company workers Lupita Bujes Maquinado y Resortes and Pepe de la Muelle Disco Ybarra. Installments in the series refer the reader to company-defined values "such as leadership, team work, or annual production goals set by management" (Ramírez Tamayo). Produced on contract with ¡Ka-boom! Estudio, the comic book characters are intended to facilitate factory workers' identification with company directives and norms. Lupita's and Pepe's extended surnames identify them with the automotive commodities produced in Rassini's factories—spark plugs (*bujes*), springs (*resortes*), shocks (*muelle*), discs (*disco*)—and the female character reflects an effort to target communication to the high percentage of female workers in several Rassini plants. Lupita, in fact, had replaced an earlier character named Pancho Socavón ("*socavón*" means mineshaft), who represented the company's mining division until the early 1990s, when the mining concern was sold to a Canadian corporation.

Lupita and Pepe can be viewed as popular cultural vehicles for what philosopher Michel Foucault famously called "the power of the Norm" (184), a principle of efficiency, productivity, and behavioral control applied systematically to the social body by modern institutions as diverse as prisons, schools, and factories. The fictional cartoon workers of *Contacto Comix* model a work ethic and personal morality that seek to fit the factory worker like a standardized gear into the company's productive machinery. Lupita and Pepe are consistently depicted peering in through windows and doors onto the private lives of Rassini employees like smiling, animated surveillance devices. It is no exaggeration to say that the comic book envisions and promotes the workplace morality preferred by company management through the same kind of panoptic visuality—Lupita and Pepe always observing and judging employees' behavior, no matter whether at home or on the job—that Foucault diagnosed in nineteenth-century prison architecture. Looked at with this normalizing function in mind, one can see in Rassini's comic a tool, or even weapon, deployed as an adjunct to labor politics—further evidence of how comic books circulate amid the clash of social class interests that occurs as a matter of course within the globalized capitalist system of production.

What of comics that stake out a position on the other side of the class divide? While the Rassini comic suggests a steering mechanism at the service of business interests who would manage workers' comportment and workplace identity, there are also comics that are representative of efforts by working-class organizations or their political allies to foment critique, popular resistance, and mass opposition to dominant business. Two interesting, albeit rare, variants in this category are comics published by labor unions and comics published by working-class neighborhood organizations. In both cases, these types of graphic discourse can directly counterbalance the social messaging of official comics, such as the Fox and López Obrador texts discussed in chapter 2, and the corporate didactics of business comics, like Rassini's workplace comic, or the monthly corporate brand comic published by the Farmacias de Similares pharmacy chain (see *Las aventuras del Dr. Simi* in chapter 7).

Graphic narrative at the service of social critique has occupied a significant niche in Mexican comics culture for some time—if a bit faded in recent years relative to its profile in the 1970s and 1980s. Comics as social critique is most notably visible in the prolific work of internationally renowned political cartoonist Rius (Eduardo del Río) and, more recently, Rafael Barajas, alias El Fisgón (The Snoop), a political cartoonist for the daily newspaper *La Jornada*. In an important sense, the work of these artists, among others, partakes of a modern Mexican tradition of socially engaged graphic arts that runs through José Guadalupe Posada's print-making in the late nineteenth and early twentieth centuries and later the radical Taller de Gráfica Popular (TGP) of the 1930s onward. Rius, in fact, pointedly disassociates himself from the Mexican comic book industry in his well-known history of comics, *La vida de cuadritos* (The Life of Comics, 1983): "the bad quality and even worse taste of Mexican comics can be attributed to its editors and publishers, more interested in selling 'popular' products than in the didactic use of the comic book form" (Priego). Barajas, meanwhile, positions his work among a long line of political caricaturists whose satirical visual art has served as "the foundation for the creation of popular political culture" since the nineteenth century in Mexico (Barajas 2000, 19).

Rius's and Barajas's works ally the authors to the bottom-up cultural activism of artists and educators who aim to *concientizar* (raise social consciousness) across a multiclass Mexican readership. In addition to publishing over the past four decades numerous book-length graphic narrative treatments of contemporary social problems, ranging from machismo to capitalism, and introductory "manuals" on themes such as Marxism, the Cuban Revolution, and vegetarianism, Rius created his first comic book series in 1965 with the social commentary offered by his characters in *Los Supermachos* (The Supermachos; Editorial Meridiano). His second series, the politically mordant *Los Agachados* (The Hunched Over), was published from 1968 to 1981. Barajas's work for *La Jornada* places his artistry as a caricaturist unambiguously in the public eye, but as with Rius, it is his graphic narrative that most clearly constructs a class-conscious view of Mexican social reality. He has authored a number of book-length graphic narratives, including several that treat the politics of globalization: *Me lleva el TLC: El tratado retratado* (Carried Away with NAFTA: A Portrait of the Treaty, 1993), *Como sobrevivir al neoliberalismo sin dejar de ser mexicano* (How to Survive Neoliberalism and Still Be Mexican, 1999), and *Como triunfar en la globalización* (2005). (He also published an English-language variant in *How to Succeed at Globalization: A Primer for Roadside Vendors*, 2004.) Unlike the work of Posada or the TGP, whose woodblock cuts and etchings adorned posters, fliers, and other print media aimed at informing and mobilizing readers, the narrative dimension opened up by sequential art has allowed the work of Rius, Barajas, and others to function in self-contained form as an alternate social and historical discourse.

The comic book in this incarnation represents an interface between a popular audience and the critical social narrative and analysis of engaged public intellectuals. The particular way that this tradition inhabits Mexico's comic book culture (that is, on the left end of the spectrum, and with a cynical view of the comic books industry) may explain why working-class organizations that have sought in recent years to use graphic narrative as a medium of popular communication for their message and values have tended to develop a relationship with an artist or artists instead of contracting the technical services of a private graphic arts studio.

In the context of rule by the Partido Revolucionario Institucional (PRI), independent barrio-based urban social movements had emerged in Mexico City after the 1985 earthquake, marking the beginning of the end of PRI dominance in the capital city. Many of the barrio organizations developed organic relationships with local visual artists, who generated much of the imagery of group identity needed for political action—ranging from street murals to pamphlets and posters and the occasional *historieta*. In the case of the southern Mexico City neighborhood organization Unión de Colonos de Santo Domingo (Union of Residents of Santo Domingo), initially founded in 1977 after one of the largest urban land invasions in Latin America (Rosales, 41–43), postearthquake organizing brought resources from international donors and resulted in a close working relationship with legendary Mexico City mural artist Daniel Manrique. Manrique's work with the Santo Domingo community in turn resulted in the publication of "La discriminación en México" (Discrimination in Mexico, 1999), a twenty-eight-page-long comic book that treats a social theme of great relevance to the working-class people of indigenous heritage who comprise the local community, and does so from a perspective critical of Mexican officialdom. The anti-official thrust of Manrique's comic is consistent with the antagonistic history of the squatters' settlement vis-à-vis government authorities.

For their part, labor union organizations have historically occupied an ambivalent position relative to Mexican officialdom. In the aftermath of the PRI's political collapse in the 2000 elections, official unions, organizations whose leadership had operated within the reward-and-punish logic of the PRI's corporatist governance since at least the 1940s, found themselves in a changed political circumstance. The new Fox administration quickly alienated rank-and-file unionists through a series of early political moves: refusing to increase Social Security benefits for working-class retirees, denying legal recognition to a month-long sugar workers strike, and declaring an increase in the minimum wage that barely kept pace with the rate of inflation, falling far short of the demands of organized labor. Although some corrupt union leaders continued to seek accommodation and patronage with the Partido de Acción Nacional (PAN) government, it had become clear that the post-PRI political landscape was not prolabor. Released from the PRI's control, if not from the tradition of upper-echelon union corruption and opportunism, the decades-long struggle for an independent labor movement was reengaged, now from within Mexico's major unions (La Botz 2001). Public sector unions, whose interests run directly counter to the neoliberal policy of selling off public assets to the private sector, had no choice but to attempt to exercise independent political muscle with respect to the Mexican government's control of economic policy.

One of the signs of this nascent independence has been the publication of a spate of graphic narratives aimed at challenging the neoliberal direction of the Mexican state. There was the *historieta* titled "Alicia en el país de la inseguridad" (Alice in Insecurityland, 2004), published and distributed by the Sindicato de Seguro Social (Social Security Workers Union) as part of a one-day work stoppage to protest a weakening of the law governing the Instituto Mexicano de Seguro Social (IMSS), Mexico's federal Social Security agency (Hernández Arana). There was "Que no nos roben la luz" (Don't Let Them Steal Our Light, 2003), published and distributed by the Sindicato Mexicano de Electricistas (SME) in response to the Fox administration's efforts to privatize the energy sector. More recently, and like the SME comic developed in collaboration with political cartoonists working for the national newspaper *La Jornada*, including *El Fisgón*, a coalition of labor unions produced "El salario actual, una infamia para el trabajador" (Current Wages, a Disgrace to the Worker, 2006). Presenting the depreciation of the Mexican minimum wage by more than 75 percent between 1977 and 2006, this most recent comic intends, according to Barajas, "to situate the theme of wages at the center of national debate" (García Hernández).

In order to better understand the political and cultural purpose of the working-class comics, one can usefully turn back to the corporate Rassini comic book as a point of comparison. A key distinguishing feature between a didactic comic book like Rassini's *Contacto Comix* and the oppositional comics published by unions and community organizations is precisely their relative position with regard to the national public sphere, the arena of public opinion and conversation regarding the country's values, identity, and collective interests. The Rassini comic is designed for diffusion among a strictly circumscribed, and globally segmented, public—the 4,550 employees (nearly 90 percent of them factory workers) of a manufacturer with plants in Mexico, Brazil, and the United States. The thematics of the comic book are also strictly circumscribed, limited to issues of immediate relevance to the collective project of directing the energies of several thousand employees toward the "shared" goal of company profitability. The corporate comic, in other words, is a cultural document of and for a specialized micro–public sphere, specifically the public sphere of the privately owned factory, where discussion of collective concerns and experience is governed in accord with the interests of owners and investors. As Negt and Kluge observed in their landmark 1972 study of the public sphere and class relations, this particular micro–public sphere is not, in fact, public at all but a privately managed arena of working-class experience. That is, the corporate arena of "public" conversation is both hierarchically controlled and largely invisible to the broader national public sphere of argument and counterargument, proposal and counterproposal, with regard to common interests and the collective good (Negt and Kluge, 49–53).

In contrast, the working-class comics are crafted for a more open and horizontal arena of public conversation, a sphere of discussion and debate that does not belong to any one interlocutor, and that cannot be reduced to either the power and influence of the state or the interests of a private business. In fact, the labor union comics are designed precisely to export issues—like health care and pension benefits, public control of assets, and wage levels—from the private enclave of the factory floor to the public arena, seeking to publicize workers' concerns to their fellow citizens, and to persuade their compatriots that these are properly understood as collective concerns. The working-class community comic book, meanwhile, is like the Rassini comic book in that it is pitched to a local audience, a micro–public sphere; but it differs in that it aims to fit this local community's experience and preoccupations into the broader context of the nation and its history. Manrique's comic serves a micro–public sphere, but a genuinely public one that exists independently of centralized controls. This difference between the public, working-class comic and the private, managerial comic—that is, between a horizontal diffusion for the public sphere versus internal, and hierarchical, pseudo-public diffusion—corresponds to the uneven public visibility of concerns about labor conditions, and of working-class perspectives generally. Although company comics of one kind or another are probably common, they operate within a privately owned social enclave, are almost categorically not reflective of the material interests of company workers, and are read backstage from the national public arena within which all Mexicans in principle have access and voice.

Alongside the contextual distinction observable between comics seeking to manage workers versus comics seeking to communicate workers' interests, there is a salient aesthetic difference. The business-friendly comic book (and one can see this also to some degree in those comics published by the Fox administration, discussed in chapter 2, which obviously do seek a national public audience for dominant business interests) tends toward a brighter color palette, a kind of "happy" realism in the representational style—with a well-lit, clearly delineated object world and simply but fully drawn human forms—and an upbeat portrayal of the thematic concerns of the narrative. This is, not to put too fine a point on the matter, an aesthetic approach consistent with a position of power and a legitimating function vis-à-vis governing authority. Authorities—public or private—commission a comic book narrative to present an official version of reality to their subordinates, and to therein cement the legitimacy of their authority and command (and subordination of the general reader). Undermining or questioning reality could lead to undermining or questioning the authority of those who govern it.

The labor-friendly comics, meanwhile, tend toward a darker optic. In part, this is due to the more economical use of a black-and-white color scheme, but mostly the aesthetic contrast results from making use of the exaggerated representational styles of caricature. And political caricature, of course, treats dominant power itself, and its corrupt misbehaviors, as a central component of reality instead of rendering it amiably invisible (à la Rassini) or pleasantly paternal (as with Fox or López Obrador). If a working-class sense and sensibility is to enter the public conversation, it must generally do so outside the workplace, and the visual "language" with which it is expressed is likely to differ antagonistically from the status quo "official speak" that seeks dominance in the public arena. Thus, in addition to comprising a more substantially public discourse than the internal company comic book, the working-class comic book is oriented toward nurturing a counterpublic—a collective opinion formation that runs decidedly against the grain of dominant interests and/or their representatives in Mexican officialdom. The counterpublic orientation of the working-class comic book is discernible in the interaction between the text's social, contextual character (that is, as speech or communication intended for a broad, collective audience) and its formal, aesthetic features (its "sense" of reality).

Daniel Manrique's "La discriminación en México" and the SME's "Que no nos roben la luz" are instructive case studies. Both were produced for politically organized working-class audiences—the first for organized labor and working-class users of public sector goods and services, and the second for an urban working-class residential group organized around elements of a self-sustaining communitarian economics (artisan workshops, a cooperatively managed restaurant, print shop, and community cultural center). Both narratives make use of popular aesthetic sensibilities, word play, and sexual metaphor in order to depict critically the interplay between economic and cultural globalization and the workaday lives of regular Mexicans. Analysis of the aesthetic dimension of these texts reveals how visual representation and discourse in these working-class critiques of globalization emphasize two dimensions of social experience that are closely managed, at times even policed, under the neoliberal model of globalization: the human body and physical desire, on the one hand, and creative appropriation as a mode of survival and resistance, on the other.

The cover page of "Que no nos roben la luz" is literally emblematic of the arguments presented inside. The cover presents a full-page, stark treatment of the title and its supporting graphic, a white, corporate-style symbol against a solid black background: General Electric, Inc.'s trademarked circular corporate seal has been altered to contain an eagle within its circumference, the same eagle that adorns the Mexican flag, where it grips a serpent in its talons. On the cover of the SME comic book, the eagle does battle with the trademark serpentine, cursive letters "GE," which in this rendering boast the fanged head of a snake. Numerous minor imperfections around the borders of the large, block lettering of the title at the top of the page, and in the contours of the emblem below, are indicative of the artisanal touch of the *grabado*, the manual woodcut transfer of ink to paper executed by the printmaker of yesteryear. Besides adding a certain visual gravitas to the title page, this *grabado* effect operates as a subtle visual marker of Mexican national identity, harking back to the revolutionary printmakers of the 1930s (the TGP in particular) and evoking the trace of a kind of manual labor in the artist's hand. The first image of the comic is thus redolent with political confrontation: the transnational giant General Electric is locked in mortal combat with Mexican labor. But the same image is also resonant with a specific kind of solidarity—nation and working class united in struggle, certainly, but collaboration between Mexican labor and Mexican artistry sealing that unity.

Developed by political caricaturists Rafael Barajas, Antonio Helguera, and José Hernández in collaboration with the SME's work to mobilize public sentiment against ongoing efforts by successive governments (first the PRI in the late 1990s, but subsequently the PAN under Fox) to open the country's energy sector to private control, the comic was published in an initial print run of 200,000 copies in 2003, and then reissued in a massive distribution of more than four million copies in 2004. "Que no nos roben la luz" was a strategic cultural instrument that aided the launch of the latest in a series of SME campaigns on the issue, and was aimed at "strengthening the level of resistance and rejection of privatization" among the Mexican public, according to SME labor secretary José

Antonio Almazán. Intriguingly, however, in interviews with the press, Almazán made a point of connecting this instrumental, political function of the graphic work with an argument for the national importance of caricature and graphic narrative in Mexico generally: "At least since the period of the Reform [under Benito Juárez's progressive administration of the 1860s], the *historieta* constitutes an effort to advance the central ideas that have moved many Mexicans to reject regressive measures, like privatization" (Martínez). Almazán's comments on this point, which closely mirror Barajas's own arguments in his *Historia de un país en caricatura*, stand alongside the cover image of "Que no nos roben la luz" as strong evidence that the collaboration between the artists and the union included a shared aesthetic conception of the project.

The 2003–4 SME mobilization, joined by numerous labor and civil societal groups in a September 27, 2003, march against neoliberal policy, responded to a Fox administration effort to amend the Mexican Constitution in order to relinquish state control over the generation of electricity, and to thereby invite private capital to take over that crucial function of the energy sector. The argument of "Que no nos roben la luz" is cut to the measure of precisely that political conjuncture, but also opens onto neoliberal governance more generally. In fourteen pages of narrative illustrated by a sequence of pen-and-ink images—each individually drawn by one or another of the three political cartoonists—the argument of the *historieta* runs as follows: The Fox administration claims it does not want to privatize the state-owned petroleum company Petroleos de México (PEMEX) or the state-owned Luz y Fuerza (Light and Power), but it is ceding business concessions to private enterprise, which is the very definition of privatization. Furthermore, the PAN government's attempt to alter the constitution is, in fact, an attempt to legalize privatization measures that would otherwise violate Mexican law. Fox administration policy, however, is simply a continuation of the neoliberal policies begun under president Carlos Salinas de Gortari (1988–94) and continued under president Ernesto Zedillo (1994–2000). The methods of these administrations have been the same for nearly twenty years— a state enterprise is allowed to deteriorate, private investment is invited to fix it, and then public monies begin to flow into private hands in order to guarantee profitability. As a consequence, workers suffer massive layoffs and mutilated wage and benefits agreements, and the government (and public) loses billions through lost revenues and corporate welfare. Recent government and business campaigns against the benefits enjoyed by unions in the health and energy sectors are a first step toward privatization.

The manner in which this argument is delivered to the reader makes effective use of the well-known prior narrative work of Barajas as a point of entry to the theme. In *Como sobrevivir al neoliberalismo sin dejar de ser mexicano*, Barajas had presented the problem of "free-market" globalization to the Mexican reader using the narrative device of a dialogue between a rural *curandera*, or medicine woman, and an unemployed mariachi, a musician-for-hire who dresses as a *charro*, a Mexican cowboy who wears distinctive black pants, boots, sombrero, and vest adorned with silver-plated buckles. This particular *charro* had lost his job in a mariachi band because the bandleader became infatuated with the Internet, cost-effectiveness, and global competition. The mariachi band was downsized, and the *charro* had no choice but to head northward across the U.S.-Mexico border in search of gainful employment. The *curandera*, representing a cultural figure in Mexico believed to possess spiritual insight and wisdom, enables the *charro* to see his situation clearly, to tragicomic effect.

The first two pages of "Que no nos roben la luz" open with this same hapless *charro* questioning the same *curandera* (Doña Beba) about the Fox administration's plans to privatize public sector companies. Whereas in *Como sobrevivir* the choice of these two characters allowed for recognizably national cultural figures to shape a Mexican (nationalist) view of globalization, in the SME comic the *charro* figure takes on an additional, politically pointed meaning. Since the 1940s, the terms "*charrismo*" or "*charro* labor" have been used to refer sardonically to corrupt official unionism in Mexico. In Barajas's depiction, the *charro*'s naive acceptance of the Fox administration's claims in the seven panels of the first two pages of the *historieta* is a satirical performance of the subservience and lack of critical consciousness of "*charrismo*." The first and largest of these panels, which occupies the top half of the first page of the narrative, portrays the *charro*, hands thrown up in frustration, demanding to know "Why do you think Fox wants to privatize electricity and petroleum? He promised during his campaign not to do it." Doña Beba, holding a handkerchief to her nose in an apparent physical gesture of disgust, whether with the *charro*'s exposed armpits or his political fecklessness, responds: "Sure, *charro*. . . . And like Fox never tells a lie" (1).

The comic book also makes effective use of the stand-alone format of the political cartoon, which is of course the artistic forte of all three contributing artists. While the first two pages are comprised of conventionally sequenced images, structured by rectangular panel frames arranged in narrative order from left to right and top to bottom, the ensuing visual presentation of the *historieta*'s argument consists of twenty-two separate images, each one a political commentary in its own right. One is reminded that the discrete visual form of the political cartoon is more often a vignette than a panel series, and relies on an especially compact economy of visual sign and linguistic text in order to engage the newspaper reader's fleeting attention. In the SME comic, the special rhetorical and aesthetic punch of the political cartoon is respected, at the same time that it is adapted to the sequential demands of a sustained discourse on a complex and politically contentious topic.

On page 3 of the *historieta*, for example, the reader encounters two distinct cartoons, each drawn by the hand of a different artist, and each depicting a different social subject. At the top of the page, Helguera offers an image of a dejected railroad worker who stands alongside a battered and broken-looking rail engine and passenger car. "Now it turns out we workers are the obsolete ones," observes the uniformed railroad man ironically in a lone dialogue bubble suspended above the neglected machinery. The image that occupies the lower half of the page is provided by Barajas—in this case, a plump and self-satisfied businessman consorting with a blond woman, who sports a fox stole and 1920s flapper-style bob. The fat capitalist's tuxedo, monocle, goblet of liquor, and female companion signify his membership in the elite leisure class, and underscore an air of special entitlement to his commentary on neoliberal policy: "Here privatizations work wonderfully: the government makes the contractual offers, and we violate the law." The explanatory text, previously introduced in the voice of Doña Beba in the opening sequence on pages 1 and 2, links these two cartoon images and makes contextual sense of their dramatic contrasts. Neatly delineating the top margin of the page, and providing a shared border between the two political cartoons, the narrative or explanatory text describes the modus operandi of neoliberal governance. The public sector (the state telephone company, the railroad system, "and 1,155 more") is left to deteriorate, private investment is celebrated as savior, and then public monies are spent to guarantee private profit. The worker's dejection and the fat cat's good fortune are facets of one and the same context.

Here and throughout the comic book, the explanatory, discursive text dispenses two functions. First, it organizes the page visually, most commonly marking the top and bottom limits of the page, and/or dividing the page across the middle. This allows for each of the political cartoons to occupy a visual and ideational space of its own, despite the absence of sequential panel frames structuring the relationship between these images. Second, the discursive text serves as an ideational hinge that allows the images to operate together as distinct elements in a kind of shared rhetorical syntax. Each image thus both stands on its own (as an individual illustration of the issue at hand) and opens onto the subsequent image (as one in a series of rhetorical maneuvers made in visual form).

This coordination strategy respects the stylistic differences discernible among the political cartoons (ten of twenty-two sporting El Fisgón's signature, and the rest divided between Hernández and Helguera). But it also affords opportunity for each author's distinctive style to reinforce the overarching argument. Helguera's cleanly and tightly rendered figures are augmented by careful cross-hatching that emphasizes the volume, texture, and solidity of the people and objects represented. His portrayal of workers on the job thereby underlines a ponderous materiality to their situation, which contrasts with the more traditional lampooning of powerful individuals in political cartoons. This effect can be observed in his contribution on page 5, where several railroad workers peer under the wheels of a locomotive after someone or something has been run over. "It's a shame about the collective contract!" declares one of the men, whose backs are turned to the reader and whose compact, dungaree-clad figures are dwarfed by the massive and impersonal engine. The vignette leaves no doubt that they have been collectively victimized, and that the damage done is appreciably physical, bodily, a result of a violent incident and not simply an abstract policy matter. Helguera's representational style aids in making this point, because by eschewing the distortion and caricature common to political cartooning, it more clearly situates bodies and things as existing together on the same plane of material reality. Emphasis on their quality as objects (solid, complete, with palpable surfaces) leaves emotional reality to the speech balloons.

El Fisgón, meanwhile, offers deceptively simple, sketched outlines in his figures, sometimes marked by smudged, ink-heavy contrasts and detail lines. This style of figuration draws attention to the artist's medium and hand, and thus to the polemical, antiauthoritarian act of his authorship. (As noted above, Barajas's polemical emblem on the cover page of the *historieta* accomplishes this same effect via a deliberate reproduction of the look of the *grabado*.) His satirical representation of authority makes use of the classical tropes of political caricature: comically disproportionate personal features, especially of the face, expose the moral failings of power, and give the lie to official pretensions of greatness. El Fisgón's corrosive aesthetic applies equally well to powerful individuals (for example, his numerous caricatures of President Vicente Fox) and to generic social types. On page 6, an obviously wealthy supporter of the PAN government faces off with a PEMEX worker. The portly PANista's angry visage takes on a snarling, antisocial quality amid the lopsided smear of the mouth and the messy convergence of slashing contour lines in the facial expression. The PANista's accusation that the PRI looted PEMEX in order to win elections is answered by the worker's apparently more objective assessment (perceptible in the far greater symmetry of his facial features and expression): "In contrast, the PAN won the elections in order to loot PEMEX." Whereas Barajas's corrosive representational aesthetics undermines the authority of the PANista speaker (revealing a resentful, skewed partisanship in the man's lopsided expression of animus), the same dishevelment in draftsmanship emphasizes an unassuming working-class subject on the other side of the political divide.

The drawings contributed by Hernández offer yet another aesthetic vantage onto the themes of "Que no nos roben la luz." Hernández's often fastidiously detailed human figures combine the intentionally mismatched bodily proportions and sketchy disarray common to political caricature with an attentively realistic treatment of selected details of those same figures. One can appreciate the rhetorical value of this aesthetic in a full-page cartoon that appears on page 9, where President Fox stands side-by-side with a young, poor Mexican (see figure 5.1). The image is framed above and below by a didactic text that reads: (above) "Throughout the world, privatizations of the electrical industry look alike; the wealthiest end up having control of the business and only seek profits. They are never concerned that those who cannot pay have no electricity. Thus, the benefits are for them and the problems for everyone else." And (below) "The electrical and petroleum industries are strategic for the country. Without electricity and gasoline, the country could be paralyzed. If private interests have control of those enterprises, they have in their hands the future of the nation. This is a loss of sovereignty." In the image, Fox calls upon the nation to "Cheer up, friends. Soon we will see the light (*luz*) at the end of the tunnel." To which the poor man retorts, making ironic use of the double meaning of "*luz*" (that is, light, but also electricity): "Yes . . . so you can privatize it."

The cartoon packs a special punch because of the manner in which Hernández combines caricature with elements of an aesthetic realism. A study in contrasts, the drawing uncovers the elitism of Fox's power and public discourse by presenting him elbow-to-shoulder with the humblest of Mexican citizens. The comparison between the powerful and the powerless is accentuated by a constellation of visual and symbolic opposites: Fox's dark suit versus the poor man's white campesino-like pants and shirt; Fox's open mouth versus the tight-lipped stoicism of the poor man; Fox's oversized, open hands versus the other

Figure 5.1. The official and unofficial bodies on display. President Vicente Fox dwarfs the poor Mexican, while the text at bottom informs the reader that privatization of the strategic energy sector leaves "the nation's destiny" in private hands.

man's modest hands-in-pockets posture; and, of course, the president's cumbersome head and gigantic stature relative to the small, and almost uncaricatured, presence of the poor man, who is subject to the PAN politician's rule. The tension between two aesthetic registers in the drawing is evident and compelling. On the one hand, political caricature portrays Fox as a patronizing buffoon; on the other, a poignantly realistic treatment of one of "those who cannot pay" reminds the reader that this is no laughing matter. Whereas Fox is treated unambiguously in the representational register of political caricature, the contrasting portrait of poverty has more the feel of a subject study for an oil painting. The humble, bowl-cropped hair and broad, indigenous cheekbones of "*los de abajo*" contrasts with the elongated cowlick that seems to leap pretentiously forward from Fox's brow and the European features of the face of official neoliberalism in Mexico.

Undeniably, across all of the stylistic and thematic differences of the *historie-ta*'s political cartoons, the body is the central figure in the text's prolabor visual discourse on privatization. As exemplified by Hernández's comparative perspective on Fox and the poor Mexican citizen, or El Fisgón's imagined exchange between the wealthy PANista and the PEMEX worker, it is not the human body in some generically humanist sense that occupies the center of visual attention in the comic. Rather, the body makes its appearance in these cartoons as the fundamental stakes of the political conflict over government policy. There are, in fact, two kinds of bodies that come into view in "Que no nos roben la luz." There is the official, dominant, elite body of the government policy makers and beneficiaries of government policy. This body is big and robust and well fed, when not downright corpulent, and its head and mouth are accentuated, as if central to its identity and function. By implication, that identity and function are not only a question of decision making (that is, "heads" of government and business) and speech making (mouth as the organ of public discourse) but also, more basely, are self-interested (big-headed egotist) and conspicuously consumptive (feeding at the public trough). Throughout the SME comic book, the excesses of this dominant body are thrown into relief via visual comparisons to the unofficial, subordinate body—a small, defiant, but ultimately abject and vulnerable organism that is frequently subject to physical violence, as with Helguera's train wreck victim, or with El Fisgón's portrayal of a worker being beaten like a piñata by a corporate executive on page 14. The diminutive unofficial body is subject to the negative consequences of the official body's satisfaction.

The aesthetic contributions of the three political cartoonists converge on the human body, a material body caught in the crosshairs of the neoliberal vision, for which the economy is a zero sum game, catering to those with the greatest desires while short-changing those with the greatest need. In the distorted political economy illustrated by the various political cartoons, the needs of the majority (electricity, telephone services, health care, and so forth) have little or no public voice or stature. The inflated body of the powerful is therefore made to signify as an adjunct to the impoverishment of the common person (see again figure 5.1). The corporal aesthesis of the SME comic book's argument allows the body to also operate metaphorically, demonstrating how the material logic of power under neoliberal rule extends beyond the concrete, human body to implicate the body politic and the nation. A cartoon on page 7 shows Felipe Calderón, then secretary of energy (president of Mexico as of 2006), fitting a headless mannequin for a set of revealing lingerie. The neoliberal functionary comments, "It's a matter of custom fitting the suit to the nation," leaving the reader with an image of the nation as a prostituted body, and of the technocrat as pimp.

As the reader is reminded by the explanatory text on page 10, "The worldwide tendency is for the large multinationals to wind up controlling the energy business. If these companies come to control energy in Mexico, they will hold in their hands the fate of Mexicans." The concern for national sovereignty is illustrated with an adjacent drawing by Hernández of a disembodied hand screwing a lightbulb into a ceiling socket. The lightbulb bears the face of President Vicente Fox, who looks out at the reader with a helpless, gape-mouthed expression. The hand holding the bulb is manicured and wears a starched white cuff and black suit coat sleeve, signs of its membership in the business class. "These companies," continues the text, "have so much power that they end up imposing their policies on local governments and even end up selecting ministers and presidents" (10). One is tempted to say that the problem of national sovereignty created by neoliberal globalization is illumined by the visual metaphor of the lightbulb, which shows the reduction of the Mexican executive—chief representative of the Mexican body politic—to an inanimate object manipulated by foreign hands.

If loss of sovereignty entails the conversion of the human body into an object or commodity, then it becomes easy to visualize a compromised national sovereignty through the depiction of the ruler's body in the same abject and vulnerable state as that of the anonymous wage laborer. There is an implicit concept of public power revealed in this image and others, like the El Fisgón cartoon on page 15 in which two burly men in suits attempt in vain to use a light switch to "turn off" a massive street demonstration against privatization. Their political helplessness is a consequence of a technocratic notion of rule and obedience. (This same concept of governance appears, in a positive light, in the Fox administration's comic "A mitad del camino" discussed in chapter 2.) As it turns out, those fat, self-interested official bodies that appear throughout the SME *historieta* are symbols of a failed, even fictional, public power that ultimately operates as a tool of foreign interests. True sovereignty would recognize and respond to the more fundamental needs of the body, the flesh-and-blood popular base of Mexican society. In the vision of the SME comic, Mexican officialdom faces a choice between meeting the needs of the Mexican people and satisfying the interests of multinationals, between serving the body in need and feeding the private sector's profit motive.

Daniel Manrique's "La discriminación en México" offers a variety of obvious contrasts to the SME comic book. Manrique's comic was, of course, authored by only one artist and contains less aesthetic variation than the SME collaboration, but it also is longer at twenty-eight pages, contains significantly more didactic text, and traces Mexico's present political situation through a long, historical view instead of the SME's focused accounting of specific recent government policies. Published with money from the municipal and community cultural program of the government's Consejo Nacional para la Cultura y las Artes (National Council for Culture and the Arts) and the Dutch antipoverty nongovernmental organization Novib, the comic book is based loosely on Jorge Paulat's book *La discriminación del indio* (Discrimination against the Indian, 1972). Using the narrative mechanism of a dialogue between two young men from the barrio, the comic describes the long historical arc of indigenous identity and subjection in Mexico, from pre-Colombian times, through the Conquest and the Spanish colonial period, and down to the present-day defender of indigenous rights and critic of neoliberalism, Zapatista Liberation Army leader Subcomandante Marcos.

Fernando Díaz Enciso, a Santo Domingo community activist and organizer of the project, intended the comic as a tool for fomenting public discussion about discriminatory attitudes toward indigenous people and heritage in Mexico. Díaz Enciso's rationale for the cultural project was clear on this point: "Discrimination is a problem that is experienced daily in the city and in the countryside," and the comic book medium could make Paulat's arguments on the issue more accessible to ordinary citizens (Jiménez). In accordance with this public-sphere function, in addition to an initial print run of 10,000 copies, the comic was also published in the form of a "*periódico mural*," or newspaper mural, and exhibited for public consumption and commentary in rural indigenous communities and urban neighborhoods, beginning with Santo Domingo itself. A subsequent printing of the comic included readers' comments from the public exhibition in Santo Domingo on the final page. The tone of the public reception of "La discriminación en México" is captured by the assessment of a local reader named Gerardo: "It is entertaining but still serious in order to see the history of our country so that we aren't made idiots [*pendejos*] with official history."

Although the specter of globalization makes its appearance more obliquely for the working-class reader of Manrique's comic than for the reader of the SME comic, the critique of officialdom is equally acute. As noted above, the comic book provides the local community with a historical overview of the relationship between "official Mexico" and the everyday experience of anti-indigenous discourse and policies. Notably, in both the visual and textual dimensions of the comic, the view of Mexico's globalized present is filtered through a popular cultural idiom—the narrator's commentary delivered in urban street *caló*, or slang, and the drawing style tending toward playful notebooklike doodles—which secures aesthetically a view of Mexican officialdom from the outside, and from below. Although globalization is never mentioned by name, in the first few pages the dialogue of the two barrio characters makes clear that the problem of anti-indigenous racism in Mexico orbits around a discourse of U.S.-led modernization, which in turn is linked to U.S. economic dominance and cultural influence. One of the characters, who wears a baseball cap backward and a "Chicago Buls" T-shirt to signify a degree of insouciant Americanization, serves as a critical foil in this regard, asserting: "We [Mexicans] started to improve when the Spanish speakers came, and we continue improving now that we've got the gringos here. The Spaniards taught us to speak, and now when we start talking [*mazcar tata cha*] in English we will be sharper [*más picudos*] and we will even use the computer and the internet, and we'll even be modern . . . it's true!" (3).

In order to debunk this self-loathing assumption about Mexico's relation to the global order, the visual premise of the narrative is one of witness: the two modern, working-class Mexicans observe and testify to the historical degradation and domination of Mexico's indigenous origins. The "Chicago Buls" character embodies that degradation as a contemporary artifact of a historical domination, now internalized and crudely parroted, that began with the Conquest, was consolidated under Spanish colonial rule, and continues under U.S. hegemony. The visual artistry of the comic not only illustrates the historical narration provided by the dialogue, it also sets the scene for a kind of time travel by the characters, transporting them (and the reader) to the time of the great pre-Colombian civilizations, and later to the scene of their subjugation. Somewhat parallel to the workers of *Contacto Comix*, the witness and judgment of the perambulating barrio duo are, as in the Rassini comic book, ubiquitous. The visual organization of the comic changes from one page to the next, accommodating a sense of movement of the barrio characters through history. On page 11 they observe the grandeur of the great Aztec city of Tenochtitlan from a perch atop one of the pyramids in the foreground of a full-page panel. On page 13 they look down on a conquistador and a Mexica warrior engaged in close combat, this time from the branches of a tree (perhaps the tree of the legendary "Noche Triste" where Hernán Cortés is said to have wept after an early defeat of his troops) at upper left, situated outside the dramatically jagged margins of the central panel. On page 18 a window frame is used in lieu of a panel frame for the two, emphasizing their role as witnesses to historical events playing out on the page below them. Elsewhere, historical experience is framed in cloud-shaped panels suggestive of the characters' own thoughts, or in dog-eared panels suggestive of manuscript pages. Despite frequently dense narrative text, Manrique's loose and mutating panel structures assure that the two modern characters, the urban working-class reader's most likely point of identification with the comic book's argument, always share the page and seemingly the historical moment as first-hand witnesses to torture, rape, cultural devastation, and slavery, peering in on scenes from the Conquest and then the colonial period.

Unlike the workers of *Contacto Comix*, however, Manrique's characters engage in witness in a juridical sense and in the manner of human rights documentation, not as agents of an individualized, panoptic superego. The judgment rendered in "La discriminación" is always a historical and political one and refers to the broader society, instead of being an assessment centered on the personal behavior of the individual in the sphere of private, interpersonal relations. Discussion of Mexico's troubled relation to its indigenous heritage is triggered after the "Chicago Buls" character brags that he is "screwing a white girl" and thus doing his part to improve the Mexican people (*"mejorar la raza"*). His counterpart, who proves to be a working-class intellectual, much like Manrique himself, moves judgment into the sphere of collective, historical meaning—"What's up with you dude [*güey*]? You talk like you don't know anything about history" (2)—and takes on the task of educating his friend about Mexican history and identity. Moreover, the witness performed by Manrique's duo is dialogical, and propositional; the knowledgeable narrator responds to his interlocutor's questions and doubts, offers evidence and rebuttal: Mexico's long indigenous heritage includes a series of important native civilizations that offered major contributions to human development, from the Olmecs and Toltecs to the Mayans and Teotihuacanos and finally the Aztecs. Or, as the narrator phrases it—among "the coolest [*chirindongas*] civilizations in all of humanity" (6).

The arguments and narrations are presented in handwritten text, in a Mexican "street" Spanish that performs a critical popular historical consciousness. The reader is reminded throughout, in other words, that instruction is not provided by an "outsider," or professional historian, or even a formally educated Mexican, but by a fellow member of the lower socioeconomic echelons of Mexican society. Alongside this popular discourse, the visual artistry of the comic is varied in order to shape the reader's perspective on the relationship between historical past and present. For example, Manrique's drawing style shifts to that of an archaeological sketch in his renderings of representative artifacts of the pre-Colombian civilizations, and then to a more starkly shaded and dramatic mode when depicting the violent moment of the Conquest. These stylistic shifts strike a contrast with the more cartoonish and facilely rendered barrio characters, and thus reinforce the idea of a narrative movement away from the private sphere of personal whimsy and ignorance where the "Chicago Buls" character's racist attitudes flourish, and into the realm of collective history. Later, as the two latter-day Mexicans bear witness to the depredations of Spanish colonial power, the stately images of indigenous power and civilization give way to another, more comically grotesque figuration: a hairy, penis-faced barbarian standing in for the Spanish colonial project (see figure 5.2). Pages 14 through 25 of the comic find the two time-travelers from the barrio gazing upon the violent spectacle of European colonial power, where representatives of church and state pillage and despoil while their penile noses point obscenely at the objects of their attention.

There is a dose of Mikhail Bakhtin's concept of the grotesque body in Manrique's representation of colonial power. What Bakhtin called the grotesque body was an unofficial conception of the body he identified in Francois Rabelais' sixteenth-century series of novels, *Gargantua and Pantagruel.* The grotesque figuration of the body emphasizes what Bakhtin called the "material lower stratum"—the consumptive, sexual, and waste elimination functions of the body as a material organism. The prominence of these "lower" bodily functions has the effect of opening the individual body to other bodies and to the surrounding object world. Bakhtin argued that this more worldly and materialist representation of the body is the expression of a collective, vital historical consciousness. The grotesque conjures "not the biological body, which merely repeats itself in the new generations, but precisely the historic, progressing body of mankind" (Bakhtin 1984, 367). The origins of the grotesque body, with its deconstruction of the separate and sovereign individual body, lie with millennial folk cultures, and stand in contrast to the individualized modern body, where a hierarchy of values subordinates the "lower" bodily functions to the symbolic dominance of the head and face. "Grotesque forms of the body . . . predominate in the extra-official life of the people. For example, the theme of mockery and abuse is almost entirely bodily and grotesque. The body that figures in all the expressions of the unofficial speech of the people is the body that fecundates and is

Figure 5.2. A penis puts a grotesque mask on official colonial power, and on the "Americanized" Mexican at upper left. The phallic face of power presides over scenes of torture, greed, and willful ignorance. Popular slang and wordplay dominate in the narrative text. From "La discriminación en México."

fecundated, that gives birth and is born, devours and is devoured, drinks, def-
ecates, is sick and dying" (Bakhtin 1984, 319). In Bakhtin's analysis, Rabelais'
novels are the culmination of this universal folk culture, and the grotesque aesthetic partakes of an irreverent leveling of official hierarchy and order.

The grotesque body is evoked in Manrique's drawings through the phallic face he gives official power. The "lowly" element of the phallus thrusts out
from the head of official power and authority; the official symbolic hierarchy
vis-à-vis the human body is violated, overturned. As visual discourse, the penis-
faced colonialist brings the Bakhtinian figure into play as a strategy for mocking
and denuding European dominion. The body "speaks" through the imagery,
unsheathing naked physical desire from behind the machinations of colonial
officialdom. Official authority—ensconced in theological high-mindedness and
racist superiority in the Spanish colonial enterprise—is thereby "reduced" to the
"body that fecundates," and foreign cultural and political penetration take on
the character of a sexual violation. Under Manrique's pen, official power, and as
a result, official history, is unmasked precisely by constructing a lurid mask for
officialdom. This same mask, the eminent sign of debasement (and of debased
eminence), appears repeatedly throughout the comic as a trace of official power,
linking the Spanish conquistadors and the Catholic church to present-day U.S.
dominion.

The phallic mask is the central visual signifier for Manrique's comic book,
its paradigmatic image of globalization, of Mexico's subjugation by external
forces, and of Mexicans' self-abnegating inferiority complex. Of course, the
contemporary globalized moment of the reader of "La discriminación" is
conjured indirectly on several occasions in the comic's text, as at the bottom
left of page 15 (figure 5.2), where the conquistador strangles a Mexica man while
shouting, "I want dollars! . . . um, rather . . . I want! Oregano! Oregano! Gold!
Gold! Goooooooold!" The conquistadors' appetite for gold (Hernán Cortés's first
carta de relación, or report to the Spanish Crown, mentioned "*oro*" more than
four dozen times) is conflated with the post-gold-standard U.S. dollar, and with
the transnational narcotics trade ("*orégano*" is Mexican slang for marijuana).
But the penislike nose is a more telling signifier, as it systematically links the
Conquest to present-day globalization. In fact, the same nose that appears on
the European conquistadors of the sixteenth century makes a first appearance
on the cover of the comic book, where a more subtly but nonetheless clearly
penis-faced Uncle Sam stands with his arm around the shoulders of a Mexican
politician, while a family of impoverished Mexicans stands in the shadow of

that official embrace. (The Mexican functionary, who stands on a pedestal in a vain effort to approximate the stature of Uncle Sam, declares, "Here in Mexico we don't have discrimination: all the foreigners are welcome. Right mister?") Meanwhile, throughout the comic book the Americanized urban working-class Mexican, whose racist commentary instigates the comic's history lesson, also sports a nose with a bulbous, glanslike tip.

Importantly, the grotesque visual image at the center of the graphic narrative also refers the reader back to the universe of popular speech, to linguistic metaphors that circulate as part of "the unofficial speech of the people." In the narrative text, Manrique's proletarian intellectual describes the techniques of social control and domination with frequently vulgar slang terminology. For example, he employs the verb root "*chingar*"—indigenous peoples under Spanish rule were nothing more than "*unas chingas*" (20); the Spaniards "*chingaron pior*" the African slaves (21)—which can translate variously as "fuck" or "fuck over." As Mexican poet Octavio Paz famously indicated in his essay on Mexican culture, *The Labyrinth of Solitude*, the verb "*chingar*" and its derivatives have myriad meanings, like striking, penetrating, opening, and violating, linking with one term power, violence, and sexuality. This is a network of meanings evoked in the not quite translatable wounded nationalism of Mexicans' unofficial self-description as "*hijos de la Chingada*" (children of the Violated One). That semantic network is one where Manrique's multifaceted visual sign of the grotesque, phallic mask finds an easy home.

But the Rabelaisian visual discourse of the penis in "La discriminación" references in image form another complex of popular meaning as well. The vulgar term "*pendejo*" and several associated terms are also employed—"Stop saying *pendejadas*," says the narrator to his Americanized counterpart (26); he later advises his friend, and the reader, to read Jorge Paulat's book "[i]f you want to know more so you can get rid of *lo pendejo*." "*Pendejo*" literally means "pubic hair," but sustains a dense constellation of other meanings: "idiot," "asshole," "dumbass," and "fool" could all serve as translations, as could the colorful Americanism "dickhead." It is in light of these connotations that the central image of Manrique's comic book takes on its full significance. The phallic mask shared by Uncle Sam, the conquistadors, and the "Chicago Buls" character makes clear for the reader that the local "*pendejo*"—the ignorant Mexican who repeats racist nostrums for what ails Mexico—is a product of the long history of Mexico's globalization, and an agent of the country's continued violation. In the final pages, the "Chicago Buls" character shows his own coming to critical awareness, or "*concientización*," when he poses the rhetorical question: "You mean, we're governed by *puro yeyo*?" (27). "*Yeyo*," a slang term for cocaine or cocaine user, but also idiot or crazy person, is also used synonymously with "*pendejo*."

Ultimately, for Manrique's "La discriminación," it is not individual comportment that is to be adjusted, but the sweeping metanarrative that now guides Mexican society. Instead of a fundamental inferiority on the part of the Mexican requiring (structural) adjustments applied first by the European Conquest and subsequently by foreign trade and technology ("now when we start talking in English . . . we'll even be modern"), the very notion of Mexican inferiority is contextualized as a notion serving dominant foreign interests. In the discourse of the comic, Mexicans are not inferior so much as they are violated and dominated; and they are not without significant strengths—not only in the majestic pre-Colombian past but also in the vitality of Mexican popular culture itself. Indeed, this latter strength is both implicitly demonstrated by the text's slang narration and grotesque visual aesthetic and explicitly developed in the final pages, when the narrator explains how informal racial and cultural mixing under Spanish rule produced "a new race of Mexicans" (24). "Mexicanness," in other words, is a popular cultural artifact, produced and reproduced historically against the grain of official power, and often by popular appropriation and transgression.

Comically, the "Chicago Buls" T-shirt of the ignorant Mexican is altered occasionally in the course of his education, as if to indicate a growing degree of separation from thoughtless acceptance of U.S. influence (that is, "*lo pendejo*"). Reading "Chicago Buls" on page 1, on page 16 the T-shirt reads "*Los güeyes de Chicago*," a play on the dual meaning of the slang term "*güey*," meaning literally "steer," a castrated bull, but also rough equivalent for popular U.S. usage "dude." At the end of the comic, his education complete, the man's T-shirt has become a scatological Spanish-language scramble of the original English: "*Chico Te Cago Bule Bulé*" (Kid I Shit on You), with *Bule Bulé* being an apparently taunting reference to the 1960s Tex-Mex rock-n-roll hit "Woolly Bully" by Sam the Sham and the Pharaohs. In both Manrique's comic and the SME's comic, appropriative visual discourse implicates U.S. economic power and cultural hegemony in the issues addressed by the graphic narrative. For the SME's *historieta*, the polemical cultural appropriation takes the form of Rafael Barajas's reconfiguration of the General Electric logo as an emblem of national struggle. For Manrique, it is a sign of American popular culture that is appropriated and Mexicanized.

In the visual field opened for the Mexican reader by these two texts, semiotic elements from the mass cultural market (the corporate logo and the iconic promotional T-shirt) are combined irreverently with recognizable symbols of Mexican national identity, masculine virility, and official authority. In the details of how these elements come together in *historieta* form, one can discern important propositional content with regard to globalization that circulates here among working-class counterpublics. A proposition, of course, is an assertion, claim, or proposal made available for reasoned evaluation. Comic books are not typically read as propositional media, but with the SME and Manrique texts this is unavoidable, because the texts were so obviously developed to function precisely as public discourse. Importantly also, both comics are the product of a relationship between individual artists and a working-class organization. As such, both arise from contact between the aesthetic and political orientation of the graphic artist, on the one hand, and the collective goals and values of the organization, on the other. Therein can be found all the discursive and aesthetic differences that matter between the two texts.

The human body and its material circumstances figure prominently in both "La discriminación en México" and "Que no nos roben la luz." But beneath this formal similarity between the two didactic comics there are other, underlying differences. A popular aesthetic is present in both, but in Manrique's comic the presence of the popular draws heavily upon popular speech, to such a degree that the central visual signifier is overdetermined by the universe of street slang. In contrast, the SME comic channels popular sensibilities through the caricature aesthetic of the political cartoon, a visual genre formally integrated to the public sphere through the medium of the newspaper. While both approaches evince a certain Bakhtinian feel, the weight of Manrique's *caló* markedly separates his discourse from "polite" society, and accents his narrative determinedly as a view "from below." From the perspective of a social semiotics, "La discriminación" is marked by "metasigns" or in-group discursive markers that make it more authoritative, more appealing, and fundamentally more accessible to urban Mexicans socialized to the informal culture of the street and the barrio (see Hodge and Kress; and Volosinov). The SME text constructs a potential affinity for a broader cross section of Mexican society, because its exaggerated imagery mainly isolates the very powerful or very rich as existing "outside" the realm of the quotidian and the normal.

These distinct relationships to popular cultural sensibilities are suggestive of the manner in which artists' collaboration with social organizations can shape artistic choices in cultural production. They are also indicative of the distinctive public character of the two comic books. While the SME comic sought a place in the broader national public conversation by giving voice to otherwise marginalized arguments, the Santo Domingo comic sought to instigate a public conversation internal to working-class communities. One can discern in each case a proposition for a particular relationship between the working-class or popular body and the Mexican state, and for a particular antidote to the threat posed to Mexican popular sovereignty by U.S.-led capitalist globalization. In "Que no nos roben la luz," national sovereignty arises from a control of material resources that attends to the needs of the working body; as a corollary to this, the diversion of resources away from "*lo popular*"—that abstract and symbolic "we" that recognizes itself in substantive demands for justice—results in a weakening of the state and a conversion of the human body into a commodity. In "La discriminación en México," meanwhile, the principal threat to national sovereignty is foreign influence over Mexican popular cultural sensibilities, an influence that strips away the nation's most profound strength, the popular cultural core of its independence, and replaces it with the *pendejo*.

MEMORIES OF UNDERDEVELOPMENT

La Familia Burrón and the Politics of Modernization

Gabriel Vargas's *La Familia Burrón* is uniquely valued as an expression of Mexican national identity that transcends demarcation between "high culture" and popular culture. The cultural imprint of Mexico's one-time extensive comic book industry is felt in the sentimental and nostalgic remembering of the golden era of the 1940s through 1960s, when series like *La Familia Burrón, Kalimán, Fantomas: La amenaza elegante* (Fantomas: The Elegant Menace), and others enjoyed mass readerships under government supports for the domestic cultural market. In one recent news article, the Mexican comic book is lamented as a thing of the past: "a species gone extinct, or like many other expressions of the heart it has become an underground voice" (Olvera and Tapia). But *La Familia Burrón* is exceptional because Mexican intellectuals, cultural institutions, and government in recent years have formally and explicitly identified Vargas's long-running comic book series with the Mexican nation's values, and with the social experience of its postrevolutionary process of modernization.

La Familia Burrón is a cultural vehicle for collective memory, what sociologist Maurice Halbwachs describes as a group's sense of the past "reconstructed on the basis of the present" (40). The reconstruction of the nation's past that attaches to the *Burrón* series holds the celebrated comic close to the post–Partido Revolucionario Institucional (PRI) present, despite the fact that its narrative and aesthetic formulae were initiated and perfected during the long period of state-led national development later mostly superseded by neoliberalism. President Vicente Fox, for example, linked the historic comic book's characters to Mexicans' social present by employing a national "we" when awarding Gabriel Vargas the National Arts and Sciences Prize in 2003: *La Familia Burrón* is comprised of "popular archetypes that are just as close to us as the people we know from our daily lives" (Presidency). As with the official comic books discussed in chapter 2, this kind of public celebration and interpretation of the *Burrón* series is evidence of the strategic importance of "*lo popular*" to both those who embrace neoliberal globalization as the new model for national development and those who are critical of the free-market model. *La Familia Burrón* offers a case study in how an artifact of popular culture, and the representation of national popular culture configured therein, can operate simultaneously within competing narratives of the national past and present, which is to say the symbolic crux of conflict over globalization.

The special place accorded to *La Familia Burrón* in early-twenty-first-century Mexican culture is, at least in part, a consequence of the series' status as not only the longest-lived Mexican comic book still in production today but also the oldest such publication in all of Latin America. Begun in 1939, the *Burrón* series was published by Editorial Panamericana until 1977, when Gabriel Vargas ceased production over a contract dispute with the publisher. Vargas subsequently began producing the comic again in 1978, in conjunction with a daily comic strip printed in the midday edition of the newspaper *Excélsior* (Hinds and Tatum). Vargas has also published and distributed a weekly installment of the comic book since 1978. At ninety-two years old in 2007, Vargas has been lionized as a national cultural treasure, awarded the National Journalism Prize in 1983, the José Vasconcelos Medal in 2003, the National Arts and Sciences Prize in 2003, a postage stamp specially designated by Mexico City's Legislative Assembly in 2004, the La Catrina Award of the International Conference of Caricaturists and Comic Book Artists in 2005, and the Pedro María Anaya Prize of the State of Hidalgo in 2006. In 2002 Spanish publishing house Editorial Porrúa began reissuing the post-1978 series in bound volumes (totaling twelve as of 2007, with plans for more to come). *La Familia Burrón* sales have declined significantly compared to the so-called golden era of Mexican comics—according to recent Vargas family numbers, distribution approximated 500,000 copies per week in the period 1950 to 1970, declining to 140,000 by 2003 (Olvera and Tapia). Interviews with Chicago-area Spanish-language retailers suggest that distribution of the comic in the United States had been significantly curtailed if not ceased altogether by 2005. Nonetheless, weekly installments in the series are still distributed to significant numbers of Mexican readers every Tuesday, and the Porrúa volumes have added the *Burrón* series to the bookshelves of many more.

The Porrúa compilations and the public commemorations of Vargas and his *Burrón* series combine to give a timeless eminence to the weekly series (the Porrúa volumes go so far as to reprint episodes without dates or even series numbers). This ambient cultural effect in turn opens the content of the series to new meaning and interpretation. Something of what this entails can be appreciated in a 2007–8 exhibit at the Museo del Estanquillo in Mexico City's historic district, which re-created the *vecindad* in which the Burrón family lives in the comic book series. A *vecindad* is a building with multiple single-family dwellings that open out onto a shared central patio space, and that share a common point of entry from the street. *Vecindades* became a fixture of social life for Mexico's urban poor ever since property owners began converting colonial-era structures to rental housing in the nineteenth century. Mexico City's historic district is known for its popular urban barrios—Tepito most notoriously—where the *vecindad* has long been fundamental to the local informal economy, neighborhood politics, and local cultural activity.

The Estanquillo exhibit on *La Familia Burrón* is noteworthy for two main reasons. Most obviously, there is something remarkable about a contemporary comic book being taken up as a museological object, a popular cultural artifact still in circulation, purchased weekly from kiosks and street-side vendors by a broad workaday public, while at the same time a prestigious cultural institution displays the comic and promotes its appreciation as a historical artifact. Meanwhile, the curatorial decision (made by none other than political cartoonist Rafael Barajas) that turns the *vecindad* from *La Familia Burrón* into the organizing principle, the very architecture, of the exhibit simultaneously bestows a special cultural value on the social life of lower-income Mexicans. The *vecindad* that appears as a two-dimensional image within Gabriel Vargas's comic book is extracted and expanded from those pages so that the comic book may now reappear inside the space of the *vecindad.* The exhibit is built up upon the historical reality of the *vecindad,* and recognizes there the social arena within which this particular comic book finds its cultural meaning and vitality.

Interestingly, the architectural premise of the Estanquillo exhibit turns on an interpretation of the *Burrón* series held by Carlos Monsiváis, considered Mexico's most influential cultural critic, and whose extensive private collection of Mexican visual culture serves as the basis for all of the exhibits at the Museo del Estanquillo. In a 1998 essay published in *La Jornada Semanal*, the weekend cultural supplement of the national daily newspaper, Monsiváis contributed his reflections to a broader retrospective on *La Familia Burrón* that also included essays by the writers Sergio Pitol, Miguel Cervantes, and Carlos García-Tort, and a poem by Hugo Gutiérrez Vega. In Monsiváis's view, "The character [*personaje*] *par excellence* of La Familia Burrón is the *vecindad*, the classic space of the popular imagination until recent times, out of which extend the poor settlements, markets, residences, pool halls, street vendors' tarps, the world in sum of the street deals, police repression, solidarity amid scarcity, the rising cost of living, petty corruption, of pressing necessities." This suggestion, that the *Burrón* series presents the *vecindad* as one of the principal agents of its humorous graphic narrative and commentary, first grants personhood to the urban social space and then eulogizes it. One might paraphrase Monsiváis by saying that in *La Familia Burrón*, there is a chronicling, a documentation and remembrance, of the *vecindad* as a central agent of Mexico's urban social life.

And sure enough, any reader familiar with *La Familia Burrón* will recognize the acuity of Monsiváis's observation, since the Burrón family and their extensive network of colorful social contacts repeatedly cross paths precisely in the patio of the *vecindad*, where the red-headed, bombastic, and absurdly long-legged protagonist Borola Burrón gossips, fights, and schemes with all those in her social orbit. But given the cast of colorful characters who comprise the social world of *La Familia Burrón*, Monsiváis's interpretation entails a sly aesthetic maneuver as well. Alongside Monsiváis's reflections on the work of Gabriel Vargas, the reader encounters an essay by García-Tort and Cervantes, "Los Burrón: Dramatis personae o un elenco cachetón" (The Burróns: Dramatis Personae or a Chubby-Cheeked Cast of Characters), which is an inventory of the comic book's main personalities. These include the nuclear Burrón family—Borola Tacuche de Burrón, "central axis of the family and antidote for the long-suffering Mexican woman"; Don Regino Burrón, Borola's "long-suffering husband" and owner and operator of the Golden Curl barbershop, who "has never been able to make any money due to his scruples and lack of audacity"; the daughter Macuca, "in constant defense of her virtue"; and son Regino Jr., alias El Tejocote, who knows "no vices, bad habits or underhanded dealings." But the cast of characters also includes Ruperto, Borola's brother, who is a good-hearted member of the criminal underworld, and whose face is always obscured by a ski mask; Cristeta Tacuche, Borola's indescribably wealthy aunt, who has "the body of a beach ball"; the ancient widow Doña Gamucita and her pathologically lazy poet-son Avelino Pilongano, both of whom subsist on the elderly woman's piecework as a washerwoman; and the drunken Don Susano Cantarranas and his equally drunken girlfriend, La Divina Chuy, both of whom earn their meager living from trash-picking. If this collection of characters were not lively enough, one could mention also the Count Satán Carroña, a vampire who lives in a gloomy mansion on the outskirts of Mexico City, and Don Briagoberto Memelas, the pistol-wielding, hypermacho cacique of the rural town of La Coyotera. Against this backdrop, to call the *vecindad* "the character par excellence" of *La Familia Burrón* is not just to personify that communal social space of Mexico's urban poor, but to animate it as yet another member of this extended family of beloved and entertaining, and fanciful, Mexican comic book characters.

Monsiváis' *vecindad*, and by extension the *vecindad* of the Museo del Estanquillo, takes on the quality of an aesthetic figure, a protagonist in a narrative. And the narrative in question is not only the long episodic trajectory of *La Familia Burrón*, it is the national story of Mexico as well. All of the essays of the 1998 *La Jornada* retrospective evince an air of nostalgia, an association of the *Burrón* comic not just with a time gone by, but also with a kind of critical leverage once exercised by popular culture on the national identity and imagination. For Monsiváis, the *vecindad* is a central character in the comic book's "portrait of popular cultural manners" (*cuadro de costumbres*), a visual and linguistic "memory of pre-modern Mexico re-created through an effective satire." The cultural critic discerns a tension between Vargas's comic book and Mexico's path to modernity: "In *La Familia Burrón*, the *vecindades* that disappear as a result of modernization come back to life"; and "*La Familia Burrón* is the extremely amusing evocation of a world that refuses to disappear." For Sergio Pitol, the *vecindad* is an island of revolt against a flawed Mexican officialdom: "The world outside that patio of poverty-stricken homes is ruled and sustained by corruption and arrogance: corrupt police, corrupt inspectors, corrupt judges, corrupt bureaucrats." Moreover, Borola herself, who has held court in the *vecindad* since the inception of *La Familia Burrón* in 1939, is the embodiment of "the imagination, fantasy, risk, insubordination." "In this world of unbearable Yuppies," observes Pitol, "the name of Borola is an anachronism. Evoking it returns me to a vital ambience long since disappeared."

This discourse about *La Familia Burrón* places the comic book in a kind of critical relationship to discourse about Mexico's modernization. These Mexican intellectuals' very public interpretations of *La Familia Burrón* look backward on Mexico's path to modernity, and seek to hold dear in the globalizing present a thing from that modernizing past. The thing in question is not solely the comic; it is an oppositional conception of "*lo popular*," of a "world that refuses to disappear" despite official corruption and abuse, a site of resistance and of alternative possibility, of imagination and defiance of official authority. To some degree, we find evidence here that *La Familia Burrón* operates as a medium of the relationship between a generation of Mexican intellectuals, on the one hand, and popular Mexican social experience, on the other; between the intelligentsia and "*lo popular*"—at least insofar as "*lo popular*" has historically embodied for many Latin American intellectuals an indispensable pressure point in opposition to, or efforts to reform, official pursuit of a "first world" model of capitalist modernity.

Indeed, over the course of the twentieth century three main intellectual and political claims on popular culture and "*lo popular*" have vied for influence over state power and official policies in Latin America. William Rowe and Vivian Schelling have usefully delineated these as centered on: the authenticity of premodern folk culture as against the degradation of community resulting from industrialization; the relative success or failure of popular culture in replicating the modern cultures of the capitalist economic powers; and the principles of progressive social transformation embedded in popular culture (1–16). The first of these is usually encountered as a conservative critique of mass culture and modernization, seeks national identity in the "pure" folkways of tradition, and often takes the political form of a populist nationalism. The most prominent variant of the second discourse is the modernization hypothesis promoted in the post–World War II period by a number of prominent U.S. Weberians, social scientists who theorized that national development could occur in the "third world" through a process of mass cultural diffusion that brought rational individualism and other principles of "first world" modernity into the national cultures of the developing world. Under this construction, cultural tradition is often an obstacle to economic and social development, and U.S. cultural norms (or their local equivalents) are the antidote. This view is retained at the core of official U.S. globalism. The third discourse often operated, in the context of twentieth-century debates over Latin America's relationship to the U.S. model of development, as an adjunct to national liberation movements and Marxist theories of economic dependency and cultural imperialism. One can sense all three of these approaches to the relationship between popular culture and national development subtly at work in recent valuations of *La Familia Burrón*.

An attentive reading encounters all three of these discourses on popular culture at work also in the comic book's presentation of the *vecindad*, of its values and behaviors, as the space of representation of Mexican popular culture. The satirical bite of the *Burrón* series shows, by turns, traditionalist, modernization-ist, and progressive colors. The central problematic, the unresolved issue around which the speech and behavior of the characters constantly orbit, is poverty. The central question raised within the *vecindad* is whether the space of popular culture, the ethos of Monsiváis's "character par excellence," is in the final analysis a proponent of or an obstacle to Mexico's national development. As we shall see, the comic's unique aesthetics resists reduction to any one ideology or narrative of development. What emerges as more important in its strategies for representing Mexican society, and poverty in particular, is its remembering of the politics of modernization, something that the neoliberal model would rather the reader forget.

In formal terms, there is nothing flashy or nuanced about the visual dimension of Vargas's comic. *La Familia Burrón* is characterized by a simple chromatic scheme in which solid colors provide "fill" for iconic figures drawn with bold, clean lines. Coloration is flat, with little in the way of shading, and the composition of figures is marked by a pleasantly rounded form. The circle is, in fact, the basic underlying structural design for the face, nose, and eyes of nearly all the characters. Even the trunk and legs extend outward from a circular rump always located at the center of the human figure. One of the first things one notices about Gabriel Vargas's Burrón family and their social cohort is precisely that: a pleasant roundness, complimented by the ubiquitous semicircle of a smile. The characters thus project an affability and sense of underlying innocence that are far more consistent with a children's comic book than with one read by a wide cross section of adults, much less one considered by prominent cultural critics to be an important satirical commentary on Mexican society.

The amiable, almost naive feel of Vargas's characters belies, however, a very worldly, and at times even wildly extreme, range of problematic behaviors. In one episode, which seems to lampoon the modern fashion of plastic surgery, Borola complains of sleeplessness because she is haunted by the knowledge of her own skeleton. So she has a surgeon remove her bones, and spends the rest of the episode slithering around the city before deciding to have her skeleton restored to its rightful place (volume 8). In another, the perpetually unemployed Don Susano, who is always accompanied by a collection of bubbles floating above his head to signify his inebriated state, tries to make some money by juggling oranges in city traffic while balancing on a woman's back. Instead of receiving money from passers-by, the two are run over by a cargo truck (#1484). Gunplay is not infrequent, nor are beatings, heavy drinking, mendacity, theft, gossip and character assassination, or the most abject laziness. But even the very embodiment of evil, the vampire Don Satan Carroña (probably the most angular of all the characters, sporting a widow's peak, pointy ears, fangs, and a football-like nose), lusts after the blood of his impoverished victims with a smile on his face. The affective envelope provided by the nearly omnipresent smile and the pleasantly rounded features of Vargas's portrayal of Mexican society serves the function of satire, but also of normalization. The apparent innocence projected through visual form in the *Burrón* series is not a foil, in the person of one character, useful for throwing into relief the foolishness of others. Rather, Vargas's visual aesthetic has an effect comparable to an inversion of the Catholic notion of original sin—the reader can sense an original innocence beneath the surface of every character's ill-conceived or reprehensible behavior.

One consequence of this aesthetic effect is that social conflict and aggression are hedged. Characters quite literally threaten and insult one another with a smile. As a result of taking the sharp edges off the visual dimension of the narrative, social division and disruption are not "felt" directly, but instead take place with a presumed rapprochement and resolution always already in evidence. The air of innocence and joviality effected through the comic's visuals turns out to be a shared and unifying trait, a quality that trumps social differences of class, age, and sex, even when such differences are performed as combative oppositions, as is frequently the case. In the January 18, 2005, episode (#1376), for example, Macuca secretly dates an extremely wealthy elderly man. Although her parents prohibit her from dating, her mother informs her (with Borola's typical mercenary manner) that when she does find a man, Macuca must first "make sure he is the owner of large properties, fabulous residencies and above all a whole lot of money" [*mucho, mucho* money] (12). Meanwhile, Macuca's brother, Regino Jr., is suspicious and, being jealously protective of his sister's honor, follows her until he discovers her suitor and confronts him. What follows is a violent confrontation, pitting the lower-middle-class Regino Jr. against the elderly ruling-class man and his burly chauffer. Through a series of eleven panels, the confrontation escalates from the young Burrón's demand to see his sister, to a brutal exchange of blows. Regino Jr. strikes the old man in the face; the chauffer punches Regino Jr. and then body-slams him to the ground; the chauffer then aggressively pounds the head of Regino Jr.'s younger brother, the diminutive Foforito, who is standing nearby. The violence is graphically reinforced with boldly lettered sound effects—"CUAS!" "CHIN!" "PON!" "JUM!"—and even described in evocative detail—"The rich man's chauffer strikes a tremendous blow to Regino's chest, which throws him backwards, making him cough repeatedly" (19). And yet the chubby-cheeked smiles of the parties to the fracas, and of passers-by who witness it, combine to contain the violence in an aesthetic envelope that lets the reader know that this is violence without greater social consequence. The chubby and childlike bodily features and generally upbeat demeanor of the characters manage to turn the reader's thoughts away from the otherwise tempting notion of class-based social strife, despite the egregiousness of the conflict and the social class extremes involved.

The same amelioration of social conflict occurs in the many episodes in which the Burróns' *vecindad* constitutes the visual centerpiece of the narrative. In one such episode, Borola engages in an armed assault on upper-class interests, but the end result is, as usual, a return to the status quo ante. Episode #1488 (March 13, 2007) begins with a full-page sociological statement formed by a half-page panel at top and side-by-side quarter-page panels at the bottom of the first page. Each panel presents a scene from Mexican society in general, rather than of the familiar characters of the *Burrón* series: first a street scene in front of a restaurant where an ostentatiously wealthy couple (he wears a top hat, she a mink stole) have just finished eating and their chauffer awaits at curbside; then the two quarter-page panels at bottom are presented side by side, one depicting a wealthy family at dinner, and the other presenting their impoverished counterparts from the lower economic strata of Mexican society. Each panel is accompanied by a descriptive text that highlights the stark social differences of Mexican society, all with reference to food. In the image at the top of the page (see figure 6.1), the distinct social classes convene by coincidence on a public sidewalk—a middle-class couple strides past a beggar woman, and a poor, working-class pair crosses paths with the super wealthy. The accompanying text does not mince words: "The social classes are very defined because there are only two: Those who have a lot and those who have nothing. Those who always walk around with their bellies shining from eating so much and those whose bellies are limp like a deflated balloon because their bellies are empty, completely empty" (3).

This materialist social axiom is reinforced by the symmetrical images in the lower half of the page, where the sumptuous "pheasant and champagne" feast of a millionaire family is illustrated comparatively alongside a working-class

Figure 6.1. Lower, middle, and upper classes share the sidewalk outside an elegant restaurant. The inset text frames the scene with a social dichotomy: those whose bellies are full, and those who go hungry. From *La Familia Burrón* #1488, 3. Courtesy of Gabriel Vargas.

family's meager dinner of stale tortillas flavored with nothing but "green chiles or a smear of beans." When, on the very next page, the reader is transported to the Mexico City *vecindad* where the Burrón family shares a patio with a number of other poor Mexican families, the effect is to contextualize the Burróns' *vecindad* in no uncertain terms as a space of stark material need and struggle for survival, and as a social site that coexists with the forms of social life enjoyed by Mexico's wealthy. As is typical of the *Burrón* series, throughout the episode the characters and their interactions are consistently situated in architectural spaces—private interiors as well as the public spaces of the street, the patio, city traffic, the supermarket—that are likely to be as familiar to the Mexican reader as the characters themselves. In this particular case, the characters move constantly back and forth in the thirty-four pages of the comic between the private interiors of the homes of the Burróns and of their neighbors, and the shared patio space of the *vecindad*. The visual dimension of the comic makes clear, in other words, that as the drama unfolds, it features as its key player the *vecindad* and the social values it embodies.

The storyline of the episode develops the initial, general portrait of Mexican social reality in the direction of an unavoidable collision of social classes. Narrated with four quarter-page panels per page—a format from which Vargas's series seldom deviates—the storyline could not be more bleak. A Burrón neighbor, Don Pepe Juan Carrión, comes home to find that his family has been threatened with eviction by the *vecindad*'s owner, unless the family can pay the more than ten years of back rent it owes. Unable to persuade his boss to give him an advance on his salary, Carrión and his family take Borola's patently absurd advice—that is, spend the entirety of the family's income on rent, and try to survive on air and water instead of food. (The children can be fed banana peels if necessary, Borola suggests helpfully.) The storyline and the explicitly delineated social context that introduces it are obviously critical of the material circumstances of Mexico's working-class families. The self-evident absurdity of Borola's advice—which she describes as a "recipe," an ironic detail that further underscores the injustice of the circumstances—gives the story a sharp, satirical edge. Here Borola's smile serves the satire.

Borola's intervention is not limited, however, to personal financial advice. When the landlord's minions arrive to put the Carrión family's belongings out on the street, Borola sends Macuca for an old musket, which she then uses to threaten the men, forcing them to leave the Carrións' home intact. By doing this, Borola is in fact reenacting a practice that was common for many years in the *vecindades* of Mexico City's poor barrios: when an eviction was under way, people from the barrio, often signaled by the launching of a bottle rocket, would come rushing to the collective defense. Although Borola is its principal agent, the *vecindad* can be seen here as resistance, the conviviality and solidarity housed in the nation's popular culture a bulwark of defense for basic economic rights like food and housing. Borola's version of the principle of class solidarity differs in that she takes up arms with a smile, and her threats are somewhat moderated by the fact that the musket balls from her firearm can be seen bouncing ineffectually off the patio floor like Ping-Pong balls. The embodiment of progressive values is thus pulled back from the brink of class warfare by the visual aesthetics of the comic. The aesthetic hedge is an effect of the comic's visual modality—a concept discussed in chapter 3 with reference to *El Libro Vaquero*—which strategically separates Borola's action from the reader's sense of reality.

The progressive moment in the narrative is further moderated by the presence of a "free-market" explanation for the Carrións' predicament. Carrión's employer pleads a lack of cash flow in refusing to advance the worker's salary, arguing, "I'm drowning in taxes. I started my factory so I could make a little money and now I'm just working for the government" (15). Public intervention is part of the problem, not the solution. In the end, Borola collects donations from all of the households of the *vecindad* in order to placate the landlord, Don Quintin Peluche. In the final four panels, everyone gathers, smiling, in the patio of the *vecindad* to present to Don Peluche a tray full of money. Borola explains the situation to the landlord: "It is necessary for you to know that all of the neighbors have sacrificed in order to help the Carrión family, who because they eat three meals a day cannot pay you the rent" (34). Embarrassed, the landlord returns the money to his tenants, and the story thereby returns the reader to the status quo. The landlord has responded to moral suasion, desisting from his plans to evict the Carrión family. But his governing interests, his class-specific interests, remain intact, and are even legitimated.

Not only is there ultimately no alternative to the problem of poverty imagined by the story, the comic's visual aesthetic unites the characters under the banner of a fundamental innocence. The ever-upturned smiles, of both the extremely rich and the extremely poor, in the face of economic injustice, and the flaccid downward arc of Borola's buckshot, are signposts of the manner in which socially justified challenges to the social order are portrayed in *La Familia Burrón*. The clash of working-class interests with the economic controls of the upper class is made painfully visible through satire, but where transformative social action is concerned, the smile signifies differently. The critical, ironic smile, which made a mockery of the landlord's demands, is first replaced, during the armed defense of the family's home, by the playful grin of a child in a sandbox dispute. The same smile then fades in the end to a conciliatory gesture. Whereas irony stirs social awareness, the smile with which the story ends draws a line beyond which challenge to the status quo shall not go. If the *vecindad* can be a progressive site of resistance against capitalist abuses, it is also a conservative site, a space for the consecration of the social order.

In much the same way, ideological differences are hemmed in, neutered, restrained from resulting in irreparable (or transformative) social division, at the same time that certain shibboleths of the national development problematic are lampooned. For example, Borola's suggestion that the Carrión family simply budget differently in order to make their monthly rent appears to lampoon the neoliberal discourse of "personal responsibility" that characterizes poverty as a consequence of irrational economic behavior and/or of a lack of individual discipline. These ideologies are not always made explicit through the speech and ideation in the comic book so much as through the behavior and attitudes of the characters. In general, the Burróns and their fellow citizens of Vargas's Mexico act out distinct ideologies or discourses of modernization in the form of attitudes, anxieties, or whims that grip them for an episode, causing them to experiment with or challenge preexisting patterns of behavior. Often implicit in these personal social experiments are competing frameworks for promoting and evaluating social and economic development or progress. In fact, if there is one concern that most preoccupies the marriage of Don Regino and Borola Burrón, it is social and economic change per se, including the all-important question of the future economic prospects of the Burrón family, but also gender roles, business practices, fashions, and the like.

Marital strife (again, always with a smile) turns out to be haunted by the politics of development. In episode #1376, as Macuca is courted by a ninety-five-year-old rich man, Borola and Don Regino quarrel over the legitimacy of the relationship, opposing monied interests to traditional values. Borola argues: "How could I be opposed when she told me that that young Porfirian [a joking reference to the rich suitor having been born during the dictatorship of Porfirio Díaz, whose rule was ended by the armed revolution of 1910] owns several buildings, haciendas, and above all, lots of jingling money" (26). And then, more to the point: "This fragile and beautiful girl will save our home from the horrible misery that holds us in its claws, by marrying an old man made of gold." Don Regino responds: "I think differently from you. If Macuca were to marry a young man and her marriage was out of love, I would not oppose her making a life for herself" (27). As is usually the case, Borola's fantasies of economic betterment are frankly mercenary and self-interested, while Don Regino's response is traditionalist, but generally reasonable. Borola's comical reference to the wealthy man as a "young Porfirian" evokes the prerevolutionary, nineteenth-century free-market liberalism of Porfirio Díaz's technocrats, thereby associating her own position in the argument with an ideology of national development that was, in theory at least, superseded by the Mexican Revolution. At the end of the episode, after a nasty brawl between Don Regino and the ruling-class suitor on the floor of the Burrón barbershop, the family awakens to discover that the whole affair was a collective dream. For Borola, it was a dream that could be made reality, and she is ready to sacrifice traditional social values and the collective unity of the family in order to send Macuca off in search of a wealthy partner. Don Regino, however, rejects the dream as ideology: "Don't deceive yourselves, we are poor and that's it" (34).

Although Don Regino's traditionalism most often wins out over Borola's wild schemes for improving the family's prospects (in one episode she sells a crude form of "cosmetic surgery" out of her home by yanking women's hair back so far that it stretches the skin of their faces taut), the tension between tradition and modernity is never resolved because the family remains plagued with the economic woes endemic to their class position. Regino's embrace of tradition is colored with a self-defeating fatalism ("we are poor and that's it"). The family's seemingly inalterable lower-middle-class circumstances meanwhile make Borola a relentless force for change. In the first ten panels of episode #1490 (March 27, 2007), she walks through the city with Macuca while criticizing Don Regino for "not having ambitions to progress" [*progresar*] (3–5). The backdrop to her comments is not the *vecindad* in this case, but in panel after panel an urban environment in which modernity and tradition coexist. Multistoried buildings, an upscale hotel (with a "Read La Familia Burrón" billboard on the side), a satellite dish atop a modernist-looking structure, and a large, well-maintained PEMEX gasoline station are displayed in separate panels as key features of the environment through which Borola and Macuca move as the mother critiques her husband's business ethic. Rendered in clean, rectilinear form, these signifiers of Mexican urbanity and modernity are interspersed with other panels containing more traditional points of reference: a shoe-shine stand, a colonial-era mission-style church, a newsboy hawking the daily paper on the street.

At the PEMEX station, Borola calmly purchases a gallon of gasoline, and then carries this to Don Regino's barbershop, which has been contextualized in the preceding panels as yet another traditional site in the cityscape. Inside the barbershop, Borola splashes gasoline over the chairs and sets them ablaze, explaining to a horrified Don Regino, "I'm doing it so that you will change your profession" (6). Borola proves, once again, to be willing to resort to violence in order to promote change, in this case lashing out as a radical proponent of market forces. "I burned your shop [because] otherwise you would be incapable of abandoning your poorly paid trade [*oficio*]" (10). The dialogue, including use of the guild-related term "*oficio*," makes clear that her act of arson was directed against failed tradition, which is, to translate Borola's comments into the language of the market, slow to respond to economic disincentives. Don Regino laments, "I feel sad to leave the shop, since for so many years we made a living from it. Besides, it's the trade [*oficio*] my father taught me" (12). At the same time, however, the visuals turn Borola into a ridiculous burlesque of the principles of modernity she enacts. The gasoline-fueled flames mostly consume her sensible outfit, leaving her exposed in bra and panties and high heels, with her hat scorched to look like a traditional brown campesino's sombrero. For the next twelve pages, she walks through the city in this surreal state with her family at her side, celebrating all the while her sudden sexual liberation as "a girl from the year 2007." "The time when we women dressed like nuns is long since past," she admonishes her scandalized family (15). Meanwhile, she and her husband discuss the necessity for Don Regino to transform himself into a modern subject. "I need time to change my character and lose the shame that has always dominated me," he confesses (18).

Borola's will to modernize prevails initially, but the return to the status quo is as inevitable as her smile. Unknown to each other, Borola and Regino both seek work as dancers in the theater, she motivated by her newfound exhibitionism and he by an old acquaintance who is now an entrepreneur running a dance school. The visual setting provided for the action in the latter half of the narrative leaves no doubt that the two have left the *vecindad* behind and immersed themselves completely in the promises of an affluent modernity. In a visual detail reminiscent of *El Libro Semanal*'s conservative critique of the urban high-life discussed in chapter 4, no fewer than nine separate panel images place the Burróns in relief against the abstract geometry of an urban skyline. Caught in the logic of a gendered double standard, Regino gets the part of an elderly gentleman who dances with a cast of young women, while Borola is rejected as too old. Borola's defeat occurs in the corporate suite on the top floor of a towering high-rise, and the unnatural imposition of the modernity it embodies is suggested by a panel image that presents the building's green exterior as a skewed abstraction against a pink sky (on page 26). Regino's triumph occurs in a dance salon decorated with what appears to be postexpressionist geometrist art. Because of Borola's vanity—which is to say, the personal flaw to which feminist modernity is finally reduced by Borola's behavior—her husband's success is intolerable. In the last panel of the story, Borola takes the family back to the scene of the fire, where she insists that Regino return to his heritage. For his part, Don Regino is now a market-driven modern man: "The show . . . was a big success. I can't abandon the entrepreneur when I know that I am good for business." Borola, on the other hand, has come to embrace tradition: "You were born a barber and you will die a barber" (34). His willingness to exhibit himself and to follow the incentives of the market comes full circle, through the affable dialectics of the comic book's satire, to confront Borola's renewed respect for tradition. Her impulse to modernize chastened, Borola returns home to the status quo once again.

Although Vargas's comic is clearly marked by a conservative orientation, Don Regino's stewardship of tradition suggests a wounded resignation in the face of modernization rather than an advocacy of alternatives. In episode #1491 (April 3, 2007), Don Regino muses about the changes to his profession brought on by global youth culture. Once again, he plays the traditionalist, bemoaning his inability to "interpret" young people's "modern hairstyles." Reluctantly, he decides to expand his repertoire of haircuts to include modern tastes, but not before the narrative and visuals have effectively identified punk and hip-hop fashions with dog grooming and the caprice of the wealthy. Don Regino discovers he had already been doing state-of-the-art haircuts whenever he clipped the pets of wealthy clients. The semiotic equivalence between hip urban youth and poodles also affords an opportunity for a conservative mockery of rebellious youth culture: "Poor doggies. Since they don't know how to speak they can't defend themselves. I've fixed them up in a thousand different ways and none of them has protested" (8). Modernity, however superficially represented, is accepted with a smile, and the market allowed to dictate cultural norms. That same smile of acceptance signifies a critique as well. The cultural effects of the marketplace are laughably ludicrous, even de-humanizing. But market-driven modernity in *La Familia Burrón* is, at the end of the story, an unavoidable concession. As the narrator's voice sums it up on the final page: "Burrón embraces his new profession as a barber of 2007, with care and professionalism, as this is the only way he can think of to save his family from hunger" (34).

The ideologies of development recognizable in the plots of the *Burrón* series—a traditionalist rejection of modernity; a modernizationist disdain for tradition; a progressive, class-based critique of capitalism; and a feminist overthrow of social convention, which Borola frequently personifies—share center stage, and by turns command the reader's attention. At the same time, however, all these political postures are stripped of their authority by the corrosive satire of the comic, and each is ultimately undermined by the overall unity and stasis of the social world the *Burrón* series depicts. Visions of social agency and progress articulated by twentieth-century Marxism and feminism are staged as absurd displays of individual whimsy or willfulness, and are ultimately "corrected" by a reassertion of more conservative collective values. Doctrines of capitalist modernization are also lampooned; Borola's embrace of entrepreneurialism is as risible as her idiosyncratic and clownish version of feminism. Despite the series' predilection for resolving its narratives in favor of the original state of affairs, even traditionalism is demoted to an inert, if dignified, adherence to custom, since Don Regino's conservatism seems to shoulder some of the responsibility for the abject economic conditions inside the *vecindad*. And all the while, those cherubic, round-bottomed fellow citizens remind the Mexican reader of a fundamental and shared innocence that belies the occasional violence and confrontation, and that unites the social world despite the economic chasm that separates the social classes.

What is the political sense of a text that appears to lampoon its characters' efforts to change their circumstances? And more to the point: where does the comic book position itself with regard to the politics of globalization in Mexico? A partial answer can be found in the arresting glimpses of the globalized present that flash up from time to time in Vargas's Mexico. These are moments in which the relatively contained and close, interpersonal world of the series' familiar characters is abruptly intruded upon by forces or events from beyond the horizon of Mexico. These are also moments when the boundaries of the nation are brought into evidence. As noted above, in episode #1491 the youth culture in question is described not only as modern, thus making Regino's defense of tradition more visible to the reader, but also as global. A series of eight dialogue-free panel images, each with a block of descriptive text, presents the barrio barber's explanation of how modern youth hairstyles came about. A half-page panel image of a street scene in England—"the original nest of kids who style their hair in a spectacular way"—joins others portraying African American street life in the United States ("Gringolandia") and a rock concert (10–13). In much the same way that the *vecindad* was framed sociologically as a phenomenon of social class in episode #1488, the neighborhood barbershop is here positioned amid global cultural influences. Just as the ridiculous modernity of "modern hairstyles" draws attention to Don Regino's embrace of tradition, the global provenance of those styles, their description as exports from other nations, sets off Regino's traditionalism as an appreciably nationalist attitude, and his barbershop as something of a Mexican popular institution.

Although such episodes are rare in the series, they are significant because they imagine global cultural or economic forces in relation to the Burróns' local, Mexican reality. In episode #1496 (May 9, 2007), the poet Avelino is invited by his friends to travel during Holy Week to Acapulco, Mexico's international beach tourism mecca. His main obstacle is that in order to afford the trip, he must convince his mother, Gamucita, to give him the astronomical sum of

30,000 pesos. Avelino's desire to live the high life for one week is at loggerheads with both Gamucita's insistence that he attend church during Holy Week and the economic misery that makes his plan little more than escapist fantasy. Lacking funds, Avelino never gets to travel to Acapulco, but as he describes his fantasy to Gamucita, a series of twenty-seven panel images transport him and his mother, to great comic effect, into the transnational space of a luxury vacation. In this image sequence, marked as fantasy by the cloudlike boundaries of the panel frames, it is as if characters of the *Burrón* series have appeared as interlopers in the pages of a *Libro Semanal* episode.

The upper-middle-class experience of transport and leisure, basic to the U.S. cultural model and presented as the "natural" environment of characters in *El Libro Semanal*, is celebrated in Avelino's fantasy as an otherworldly modernity. The comic book's central contrast between modernity and tradition is here globalized in an important sense: Acapulco versus Holy Week, international luxury enclave versus the barrio. In one panel image, Avelino and his elderly mother rush breathlessly through the airport as he warns her against arriving late to the plane: "Nobody waits for you here. . . . Without compassion, they will leave you." In another, the airplane, or "*aeroplátano*" (*airbanana*) as Avelino calls it, is a "colossal apparatus, which carries in its belly more than three hundred people" (15). Other images show the impoverished pair water skiing, dancing to rock music on the deck of a cruise ship, dining on a side of beef, and watching a cabaret. The absurdity of Avelino's fantasy is premised on an insurmountable boundary—symbolized visually by the "cloudy" panel frames that partition the fantasy sequence from the rest of the story—between the economic reality of the *vecindad* and the globalized tourist economy of twenty-first-century Mexico.

At times the juncture of the global and the local is tragicomic. In episode #1484 (February 13, 2007), the reader encounters the lumpenproletarian Don Susano Cantarranas struggling to find a way to earn a living. Don Susano lives in the grinding poverty of the *arrabal*, the outskirts of the formally defined urban area, where immigrants from the countryside and emigrants from the urban core come to build ramshackle housing in the mud after being displaced by either rising urban rents or declining rural income. He inquires of his equally impoverished neighbors as to how they make a living, and based on what he learns decides to earn money as a street performer, juggling oranges at a busy intersection in the city. (One of his neighbors had recently given up the "performing arts"—blowing fire by spitting kerosene—because his wife complained

Figure 6.2. A "Transports of the North" truck runs over the Mexican subaltern. "Goodbye, ungrateful world!" shouts one of the victims. From *La Familia Burrón* #1484, 34. Courtesy of Gabriel Vargas.

that his lips were always swollen up like balloons.) Implicitly refuting the image of the lazy, undeserving poor, Don Susano dutifully trains at his chosen art. He finds a partner, Doña Clotilde Mascorro, who will allow him to stand on her back as part of the spectacle. When their pathetic scheme is finally put into practice, it is quickly and unceremoniously ended by "a heavy sixteen-wheel trailer, running them down in an ugly manner" (34). And there, in a single half-page panel on the final page, appears the specter of Mexico's globalization. The side of the truck is emblazoned in big, bold lettering with a legend that resonates with a post-NAFTA Mexico and its increased commercial traffic from the United States and Canada: "Transportes del Norte" (Transports of the North). Above the cab of the truck is painted, ominously, "El Rey del Camino" (King of the Road) (figure 6.2).

As a reading of the comic book shifts its analytical lens from the state-led modernization paradigm of the PRI to the market-led modernization paradigm of the globalists, the margins and limits of the nation come into view in *La Familia Burrón*. The social world of the *vecindad* and the daily problem of poverty continue to contradict official doctrine. A sense of resistance, à la Monsiváis, is still present in this social world's refusal to disappear under the weight of the official development paradigm of the moment. But in those occasional moments of intrusion where the global comes into contact with the space of the popular, this latter ceases to be coextensive with Mexico. The space of popular experience is diminished and humbled by the expansiveness, inevitability, and speed of globalization. Where the enormous breach between social classes can still be bridged by the affable goofiness shared by all the *Burrón* characters, the gap between the local and the global is instead often colored by dehumanization: witness the poodlelike modernity of global youth culture; the cold, compassionless logic of the airport; and the accidental brutality of the cargo truck. The Burróns of the PRI period represent a Mexico that gives the lie to the government's discourse on national development. In contrast, the post-NAFTA Burróns represent a social world in danger of being left out and left behind by the globalization of the nation's economy.

Given the long life of *La Familia Burrón*'s aesthetic formula and narrative preoccupations, analysis of the comic book's politics is a historical as well as a contemporary matter. What is most politically meaningful about the comic book can be located in the juncture of the national present and the national past, in the relationship between the Burróns and the work of collective memory. Theorist of social memory Maurice Halbwachs offers a useful caution in this regard: understanding the "reshaping operation" of a social group's memory requires that "we do not forget that even at the moment of reproducing the past our imagination remains under the influence of the present social milieu" (49). The antics of the *Burrón* series' large cast of characters, including the *vecindad*, are unavoidably read at the beginning of the twenty-first century against the backdrop of the "postnational" horizon projected by neoliberalism onto Mexico's process of modernization. At the same time, under the weight of that present, the same text recalls the tarnished luster of a narrative about Mexican national development authored by decades of technocratic governance and official discourse about modernization under the PRI.

In that earlier story, the hero was the PRI cum state, and the nation's popular culture was meant to play a supporting role to an official emphasis on massive public works projects intended to conspicuously demonstrate the country's modernity. In the postrevolutionary period (that is, after the end of Lázaro Cárdenas's administration in 1940), the PRI's monumental paradigm of modernization led, of course, to colossal tragedies. Prior to the 1968 Olympic Games, the Díaz Ordaz administration remade entire sections of Mexico City in order to project a sense of Mexico's urbanity to the world. The same logic led Díaz Ordaz to order the massacre of hundreds of students at Tlatelolco on October 2, 1968, after mass demonstrations against official authoritarianism threatened to disrupt the government's carefully managed international image of Mexico. A few years before this, the same Díaz Ordaz administration had censored U.S. anthropologist Oscar Lewis's book *Los hijos de Sánchez* (The Children of Sánchez, 1961), saying the book, which developed the concept of the "culture of poverty" based on *vecindad* life in the barrio of Tepito, was immoral and a "denigration" of the Mexican nation. To talk publicly about the reality of widespread poverty in Mexico, and to theorize a popular culture mired in self-defeating pathology (the "culture of poverty" thesis in a nutshell), simply cut too deeply against the grain of official discourse about a successfully modernizing Mexico. The Burróns' *vecindad* and the recalcitrance of its economic misery similarly contradict the official story, but under the protective veil of the joke and with a far more ambivalent representation of popular culture.

As the hegemony of the PRI suffered a slow but certain collapse in the aftermath of NAFTA's implementation in 1994, it was to be expected that the enduring elements of the nation's popular culture would be politicized, or repoliticized, and be made meaningful in new ways. The *Burrón* series takes on new cultural life in part because critics of the PRI's model of governance find in this comic book, which accompanied PRI rule for sixty years, an image of poverty and official corruption that retroactively discredits PRIismo. While Monsiváis and Pitol see in the Burróns and their *vecindad* something more progressive than the modernization-at-all-costs paradigm of the PRI, Pitol's reference to "Yuppies" indicates that the *Burrón* series also takes on new meaning in the context of the epilogue to the PRI's rule: that is, neoliberal talk about how free-market globalization is the inevitable successor to the state-led modernization programs of yesteryear. For this neoliberal storyline, the corrupting power of the state is the villain, the primary obstacle to national development, and the principal author of the nation's poverty. The protagonists of the neoliberal narrative are capital and economic rationalism on the macroeconomic plane, and the self-interested, entrepreneurial individual at the microeconomic level. The Burróns' *vecindad* is an ambivalent figure for this storyline: on the one hand, the moral distance between social life in the barrio and the state could not be greater; on the other hand, Borola's interpretation of a market ethos more often than not results in terroristic assaults on the social fabric.

Nonetheless, reading *La Familia Burrón* in the context of the neoliberal paradigm for globalization raises a political valence for the comic book that is distinct from the earlier antigovernment critique of PRI rule. Specifically, the post-PRI cultural vitality of the Burróns arises from the manner in which the comic book conserves an image of a pre-NAFTA Mexico. As noted, the series' aesthesis of ideology—its translation of abstract social doctrines into concrete visual and narrative forms—corrodes and undermines a range of ideological positions, exposing them equally to ridicule by converting them into questionable behaviors, absurd social postures, or exercises in futility. Because of this, one could be tempted to conclude that, inoculated by its own satire, the comic book is immune to politics in general—that is, if not for the unitary and immovable sense of the social world that the comic book projects through its visual and narrative aesthetics. The fact that conflicting ideologies of development are both visible and risible in *La Familia Burrón* is consistent with the logic of the social and political environment for which the comic book was produced for six decades. If the conjoining of mutually discrepant ideological positions into a unified whole is a hallmark of political corporatism, then *La Familia Burrón* bears the clear imprint of the political history it traversed from its inception until the political defeat of the PRI. Indeed, the inclusion of the social class extremes of the superwealthy Cristeta and the dirt-poor Don Susano, and of the rural-urban polar opposites of the remote pueblo La Coyotera's cacique Briagoberto Memelas and Mexico City's Burróns, traces the breadth of the once-totalizing PRI coalition, bundling all of these diverse social actors together under the same familial banner. In fact, the aesthetic decision to create a cacique character—the corrupt and authoritarian Don Briagoberto, who swills *pulque*, the fermented sap of the maguey plant, with his poncho- and sombrero-clad compatriots in Coyotera's municipal palace—meant inclusion in the series of a key mechanism of the PRI's political control over rural Mexico.

La Familia Burrón was initially elaborated for a national context for which a drive toward modernity was the primary *razón del estado*, the first and final measure of the state's purpose and legitimacy. The comic developed its forms in the shadow of a political system capable of absorbing and rendering inert each and every social movement and doctrine to come into contact with it. *La Familia Burrón* projects a commensurate obsession with modernity, and a similar unitary inertia to that of the PRI's postrevolutionary hegemony. This is not to say that the comic book series should be read as a simple reflection of that former political reality. Rather, the insistent foregrounding of *lo popular* in the comic's explicit emphasis on the persistence of poverty has always critically distinguished its discourse from that of contemporary officialdom. And importantly, the Burróns' world is a world without an authoritative social or political discourse; there is no room for the "revolutionary" nationalism of the PRI, or for uplifting talk of modernity and globalization in the *vecindad*. Insofar as the *vecindad* is simultaneously a premodern vestige, a bastion against institutional corruption, and a space of imagination and resistance, it becomes a multivalent signifier of a national condition vexed by the question of modernity.

It is as national, collective memory that *La Familia Burrón* occupies its own distinctive political position in a Mexico troubled by globalization. As Halbwachs reminds, "What a group opposes to its past is not its present; it is rather the past . . . of other groups with whom it tends to identify itself" (184). Those social groups who favor the private sector interests of capital can revel in the *Burrón*'s representation of twentieth-century popular social experience, seeing there a repudiation of the state-led economic model of the past and an opportunity to associate themselves with the special moral authority of *lo popular*. This neoliberal triumphalism, however, separates and excludes history from the present; this reading cannot recognize in the *Burrón* series the unresolved problems of Mexico's present. (A commonplace of neoliberal thought, the same ideological maneuver is the basis of Francis Fukuyama's famous essay "The End of History.") Critics of neoliberalism, in contrast, can find in the Burróns' misadventures a remembrance of an as yet unfulfilled collective project, projected into the historical gap between the authoritarian modernization paradigm of the PRI era and the postnational "free market" of neoliberal globalism. What is inconvenient for the neoliberal use of the comic book, however, is the social framework that structures the aesthetics of *La Familia Burrón*, with its inalterable unity of the social world. One can recognize there a collective memory of the PRI's long rule. But what is remembered is not the PRI's version of social reality. Rather, the contradiction between the pleasantries of the comic's visual aesthetics and the violence and social tensions of its plots exposes fissures within the once-dominant corporatist model of nation and modernization and preserves them for the present.

What is remembered is the fractious struggle over the terms of the nation's modernity. The petit bourgeois conservatism of Don Regino, an authoritarian *caciquismo* in the countryside, pent-up demands for social justice among the urban poor, an enormous breach between rich and poor, and foreign cultural influence are copresent in a national reality once obscured by official representations of the nation. If, as Halbwachs argues, "the most painful aspects of yesterday's society are forgotten because constraints are felt only so long as they operate" (51), then what is remembered in the *Burrón* series is not PRI dominance and failure so much as an evocation of enduring national unity around the shared problem of economic progress. It is the PRI turned inside out—a collective struggle for national betterment, embracing the whole of Mexico's uneven social development and the full range of class and ideological conflict, unadorned by a dominant discourse. And all of the conflicts and tensions that come with the total social package are included in the *Burrón*'s image of the collective project. What the comic book makes difficult to forget, in other words, is the fundamentally political nature of national development.

CAPITALISM'S HERO

Las aventuras del Dr. Simi

Dr. Simi is short, and his round bald head, snow-white eyebrows, and handle-bar mustache indicate that he is elderly as well. His demeanor is generally pleasant, and understandably so, since he lives a life without personal adversity. He has access to unlimited means of travel—late-model cars and trucks, helicopters, and even airplanes—and is always accompanied by beautiful women, who form his "Team Simi." He is worldly and well-read, travels constantly, revels in competition as an end in itself, and celebrates "cultured" knowledge (for example, Shakespeare, Gandhi). His style of dress is modestly formal, except on special occasions, when he dons an all-white suit and a black tie. A man of constant ethical reflection, he is quick to recognize injustice or social need. Like many comic book heroes, he is a man of action, though he mostly relies on moral suasion to turn the will of others to the side of justice; when a display of power is needed, he calls upon allies in the business world, chief among them the Mexican entrepreneur Víctor González Torres, who heads the generic drugs pharmacy chain Farmacias de Similares. Dr. Simi believes in teamwork, and is not averse to speaking directly to the comic book reader about his values and social vision: "One of our missions is to help those who have least," he declares, looking out from the comic book panel directly at the reader. "And you too can do it! We have to make of this world a more just place for everyone" (#59, 10). In sum, Dr. Simi is a compassionate globalist and free-marketeer, a social reformer who promotes competition and private sector investment for the betterment of humankind.

Dr. Simi is the protagonist of *Las aventuras del Dr. Simi*, a comic book series created in 2003 as a commercial marketing tool, and eventually electoral campaign propaganda as well, for Víctor González Torres, founder and president of the pharmaceutical chain Farmacias de Similares and 2006 minor party Mexican presidential candidate. The monthly installments of the glossy, full-color *Las aventuras* are produced for the pharmaceutical company by Art & Talent International Media, with a segmented division of creative labor common to the comic book industry: Sixto Valencia in charge of drawing, Francisco Reyes Hernández responsible for graphic design and color, and Benito Taibo and Arturo Martínez managing the storyline. *Las aventuras* is a conventional comic in that it comprises a twenty-two-page-long comic book narrative displayed in standard rectangular panels, arranged five or six to a page. But the cover design and inside front and back pages include photographs of people who appear as drawn characters in the comic book narrative—making the series a hybrid species of graphic narrative and photographic and hand-drawn visuals combining to project an image unique to the Dr. Simi construct. With a print distribution of 100,000 copies per month, and occasional issues published online, the comic book's peculiar combination of photos and cartoons presents to the Mexican public the philanthropic exploits of Dr. Simi, who serves as the avuncular, mustachioed mascot for the pharmaceutical chain, and pseudonym for González Torres himself.

The extensive network of Farmacias de Similares in Mexico provides low-cost generic drugs and basic medical treatment to Mexicans who cannot afford brand name pharmaceuticals and adequate health care. González Torres campaigned for the presidency in 2006, primarily as an antagonist to the left-of-center candidacy of Andrés Manuel López Obrador. His public discourse combined attacks on the mayor of Mexico City; rejection of "populist" politics; allegations of corruption and incompetence leveled against the Instituto Mexicano de Seguro Social (IMSS), which operates the government health care system; and promotion of the private sector as an answer to the country's problems. His political agenda, which he has called, bizarrely in the context of his policy positions, "moderate socialism," is backed by the Grupo Por Un País Mejor (Group for a Better Country), an alliance of his pharmacy chain and philanthropic organizations founded by him. In this context, *Las aventuras del Dr. Simi* fuses the marketing function of an advertising tool with the personalized public relations maneuvering of a political campaign.

Gónzalez Torres's Farmacias de Similares has a long family lineage. Víctor and his older brother Javier inherited the family's pharmacy chain, which dated back to a great-grandfather's first pharmacy in 1875. The family business had benefited from Mexico's public sector investments in medical care under the rule of the Partido Revolucionario Institucional (PRI). Due to disagreements with his brother, who now owns Farmacias El Fénix, Víctor bought out his father's control of Laboratorios Best, a generic drugs manufacturer whose products were only sold in public sector clinics. In 1997, now operating in the post-NAFTA environment, the younger González Torres began to sell generic drugs directly to the consumer. But he has not been shy about seeking government supports for the business, including intense lobbying in 2003 for legislation that would establish compulsory licensing for certain patented drugs, allowing Mexican generics manufacturers to define the market for AIDS and cancer drugs. Farmacias de Similares is viewed as significant regional competition for major European and U.S. pharmaceutical companies like Eli Lilly, Merck, and Pfizer, whose claims that González Torres's generic drugs are low-quality rip-offs are likely motivated more by concerns about market share than about consumers' well-being (Luhnow; Smith). The Similares chain grew quickly to comprise a network of more than 3,700 pharmacies in Latin America, heavily concentrated in Mexico and Central America, and targeted to the poor (Guerrero, 26–27). González Torres's cartoonish alter ego, the protagonist of *Las aventuras del Dr. Simi*, appears designed with just that audience in mind. The businessman describes his marketing icon as "a symbol for the poor" or "the Virgin of Guadalupe's nurse" (Guerrero, 29).

Dr. Simi is, in some respects, cut to the measure of U.S. neoliberalism. The U.S. cultural model, discussed in chapter 4, resonates in the figure of the good doctor of the pharmaceutical company's *Las aventuras*. Viewed as a kind of capitalist hero, Dr. Simi could easily be a figment of the same social imaginary, the same system of social meanings, that lionizes powerful capitalist elites like Donald Trump of Trump Enterprises or Bill Gates of Microsoft. These kinds of cultural icons personify success within a market society, lending the credibility of a personal biographical narrative to the cultural model's promise of material rewards for hard work, risk, and ingenuity. But these figures also personify capital, bringing the abstraction of an inescapable economic order based on private wealth and competition down to earth, giving it a face and personal style, a sense of humanity, and a purpose. The oafish and self-aggrandizing Trump is celebrated in part because his "low-brow" embodiment of capitalism is symbolically more democratic, more brash and rough-and-tumble, than the effete "old money" aristocracy of the Rockefellers. Gates is the capitalist "brain," the middle-class nerd who conquered the world without charisma or inherited capital. In both cases, whether in real estate or information technology, these capitalist heroes are world transformers, agents of change. Dr. Simi, as González Torres's surrogate, could be considered on first gloss to be a figure in the same pantheon.

And yet González Torres's Dr. Simi character deviates from this cultural and ideological template in important ways. Although the doctor is a stand-in for González Torres—and functions publicly in this role to such a degree that the owner of the pharmacy chain is often referred to as "Dr. Simi" in the Mexican press—the comic book character constructs a public image for the capitalist that operates at one remove from capitalism. The character is a doctor, and spends his time in nonprofit endeavors, raising money, traveling, and/or educating people about his social causes. He has no apparent source of income, and when at home lives a modest middle-class lifestyle, as if retired. He thus embodies capitalism in an ambiguous manner. The doctor is both a shill for private enterprise (specifically for González Torres's pharmacy chain) and a doctor concerned for the welfare of others. He even does moral battle against devious forms of self-interestedness, such as theft, profiteering from the circumstances of others, or the underhanded scheming of his nemesis Señor A, who is always seeking unfair advantage over others. Dr. Simi's own deviation from the profit-based logic of market capitalism can be seen in his promotion of altruistic behaviors that have no clear market reward.

In this sense, Dr. Simi operates as a supplement for capitalism in the social message of the comic. In other words, rather than an embodiment of the economic order that he avidly embraces, the doctor is a compassionate and socially concerned complement to capitalism's self-interested, private wealth-oriented ethos. As Jacques Derrida's deconstructivist notion of "the supplement" reminds us, however, this also means that the doctor is at the same time an unavoidable prompt to recognize what capitalism cannot be if left to its own logic—which is to say compassionate and socially concerned. Cultural critics familiar with Derrida's philosophy of deconstruction will also recall that one of his earliest efforts to demonstrate how this kind of supplement works was a 1968 essay titled "Plato's Pharmacy." Ironically, given the present discussion of the pharmaceutical chain's Dr. Simi, the supplement was understood there, following Plato's original Greek, as the "*pharmakon*"—a remedy, or poison, that comes in from the outside, in effect an alteration or distraction in the manner of a drug. Although for Derridean deconstruction the most culturally significant supplement is the relationship between writing and speech, in the *Dr. Simi* series one can identify this same ideological function in the relationship between the do-good doctor and what he represents.

Dr. Simi is supplemental to González Torres's public image. The figure of the comic book doctor bridges the social class gap between the wealthy capitalist entrepreneur and the mostly impoverished consumer base for his enterprise, and offers a public service adjunct to promote the businessman's private interests. In the United States, this kind of ideological bridge between the interests of economic elites and the values of the nation's popular culture has been constructed with cultural materials such as a Protestant Christology, or interpretation of the life of Christ, which emphasizes a radically individualist concept of morality and personal responsibility, thereby squaring (particularly in the public discourse of the U.S. Republican Party) public ethics with the neoliberal defense of private interests. But despite major advances for evangelical Protestantism in Latin America in recent years, there remain significant and unavoidable tensions between the cultural figurations of U.S. neoliberalism and certain elements of Latin American public culture (see, e.g., Wiarda). In Mexico, a neoliberal ethics must respond to a different concept of state and church that operates through the country's popular culture, including a moral authority for the poor nearly absent in U.S. public life, symbolized in the iconic Virgin of Guadalupe, and a Thomistic concept of the state that presents the common good as the ultimate standard for good government, as St. Thomas Aquinas did. In the end, the cultural figure of Dr. Simi therefore looks a lot more like Mother Theresa than like Donald Trump, even though the doctor is a deliberate marketing construct of a for-profit enterprise.

What is aesthetically unique about the *Dr. Simi* series is the supplemental structure of its visual representations. It is not just that Dr. Simi supplements the public image of González Torres, although this is a core function of the comic, or that altruism supplements self-interested competition in the social message of the comic. The visual dimension of the comic book is itself organized around a supplemental logic: the photographic image and the cartoon figure complement one another, complete one another, and distract from one another in ways that reinforce the moral authority of the entrepreneur as an agent of progress, and thus as the incarnation of morality in the context of Mexico's national striving for modernity. Two components of the Dr. Simi construct interact in projecting a view of a globalized Mexico for the Mexican reader. First, the photograph—the root medium of mass entertainment media—bolsters, and delimits, the sense of reality established in the cartoonish visual forms of the comic book series. Second, the Dr. Simi character, a complex visual signifier or unit of meaning, literally masks and enacts the public authority of a real-life social actor, the neoliberal González Torres.

Analysis of the comic book centered on these aesthetic elements reveals, in turn, two related ideological dimensions of Dr. Simi's adventures. First, there is a model of public agency and authority structured into the Dr. Simi figure. The doctor's altruistic corporate Team Simi comprises a private sector variation of the political corporatism of the once-dominant PRI. The paradigm of governance implicit to Dr. Simi's exploits combines traditional *machista* gender roles (Dr. Simi surrounded by beautiful female assistants), an aura of technological and social progress (female professionals and modern transportation and communication technologies power the team), and the elevation of the individual capitalist to the status of enlightened father figure. Second, the doctor's adventures in Mexico, and in Latin America more broadly, often entail a narration of Mexican history and society that reimagines historical and social experience to fit with Dr. Simi's optimistic globalism. This requires a highly attenuated sense of social reality. Thus the figure of Dr. Simi recycles elements of the Mexican mass cultural environment, combining photographic images of television actresses with the doctor's cartoon "reality," in order to secure a portrayal of private sector economic leadership in a popular cultural medium, while carefully managing reference to the dire economic conditions experienced by a majority of Mexicans.

Dr. Simi is a curious vehicle for promoting neoliberal politics and ideology. As noted in chapters 2 and 5, the deployment of comic books in the Mexican public sphere for specific political ends has been commonplace in recent years. Alongside graphic narratives distributed by the Partido de Acción Nacional (PAN) presidency under Vicente Fox, the Partido de la Revolución Democrática (PRD) government of Mexico City under Andrés Manuel López Obrador, and union organizations, among others, *Las aventuras del Dr. Simi* represents an intriguing private sector vehicle. *Las aventuras* is perhaps most similar to the López Obrador administration's *Historia de la ciudad*, at least insofar as the latter was also published as a series, elevated one man's moral authority above all others, and effectively doubled as a story about collective values and as promotional literature for a political candidacy. The differences, however, are numerous, including the fact that the Dr. Simi comic is also a "branding" vehicle, promoting the Farmacias de Similares label and trademark with every episode.

Although presented on the Farmacias de Similares Web site as a children's publication (information about the comic book is available under the "Simi Niños" heading), the comic possesses a number of obvious adult qualities, such as a text-heavy presentation and the use of attractive female models in a glossy, magazine-style layout. The panel construction and sequencing in the *Dr. Simi* series is conventional in most respects—rectilinear and rectangular frames arrayed for reading left-to-right and top-to-bottom—but the comic's dialogue-driven story arcs require the characters' thought and speech bubbles to crowd the panel images, and frequently to extend beyond the individual frame. In fact, insofar as there is rupture or variation within the panel formatting, it arises from tension between image frames and speech balloons. These latter spill into adjacent panels or squeeze the visual image out of view in a given frame.

The grammar of the comic book's visuals—the implicit rules governing its visual composition—seems to include an adult optic alongside more child-friendly details. The Dr. Simi character and Simidog, his pet dog, for example, are both drawn cartoonishly with simplified and enlarged facial features, in a style of visual representation likely appealing to children. Both have noses that are little more than prominent ovals in the center of a disproportionately large head, and the few hairs left on Dr. Simi's otherwise bald head extend as three crooked lines from each side of his face, like six symmetrical and stylized insect legs. At the same time, however, the other members of Team Simi are drawn with a normal human anatomy, and their facial features are more naturally detailed. Their faces include lips, nostrils, and eyelashes and fully articulated eyes, where Dr. Simi lacks such details. Photographic portraits of these other, generally female, characters' "real-life" selves highlight their sexual attractiveness, in a manner likely appealing to an adult reader. With regard to this central aesthetic contrast, Sixto Valencia's rendering of Dr. Simi and his social milieu parallels the same artist's work on the *Memín Pinguín* comic, where the eponymous black child character is iconic, even racially stereotyped, against the backdrop of a relatively naturalist depiction of his social environment. (Memín Pinguín's exaggerated racial features, such as absurdly thick lips consistent with racist U.S. portrayals of African Americans, occasioned a scandal in the NAFTA alliance in 2005 when the George W. Bush administration objected to the character's selection for an official Mexican postage stamp, arguing the image was offensive.)

The adult outlook of the Dr. Simi comic became most obvious in the comic's content as González Torres geared up for a campaign for the Mexican presidency. Electoral politics is obviously not a typical "hook" for marketing targeted to children, since the very young are ineligible to vote and are extremely unlikely to offer resources to a political campaign. Nonetheless, the installments in the *Las aventuras* series that were published in the lead-up to the 2006 Mexican presidential election were heavy with political discourse, albeit immersed in Dr. Simi's sometimes fanciful world. In episode #39, "Peces" (Fish, May 2005), for example, Dr. Simi takes his Team Simi to the city aquarium because biologists are reporting strange behavior among the fish. With the aid of the doctor's latest invention—a drug called "*oxigomita*," which allows a person to breathe underwater—Team Simi swims among the fish, and discovers that the problem is a political campaign headed up by a large garfish called "El Peje" (the nickname of Mexico City's mayor and PRD presidential candidate López Obrador). As it turns out, "El Peje" is making promises "he knows he cannot fulfill," just like "all politicians" (8). Confronted by Dr. Simi's meddling, the garfish orders his lieutenant, a menacing piranha named "Marcelo" (Marcelo Ebrard succeeded López Obrador as mayor of Mexico City), to set "the riot police" (swordfish, in this case) on Team Simi.

Episode #52, "Motivos para luchar" (Reasons for Fighting, June 2006), brings González Torres directly into the picture alongside Dr. Simi—to whom he refers as his "twin soul"—in order to promote the businessman's candidacy for president. After a series of portrayals of González Torres and Dr. Simi together on the campaign trail, a splash panel on the penultimate page departs from the typical formatting of the series. Instead of employing a series of rectangular panel frames, the page presents Dr. Simi within a circular frame, inset in the upper third of the full-page panel (see figure 7.1). The circular frame at the top of the page allows Dr. Simi to be foregrounded as the emcee who introduces "for the first time in the history of comics" a musical conclusion to the episode, while the full-page panel surrounding him offers an image of the ensuing musical event—a female singer in Mexican cowboy-style dress belting out a ballad to a raucous concert audience (21). This visual organization of sequential events (that is, introduction and subsequent concert collapsed into a visual simultaneity) allows Dr. Simi to appear twice, once as emcee and once as member of the audience, once above the singer's head and once below, within the same full-page panel. The effect is to twin the image of Dr. Simi and position him simultaneously as a muse who floats above the singer's head, and up to whom she looks as she croons, and as a fellow citizen clapping happily among the masses below the singer's feet. The visual management of temporal sequence,

Figure 7.1. Dr. Simi above and below, "twin soul" of Víctor González Torres. At upper left, Dr. Simi introduces the spectacle: "For the first time in the history of the historieta, we're going to end this special issue with a song: 'The Ballad of Víctor González.' Enjoy!" From *Las Aventuras del Dr. Simi* #52 (June 2006), 21. Reprinted by permission of Farmacias de Similares.

in other words, also affords the visual management of social hierarchy. Dr. Simi can be presented as a "man of the people" while retaining his status as someone to look up to.

The lyrics of the song being performed, "The Ballad of Víctor González Torres," are arrayed in six complete stanzas at the top, left, and bottom margins of the page. The irregular form of the speech balloons employed for the lyrics, and the colorful musical notes that accompany the words, set a contrast with Dr. Simi's speech as emcee. The "wall" of lyrics at left pushes the reader's gaze toward the singer and the concert scene. The chorus itself is a conflation of political and commercial propaganda, and plays on the dual meaning of "*similares*" with reference to the pharmaceutical company and its owner:

> *Víctor, Víctor, Víctor*
> *Víctor González*
> *Es el remedio para*
> *Todos nuestros males*
> *Víctor González Torres*
> *Porque ricos y pobres*
> *Todos somos similares.*

> *[Víctor, Víctor, Víctor*
> *Víctor González*
> *Is the remedy for*
> *All of our ailments*
> *Víctor González Torres*
> *Because rich and poor*
> *We are all similar.]*

A national politics is obvious here, and betrays the presentation of *Las aventuras del Dr. Simi* as a children's publication. The musical *corrido*, or ballad, form is a traditional popular cultural medium in Mexico, and has been used historically to lionize the likes of Pancho Villa and Emiliano Zapata, leaders of Mexico's armed revolution of 1910. It is hard not to read in the "Todos somos similares" line at the end of the stanza a crude commercial appropriation of the neo-Zapatista movement's defiant antiestablishment slogan, "Todos somos Marcos," which proclaims an identification between the average Mexican citizen and Subcomandante Marcos, the masked spokesperson and hero of the prodemocracy and anti-free-market neo-Zapatista movement that began in the southern state of Chiapas in 1994 in response to the implementation of NAFTA.

Such populist rhetorical strategies are indicative of a discourse that is designed to evoke the nation. But Dr. Simi did not discover politics only as a function of the 2006 electoral contest. In fact, a clearly defined globalist viewpoint and a particular political sensibility were evident in the *Las aventuras* series long before González Torres declared himself a presidential candidate. Episode #33, "Carrera por la vida" (Race for Life, December 2004), opens in typical fashion with the unassuming Dr. Simi reading a biography of Mahatma Gandhi and lecturing to his pet dog Simidog on the principle of nonviolence. What follows in the body of the comic are two storylines, each describing Dr. Simi's involvement in life-saving good deeds. The doctor transports to the hospital first a motorcycle accident victim, then an impoverished boy found unconscious in the Baja desert in northern Mexico. This vital intervention is not an individual project, however, but involves, as usual, the concerted action of Team Simi. Under the paternal supervision of the good doctor, Team Simi includes in this episode three Mexican women with prominent public profiles: actress Marifer Murillo; soap opera star Luz Elena González; and race car driver Elizabeth Wayas, who makes a special guest appearance in this episode of the comic. (Marifer Murillo has been a fixture of the series throughout its run.)

The team represents the globalist promise of modernity in a number of ways. Whether by car (driven expertly by Wayas) or by corporate jet (the SimiJet), the team moves with speed and facility from one place to the next, within a narrative that emphasizes the power and importance of transportation technology in collapsing space as an obstacle. The consistency with which the *Dr. Simi* series visualizes speed and transport as signifiers of modernity shows a kinship with the *Libro Semanal* series discussed in chapter 4. Meanwhile, the virtues of the proper social order expressed by Team Simi show a clear affinity for those values articulated in the U.S. Department of State's *Country Commercial Guide*, even going so far as to make repeated mention of the value of punctuality and efficiency. (The front cover of the episode shows Dr. Simi gesturing to a stopwatch, with the Simi women posing in the background next to Wayas's race car.) Luz Elena, who is studying Japanese, declares, "Since I've been with [the Team] I've had more and more desire to learn" (13). In a discussion about the conservation of natural resources and the environment, the women decide that "if things are done well and in an orderly fashion, there's no problem" (18).

Figure 7.2. Team Simi en route to the duty-free port city of La Paz. "Like Dr. Simi says, punctuality is a special virtue!" observes Marifer, as Simidog thinks about eating and Dr. Simi holds forth on the colonial history of the port city of La Paz. From *Las Aventuras del Dr. Simi* #34 (December 2004), 16. Reprinted by permission of Farmacias de Similares.

The characters' affinity for Mexico as a nation is also subordinated to a globalist worldview. The only reference to the historical specificity of Mexico as a nation occurs when Dr. Simi discusses with Team Simi the history of the port city of La Paz in Baja state. The panel frame in which the discussion appears is horizontal and extends across the top third of the page, balanced by an identically sized panel at the bottom of the page that contains an image of the sleek exterior of Dr. Simi's private jet. The image of the team affords a view of the entire group inside the "SimiJet," an image of unity and order in the present as Dr. Simi identifies the history of the port not with the nation but with a history of globalization that predates the formation of the Mexican nation (see figure 7.2). "The bay of La Paz was discovered on May 3, 1535 by Hernán Cortés. At the beginning of the 18th century a Jesuit Mission was established there and at the beginning of the 19th century a city was established there" (16). Dr. Simi's historical overview ends prior to Mexico's national independence in 1821, and omits nearly 200 years of national history in order to emphasize the port city's connections to Europe. The point seems to be that La Paz has always been what it is in the present, a globalized enclave, graced by the touch of European modernity. In the frame immediately following Dr. Simi's minilecture, Elizabeth Wayas is the central focus of the panel, lending her celebrity to an exultation about the city's status as a duty-free port, where "[o]ne can buy a lot of imported items at a very good price" (16).

Within this proglobalization arrangement of the national, one finds the popular dimension of the nation mostly relegated to a minor and abstract supporting role in constructing a collective, modernizing agency embodied by the corporate team. Dr. Simi's pet dog, Simidog (the English term invoking U.S. influence, while symbolically domesticating it), communicates telepathically with the team members and perseverates incessantly about his desire to eat. His bottomless appetite, his lack of education, and his subservience to the enlightened Dr. Simi together comprise a metaphorical reminder of the presence of the subaltern—a class equivalent, subject to constant instruction by his corporate master on the proper use of language and the immorality of violence. The social class metaphor is reinforced by the formulaic use of Simidog in the introductory panels of each episode. The first page nearly always includes a dialogue between Dr. Simi and Simidog, and this conversation always entails an effort by the doctor to educate the canine in proper etiquette, diet, use of language, or even cultural "taste." In one episode (#60, "¡Cacería!" or Hunting! February 2007), Dr. Simi explains Leonardo Da Vinci's *Mona Lisa* to the dog. In another (#62, "El día que me quieras . . . ," or The Day That You Love Me . . . , April 2007), the doctor instructs the dog on the importance of William Shakespeare's *Romeo and Juliet.* When, on the first page of episode #59, Dr. Simi angrily scolds the dog for eating garbage (and this while lecturing the animal about the environmental value of composting), there is no doubt that the enlightened doctor is an agent of civilization and moral betterment, and that the lowly dog is a stand-in for an undignified impoverishment.

This marginalization of "*lo popular*"—of popular sectors of Mexican society, and of demands for social justice arising from those lower strata of national society—is reinforced by a hyperrealism in the comic book's format, which supplements cartoon renderings of real people with photographs of them. On the one hand, the photographs provide an empirical referent for the drawn visual representations of the comic book narrative, boosting the latter's claim on reality. On the other hand, the reader's sense of social reality is strangely attenuated by placing visual representations and their referents within the same glossy world of fantasy. The "real world" outside the comic book text is referenced with the photograph's authoritative relationship to empirical reality. But the "real world" referenced by these photographs is little more than another figment of the mass culture industry, or of the deliberate public relations strategies of the corporation. Posed portraits of the sexually attractive Simi women, with wind-swept hair and revealing styles of dress, are presented inside the front and back covers against a "wallpaper" backdrop of floating Dr. Simi logotypes. The women's photo portraits are also accompanied by fortune-cookie style epigrams, most often referring to internal, psychological realities. In one such display, showing Marifer Murillo in tight leather pants and with cleavage exposed, the reader is informed that "fantasy is one of the best tools the imagination has to learn to enjoy the world" (#58, December 2006). The presence of the photographs does not refer the attention to social reality as a "ground" for the comic book narrative; instead, the photographs ground the comic book characters and storyline in the sense of reality offered by mass cultural mediation.

This is true even in the case of the goofy-looking Dr. Simi character, who makes a real-world appearance in a photo-documentary insert in the "Carrera por la vida" episode. The photographic insert documents a publicity event connected to the inauguration of ten new pharmacies in Argentina in 2004. The fatherly Dr. Simi—an employee of Farmacias de Similares encased in a life-size body suit of the good doctor, handlebar mustache, basketball-size head and all—appears in photographs alongside Mayan activist and 1992 Nobel Prize recipient Rigoberta Menchú, an advocate of the generic drugs distributor in Guatemala, the corporate owner Víctor González Torres, and others. The doctor's "real world" appearance is an extension of the comic book's fantasy domain, but implicitly draws everyone else who appears in the photo spread back into the imagined world of the comic, lending Dr. Simi's cartoon adventures the authority of real life. Life as we otherwise know it, meanwhile, shrinks to fit Dr. Simi's world.

Conspicuously, the impoverished boy rescued from certain death in the Baja desert in "Carrera por la vida" has no photographic counterpart, no empirical datum reinforcing or demonstrating the national realities to which his character might refer. In fact, although the reader of the comic will reasonably conclude that the child is lying near death in the desert because of a failed effort to cross the treacherous U.S.-Mexico border, Dr. Simi offers no insight as to who the boy is or what he was doing in such a desolate place. Reality on this point (that is, emigration to the United States as part of Mexico's concrete experience of globalization) is glossed over, while the strategically placed portrait photos of the celebrity women on the cover, and in the publicity insert with the full-color photo display of the corporate publicity event, refer the comic book reader to the "real" presence of the main characters in the nation's commercialized public sphere. This hyperrealist presence in the comic narrative—the ersatz reality of television and mass entertainment culture—is the grounding for both the globalization-friendly portrayal of Mexico in the comic book and for the peculiar political authority constructed for Dr. Simi.

Dr. Simi's adventures are the exploits of a denizen of hyperreality. As the Italian semiotician Umberto Eco explained the concept with reference to the ersatz mass culture of the United States, "The aim . . . is to supply a 'sign' that will then be forgotten as such: The sign aims to be the thing, to abolish the distinction of the reference, the mechanism of replacement. Not the image of the thing, but its plaster cast. Its double, in other words" (7). Stated another way, hyperreality stands in for the concrete empirical referent it pretends to represent, but also pretends to represent nothing other than itself; it is reality supplanted by an image of reality. The empirical authority of the photograph allows the "Simi-chicas" (as the women are called) to document as "real" the relationship between three-dimensional Mexican society and the characters whose adventures unfold in the two-dimensional space inside the comic book. Via sharp contrast with the hand-drawn figures of the comic, the photographs of Team Simi, and the appearance of team members at public events (or the photographs of those appearances), find their authority as faithful representations of reality enhanced, made larger-than-life. And in the semiotic connection, in the relationship between the two kinds of visual signs, the cartoon lives of the same characters receive an extra charge of the real. In the end, within the tightly self-referential system of visual signs of *Las aventuras del Dr. Simi*, it is no longer at all clear which is the referent for which. Do the photographs represent the comic book characters, or do the comic book characters represent the people who appear in the photographs? Just as with the supplemental relationship between Dr. Simi and Víctor González Torres, each is, as Dr. Simi would have it, the "twin soul" of the other.

The resulting semiotic house of mirrors lends itself to the ideological and political work of the comic book. The hyperrealism of the *Dr. Simi* series corrals the reader's awareness of the social world within the communicative norms of mass visual culture—that is, the airbrushed pinup photograph, the carefully managed celebrity image, the corporate marketing emblem, and the sexualized female body as an intimation of power and luxury. The mass cultural sign system underlying the Dr. Simi figure is thereby also foundational to the ideological function of the philanthropic hero. The aesthetic and semiotic elements of the mass culture industry make possible the comic book's hyperreal evasion of the lived social world of its readers. With Dr. Simi as their center of gravity, these same elements orbit around a marketing symbol that operates as a public mask for the wealthy capitalist's agency in the national political arena (see figure 7.3). If the point is, as Eco notes, to supply a sign that is forgotten as such—an

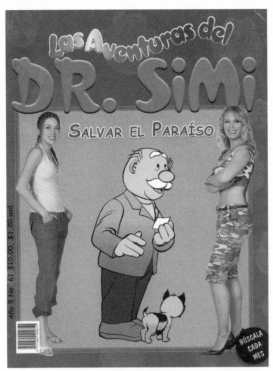

Figure 7.3. Dr. Simi's hyperreality: the comic book hero and Simidog framed by real-world "Simichicas." The cover of *Las Aventuras del Dr. Simi* #61 (March 2007). Reprinted by permission of Farmacias de Similares.

animated double with a "real" life of its own—then Dr. Simi's mass cultural supports make possible a figure who speaks with as much or more public authority as his capitalist double.

A closer look at the image of that authority illustrates this point. In episode #61, "Salvar el Paraíso" (Saving Paradise, March 2007), Dr. Simi is encountered explaining scientific progress to the ignorant Simidog. As Team Simi prepares to sally forth for a day of volunteer work in "one of the poorest but most emblematic neighborhoods of the city," Marifer Murillo arrives with the disturbing news of a real estate developer's plan to tear down the "Paradise" movie theater. Horrified that the old neighborhood theater could be destroyed to make room for a parking lot, the team decides to swing into action. Explains Dr. Simi: "I believe [destruction of the theater] is something we should not permit. We are talking about our culture, our identity, our patrimony" (3). Dr. Simi's point of entry into the problem of the moment links social class with cultural patrimony, or common cultural heritage, conjuring a vague sense of "*lo popular*" as the symbolic seat of national identity, the barrio as a social site of conflict wherein the political stakes are of national interest. To reinforce this, a strategically placed panel on page 2 visualizes his enlightened leadership on behalf of the poor. When Dr. Simi wonders aloud whether destruction of the theater is part of a larger plan to remake the area for the rich, the doctor's speech bubble above is balanced by Simidog's thought bubble below. Looking obsequiously up to the doctor, the dog's thought bubble seems to read the mind of the (in all likelihood poor) client of Farmacias de Similares as he or she reads the comic book: "As always, the winners are those who already have the most" (2).

And yet "*lo popular*" (both as class-specific basis of collective identity and as moral claim on social justice) is subsequently transferred entirely into the celluloid territory of mass culture, and national identity is supplanted by global media culture. Dr. Simi and his team are initially concerned with the possibility that the developer's designs on the movie theater are part of a plan for gentrifying the barrio. ("Why do they want a parking lot in a place where people don't own cars to park?" Dr. Simi remarks on page 2.) But the ultimate cause for political mobilization is not the economic marginalization of an urban neighborhood, whose residents must accept the consequences of decisions made by a propertied class living elsewhere. Instead, the movie theater is the rallying point and impetus for action. Immediately following Dr. Simi's declaration regarding the movie house's status as cultural patrimony, he launches into a detailed discussion of the U.S. and French genesis of film technologies, thereby undermining any notion of national heritage in play. The visuals for this moment in the narrative serve to transport the reader out of the social class context of the barrio and into the movie theater as the site of conflict. The three panels that present the doctor's disquisition on the history of moving pictures break with the norm for the series. In contrast with the more typical six square panels per page elsewhere in the story, these panel frames are unequally sized and are displayed vertically. This aesthetic choice allows for the two largest panels to accommodate representations of a movie theater's interior, where the movie screen appears as a kind of panel-within-the-panel. The reader's eye is literally drawn into the theater as Dr. Simi talks about the work of Thomas Alva Edison and the Lumiere brothers, and their contributions to "one of man's great inventions with respect to entertainment" (3).

Alongside the displacement of "*lo popular*" by mass media culture, the social significance of the profit motive is managed carefully by the storyline so that "community interest" can be taken into account in a moral resolution of the conflict. As the story plays out, there are two capitalists who vie for control of the Paradise, one who wants to rehabilitate the old theater, and one who wants to tear it down. These two investors are twin brothers, but the destructive capitalist is a deviant who ends up kidnapping SimiJunior, the adolescent girl member of Team Simi, in an effort to prevail in the struggle over the fate of the movie house. That the emblem of "our identity, our patrimony" selected for the storyline is not the barrio but the cinema diminishes to the vanishing point any possible contradiction between the public interest and the profit motive: the Paradise theater is, after all, a business. At the same time, the collective imagination, the utopian impulse to contradict and think outside or beyond a flawed social reality, is reduced to a local retail operation in the mass culture industry. Dr. Simi's declaration on the final page that "Paradise" has been saved seems a dystopian inversion of utopian desire for social change.

The comic book's visuals consistently underscore a mass mediated concept of the public interest and public agency. When Dr. Simi calls a news conference to draw public attention to the issue of the movie theater, the iconic doctor appears to look directly out at the reader, as he does in most episodes when he makes a moral appeal to the reader, and hence to the general public. On this occasion, however, his gaze out at the comic book reader is framed at the bottom of the panel image by a row of microphones marked "TV," creating the impression that the reader is looking into the rectangular image projected by a television set instead of a comic book (13). Surprisingly (or perhaps not), in the end Simi-Junior is liberated from her evil captor by none other than Zorro and Tarzan, figments of U.S. popular culture elevated to savior status on a par with Dr. Simi himself. "Me Tarzan, you SimiJunior," says the Lord of the Apes in a moment of mutual recognition between figments of the mass cultural imaginary—with that one salutation enacting as reality a globalized Mexican cultural imagination. Zorro, the more articulate of the two liberators, offers the metacommentary: "I am not a vision. I am Zorro. I live here, with many of my friends, thanks to the magic of movies. If you have not forgotten me that means I am alive, more alive than ever" (20). The comic book's "reality," and Dr. Simi's heroic dramatis persona, is relayed through the television and movie screens of mass entertainment culture.

If Dr. Simi's model of heroic, and thus moral, public agency is filtered through the modern mass cultural image, the model of public authority he embodies draws on a premodern standard. In an important sense, what one observes in the figure of Dr. Simi is a phenomenon akin to Mikhail Bakhtin's problem of the discursive mask—the social ordering of discourse and its power through historically and culturally predetermined forms of authorship. After all, Dr. Simi is a corporate logo that speaks and that stars in his own dramatic narrative. He is, in a very practical sense, the mask through which the pharmaceutical company hails its users, and through which Víctor González Torres speaks as a moral agent in the public sphere. Bakhtin centers many of his observations regarding types of speech and interpersonal communication on the social relation between authorship and authority, or as he puts it, between "the form of authorship and the hierarchical place (position) of the speaker" (Bakhtin 1986, 152). The basic insight for cultural analysis offered by Bakhtin is that premodern forms of social authority can outlive, through cultural texts, the flesh-and-blood social actors who had once embodied them historically. "The speaking subjects of high, proclamatory genres—of priests, prophets, preachers, judges, leaders, patriarchal fathers, and so forth—have departed this life. They have all been replaced by the writer, simply the writer, who has fallen heir to their styles" (Bakhtin 1986, 132). That primitive aristocrat, the Lord of the Apes, explains this succinctly to SimiJunior in episode #61: "Not die, live forever" (21).

Dr. Simi's adventures balance those "high, proclamatory genres" with modernity's promise of social and technological advancement. Repeated allusions in the series to nonviolence, environmentalism, and equality for women imbue the teamwork with an aura of progress. But these values are subordinated to the machismo of the doctor's undeniably patriarchal relationship with the younger, attractive women, and by the greater emphasis on fantasy, technology, and celebrity in the stories. Episode #59, "Vidas Sencillas" (Simple Lives, January 2007), begins with Dr. Simi explaining the importance of composting to Simidog. After both Marifer Murillo and SimiJunior arrive with complaints about modern life (a traffic jam, limited cell phone service, a malfunctioning printer), Dr. Simi decides the team should embark on an educational adventure to rediscover the simple things in life. The lesson has two parts: first, a trip to a prehistoric past without conveniences of any kind; and second, a trip to an underdeveloped locale somewhere in Latin America. While the first trip allows the team to rediscover the natural world, the labor-intensive experience of survival in a premodern state of nature mainly serves as a reminder of the value of modernity and technological progress. Revealingly, stripped of his access to technology and to his contacts in the business world, Dr. Simi's authority under those premodern circumstances becomes impossible to differentiate from that of a tribal patriarch. He is the revered elder, the unchallenged patriarch responsible for group survival, offering his teachings as guidance.

On the second leg of the team's journey, where the state of nature is associated with the socioeconomic condition of underdevelopment, Dr. Simi's model of authority comes into conflict with an oppressive local authoritarian—a classic cacique, or traditional rural boss who controls the community through control of its access to resources. Although the reader has now been transported back to the modern present, the circumstances are as postnational as the state of nature was prenational. "Where are we?" asks SimiJunior, to which Dr. Simi replies: "It doesn't matter. It could be Mexico, Argentina, Chile, any country of the American continent" (9). After discovering a small village with no running water, on the bottom of the next page Dr. Simi and SimiJunior each speak directly to the reader from parallel panels, calling for "technology to serve everyone" (10). This moral and political principle runs headlong into Don Fernando, who is owner of the sole telephone and electrical lines in the "forgotten town" of San Quirino. Don Fernando also controls access to the town's only source of water, and owns the only store in the area. He uses his monopolistic position to exploit the locals, charging them for basic amenities like water, and punishing them by withholding resources when they complain.

Don Fernando's miniregime is overthrown by Dr. Simi's new world order. Using a Global Positioning System and satellite technology, Dr. Simi locates an alternate water source and digs a communal well. Using his business contacts (that is, González Torres) and a cellular phone, he calls in the necessary capital investment for bringing electrical service to the whole town—"Yes, Don Víctor, we urgently need a solar energy plant" (15). "And thus," announces the narrative text in a pair of side-by-side panels depicting the morning sun rising over the humble town, "arrives a new and splendorous day full of possibilities" (18). The visual imagery of the narrative leaves no doubt that the town has been liberated by technology. Eight separate panels show Team Simi with a Sport-Utility Vehicle. Four more panels show Dr. Simi with Global Positioning System equipment, and an additional two panels feature his cellular phone. Other panels center on solar panels, a bird's-eye view of the town's electrical cables, and even a helicopter dispatched by González Torres to aid in the town's development. In contrast, the only technology referenced in the visual presentation of the cacique Don Fernando is a pistol tucked behind his belt.

The lines of conflict over authority are so clearly drawn that episode #59 might easily have been titled with superhero comic book boilerplate like

"Dr. Simi versus the Cacique." The avuncular, visionary embodiment of free-market globalism takes on, and defeats, the local strongman and his unjust patron-client system of monopolistic economic controls. The manner in which Dr. Simi serves as a discursive mask for Víctor González Torres (and even for the corporate entity Farmacias de Similares) can best be appreciated by reading *Las aventuras del Dr. Simi* in the broader social and political context of Mexico's public conflicts over the character of state power, local versus global control of economic resources, and even the politics of gender in the public arena. The image of legitimate authority projected in the episode turns, at least in part, on the fact that the long-governing PRI's single-party hegemony, from 1929 to 2000, was premised on the cacique's ability to deliver the vote and relative obedience of a local population reliant on his control over land, livestock, water, and other resources.

The public image conjured by González Torres's "twin soul" Dr. Simi links two subject positions, both of them gendered. The dominant authorial or discursive mask is that of the patriarch: Dr. Simi plays the benevolent political father to a team of individual women, each of these a professional urbanite, committed to self-improvement and personal success. These women are recognizably modern in part due to their status as features in the mass entertainment environment accessed by Mexican consumers through television, film, and the Internet. And yet their modernity (their individualism, urbanity, worldly competence) is consistently shaped and guided by the paternal Dr. Simi. On the one hand, these women speak as recognizable modern subjects; on the other hand, their recognizability is conditioned by their subservience to the fatherly "visionary." He, meanwhile, is recognizable as such because his women look to him for direction. Their modernity is his accomplishment. But his own modernity (problem-solving promoter of economic development and technological advancement) resides in traditional patriarchal form. The doctor even cross-dresses as a premodern authority on occasion: a medieval wizard in episode #58 ("Dragones y Princesas," or Dragons and Princesses, December 2006), a Scottish clansman in episode #62 ("El día que me quieras . . . ," or The Day That You Love Me . . . , April 2007), a magician in #53 ("Magia," or Magic, July 2006), and an armored knight in #46 ("Un mundo de libros," or A World of Books, December 2005).

Through the actions and attitudes of the characters of *Las aventuras del Dr. Simi*, and, most important, through its imagery, the comic book narrative constructs what might be called a corporate corporatism, a hierarchized and paternalistic bundling of multiple subjects under one private sector authority.

This is the PRI's model of corporatist governance but privatized. One can usefully return to the concert splash panel from "Motivos para luchar" (figure 7.1) in order to see this model of public authority concretized in a visual image. Or one can note the collective subject of Team Simi (figure 7.2), united under one iconic signifier—the Dr. Simi emblem on their caps (and on the backs of their uniforms) marks them not as a conspiracy of equals but as subject to the governance of the one true leader. What these images share in common is a twinning of Dr. Simi, his double apparition as both peer and superior, as both coequal and ruling principle. (Which of these "twins" is Víctor González Torres, and which is his supplement?) The prominent contrast between the cartoonish style of aesthetic representation employed in the Dr. Simi character and the more conventionally human figuration of the other characters comes into play as well: Dr. Simi and his corporate logo (the corporate logo, in fact, of Farmacias de Similares) are indistinguishable. His iconic caricature floats easily across the surfaces of a globalized mass media environment that the comic book references visually, and performs.

OPERACIÓN BOLÍVAR

The Work of Art in the Age of Globalization

"When our Spanish ancestors arrived on the continent," reads the brief introduction to Edgar Clement's graphic novel *Operación Bolívar*, "they did not come alone, with them came their gods and their armies of armed angels. For our indigenous ancestors these angels were not the incense vendors of the present day, they were emissaries of destruction. Between the sword of Cortés and the sword of Saint Michael the Archangel there was no difference" (1). In response to fierce resistance from the indigenous *brujos* (medicine men) and *nahuales* (guardian animal spirits), "the Holy Inquisition closed ranks with the archangels in the persecution of the *nahuales*, eliminating the most dangerous ones, mixing with the most capable, isolating the holdouts" (1). Historical traces of this holy war, asserts the introduction, are lost to the faded memory of Mexico's mestizo majority, but live on in the modern descendants of the *nahuales*, who have inherited the ability to "touch the gods and their emissaries," and hence the ability to kill angels (1). The 160-page, black-and-white graphic novel *Operación Bolívar*, the reader is informed, "is the first story about the angel hunters and their complex relations with the children of the gods and the children of men. Each one of these chess pieces has a past, present and future: RECUPERATION OF CONSCIOUSNESS" (1).

Operación Bolívar was published in installments in the Mexican magazine *Gallitos Comics*, and again as a graphic novel in 1999 by Ediciones del Castor and the graphic arts collective Taller del Perro (Dog's Workshop), with a distribution of 1,000 copies. Caligrama issued a new edition in 2007. Artists consider it the most important work of graphic narrative art in Mexico in the last two decades. According to fellow graphic artist José Quintero (author of the *Buba* series): "*Operación Bolívar* is the only work to date that has approached the graphic novel format in an intelligent, humorous, critical and virtuoso manner" (Reyes). The premise of the novel is at once mystical and bloody: there are angels, and there are angel hunters who historically have had the ability, inherited through indigenous ancestry, of killing angels. The hunt for the mythical beings follows an economic logic, because angelic body parts possess an array of instrumental values. For this reason (and because one of the use values is a powerful narcotic known—in a literalization of a metaphor of the real-world drug culture—as "angel dust"), transnational corporations and the Central Intelligence Agency (CIA) are also interested in the angels, hoping to monopolize this supernatural resource in order to enrich themselves, and to strengthen their own technological development, their market position, and/or the national security apparatus of the United States.

Narrated by an angel hunter, the story recounts how he and his partner, a brutish judicial police agent named Román, uncover and attempt to thwart a U.S.-based plot to massacre angels as a first step toward establishing total control over the global narcotics market, and thereby cementing unchallenged political control over the hemisphere. Behind the novel's unique narrative premise is a long view of globalization in the Americas, from the European conquest of native peoples in the early sixteenth century, to the subsequent forceful imposition of a Eurocentric mercantilism by the colonizing powers, to the transnationalization of domestic markets under the twentieth-century hegemony of the United States. This regional story of globalization is the backbone of *Operación Bolívar*'s plot, the operational context for its angel hunters, and the historical circumstance that motivates the story's proposed recuperation of the relationship between "past, present and future." The introduction carefully binds the reader's attention to how Clement's novel fits into the much-vaunted contemporary "global moment," because it announces the novel as a graphic counterpart to a centuries-long war for material and spiritual control over the Americas.

Two important threads of this connection are immediately apparent: first, collective historical memory is posited as the political stakes of the work, and second, the work reaches back across 500 years of history in order to present its own genealogy, in order to construct itself as legatee of a historic struggle still unfolding in the modern present. Intriguingly, Clement's work of fantasy does not sound so fantastic when read against the backdrop of the chronicles of the

Spanish conquest of Mexico. The historical record is, as a matter of fact, rife with evidence of warring angels, gods, *brujos*, and *nahuales*. In executing their evangelism of the native "idolaters," Fray Toribio de Benavente (aka Motolinía) noted with military zeal in his *Historia de los indios de la Nueva Espagna* (1541) that the Franciscan monks "took the glorious St. Michael as their captain and *caudillo*, and sang mass to him, along with St. Gabriel and all the other angels" (62). The Franciscan Fray Bernardino de Sahagún recorded in his *Historia General de las cosas de Nueva España* (1569) native testimony of the Conquest that describes "how Moctezuma sent magicians and sorcerers [*brujos*], forgers of evil spells to cause harm to the Spaniards" (766). Sahagún's notes for his twelve-volume chronicle of indigenous culture and worldview include references to "evil men" and "evil women," among whom are listed the *nahuales* (904). The conquistador Bernal Díaz del Castillo, who accompanied Hernán Cortés in his war on the Aztec empire, related how the native peoples viewed the Spaniards as gods, addressing them with the same word used to refer to their own religious statuary: *teules* (Castillo). A recent U.S. exhibit of colonial Latin American art included a large oil portrait of the angel Asiel, dressed as a Spanish militiaman and with silver-plated harquebus in hand. Painted by an anonymous artist from La Paz, Bolivia, the image of the warring angel was a commonplace in South America, where "Catholic teaching faced indigenous cults dedicated to celestial phenomena," and "images of conquering angels helped change their minds" (Knight).

The imaginative impact of Clement's novel turns on this genealogy, both as narrative and as visual display. The genealogical relationship implicated in Clement's introductory narrative, a relationship between the "story about the angel hunters" and the story of the Conquest, between the military and spiritual war of the past and the heretofore untold story of the present, extends also to the graphic medium that delivers the latter-day story. The introduction is carefully visually constructed to effect the appearance of a sixteenth-century publication: a stamped decorative border delineates the margins of the introductory text, the opening paragraph bears a monarchical seal of authority (the Christian cross and a sword capped by the Crown), and an oversized capital letter draws the reader's eye to the first word of the first sentence. These colonial-era signifiers are accompanied above by a period-appropriate block print title (including the antique "V" in "INTRODVCCION") addressed "to the profane reader," and below by a menacing winged cherub brandishing a very modern-looking shotgun. The next page presents for the reader's contemplation a reproduction from the Ramírez Codex (circa 1532), one of several records of the pre-Colombian indigenous societies and their subjugation, typically incorporating pictography authored by indigenous artists in the aftermath of the Conquest, but redacted under the supervision of Christian monastics. The image is simple and emblematic, a graphic herald of war, cultural domination, and colonization: a winged angel astride a winged horse emerges from a winged ship.

In the visual juxtaposition and narrative alignment of these images, the prehistory of Clement's graphic novel is traced back to the visual ammunition of the long war between European colonizers and the indigenous resistance: on the one hand, Catholicism's propagandistic visual armory—hagiography, icons, illuminated manuscripts, the greater authority of the written word—and, on the other, the narrative and religious visual arts of the Mexica, Mixtec, Zapotec, Mayan, and other local peoples whose civilizations came under assault by the European invaders. Motolinía, in his sixteenth-century chronicle of the Spanish conquest of Mexico, unwittingly presaged Clement's late-twentieth-century graphic project, as well as its pointed provocation of historical consciousness, when he wrote of the native pictography encountered (and destroyed as idolatry) by the European invaders—"the ancient books that the natives had with characters and figures, as this was their writing, because they had no letters, but characters, and the memory of men is weak" (Benavente, 42). Within this pre-Colombian graphic tradition "figured the deeds and stories of conquests and wars, and the succession of the principal lords; the seasonal and notable signals of the heavens, and general pestilence; when and how they happened; and all the lords who ruled this New Spain until the Spaniards came to it" (Benavente, 43).

The conquering Spaniards all but eradicated the indigenous graphic record in a "war of images" that accompanied the holocaust unleashed on the region through much of the sixteenth century. In its engagement with historical memory as a political objective, Clement's *Operación Bolívar* is a modern adjunct to that largely obliterated subaltern visual and narrative tradition. At the same time, the visual idioms organized in the work draw heavily from the cultural record of dominant institutions—political, religious, economic—that have accompanied the long, troubled march of globalizing forces through the Americas. While the aesthetic affinity of the work is with the subaltern, the forms of visuality deployed in the novel represent the victors in the long "war of images" that began with the Franciscans' destruction of pagan American "idols" and continues in the latter-day image-saturated "Westernization of the planet," in the words of Serge Gruzinski. Thus it is as an aesthetic hybrid—as a synthesis or fusion of previously distinct or even rival cultural elements or practices into a new form, as Néstor García Canclini has described the phenomenon of cultural hybridization (2005, xxv)—that Clement's project can best be read. It has been argued, of course, that García Canclini's concept of hybridity arises precisely from the mechanics and effects of globalization (Kraidy; Nederveen Pieterse). Appropriately, therefore, the complicated visual and aesthetic hybridizations that characterize *Operación Bolívar* can be viewed as a deliberate strategy for opening a critical view onto the so-called age of globalization in which we all live, but viewed from inside the forgotten cultural interior of the global order, and on local (that is, national) cultural terrain. This image-centered strategy for—quite literally—visualizing globalization from within Mexico's history also lends graphic support to a narrative that deploys Mexico's more recent conflictive political history (1968–present) as the latter-day collective point of reference for memorializing globalization as conquest.

The view of U.S.-led globalization that materializes in *Operación Bolívar* is stark and unforgiving. The action of the graphic novel takes place in a fictional country, Angelopolis, where premodern and hypermodern cultural materials are syncretized in the urban landscape—colonial churches alongside skyscrapers, indigenous traditions adjacent to advanced technology. Here, the angel hunters ply their trade as artisans, much like a deer hunter who hunts, shoots, and "dresses" the kill in preparation for consumption, or for the market. The story opens with an arresting full-page panel image: angels in flight around the bell tower of a colonial cathedral appear as ethereal, luminescent butterflies, white airbrush bursts against the gray-black photographic image of the Baroque stone tower. A turn of the page draws automatic weapon fire—"KRAN KRAN KRAN" says the text—and a female angel, mortally wounded, plummets to the ground in front of the cathedral's main doors. The narrator moves in to finish her off, quickly severing her head with a machete blow. "Killing angels might seem somewhat repugnant . . . and it is," the narrator comments (7–8). The murderous act does not represent a perversion or sacrilege, but an incontrovertible fact of supply and demand economics. "Selling angels might seem dirty work . . . and it is. . . . But it is the only thing we know how to do; and we will do it as long as there are people who will pay" (15).

The "first story about the angel hunters" ever told is thus a tale of business. There is, of course, competition for the market. After a sequence of panels that depict the narrator butchering the angel's corpse as he describes his inherited trade, the angel hunter encounters the indigenous Juan Grande, the oldest of the angel hunters, playing a trumpet for change on a desolate city street corner. The two men argue briefly over Juan Grande's presence in the city, in an exchange designed both to remind the reader of the indigenous lineage of the angel killing trade and to establish the entrepreneurial self-concept of the narrator. The economic nature of the social interaction is underscored visually by the narrator's flipping a coin into Juan Grande's cup, a gesture depicted in a series of four vertical panels of equal width that span the page and track in cinematic close-up the causal link between hand, coin, and cup. The panel sequence enables this gesture to bisect with precision twin horizontal panels above and below showing the two characters standing together under a streetlamp. The dispute over turf, and the coin the narrator drops into Juan Grande's plastic cup (branded as a Tupperware product across the bottom), underscores the extent to which this social relationship, and the practice of killing angels, pertains to the capitalist order.

But local market activity, however gruesome, finds itself eclipsed by brutal global market mechanics. Immediately following the encounter between the two local angel hunters, Juan Grande is accosted by gangsterlike figures, accompanied by a muscled and leathery guardian angel, who viciously amputate both of his hands. As it turns out, the grotesque assault on the indigenous Juan Grande is motivated by a plan, concocted by a U.S. plutocrat, to corner the market on angel-derived products, with a strategic interest in the narcotics market. Although the "gift" of killing angels is a genetic endowment of those with indigenous blood, the reader later discovers that the severed hands of an angel killer can be retrofitted for use by elite U.S. combat troops, thereby giving them the ability "to kill anything on heaven and earth." The elimination of the local competition is simply an added benefit.

While in Dr. Simi's adventures (see chapter 7) globalization extends happily from the prenational past into the postnational present, in *Operación Bolívar* the long history of globalization intervenes conflictually in the local traffic in goods. That is, the representation of globalization includes asymmetrical conflict between transnational and local actors—the indigenous "small producer" versus the U.S. capitalist, the CIA, the Pentagon, and so forth—amid market practices that appear largely unchanged in the more than 500-year history of globalization in the region. Anyone familiar with the chronicles of Columbus and Cortés, or the denunciation of genocidal tactics by Fray Bartolomé de las Casas in his *Brevísima relación de la destrucción de las Indias* (1552), will recognize the amputation of the indigenous man's hands as the standard modus operandi of the early Spanish colonizers. One can recognize here a representation of globalization that includes in the capitalist market logic the brute coercion of "primitive accumulation," snatching productive capacity by force instead of by trade, practices that Karl Marx had identified as belonging to the premodern origins of the capitalist order.

This is the most critical point that distinguishes *Operación Bolívar* from other Mexican comics that treat the global order. At the heart of the novel's representation of the phenomenon of globalization is its representation of commerce, the activity positioned at the center of the U.S. cultural model legible in the *Country Commercial Guide* (see chapter 2) and at the core of its promise of modernity. In *Operación Bolívar*, just as with globalist discourses, wealth and modernity are associated with technology and movement, but in this case wealth and technology, indeed modernity itself, are generated through violence. The body, whether of angel or human, is presented as an object caught up in a machinery of physical repression and bloody extraction of surplus value. In an image of the narrator harvesting body parts, Clement's portrait of the character at work is combined with reproduction of anatomical drawings borrowed from nineteenth-century medical science, suggesting a studied, clinical quality to the macabre dissection on display (see figure 8.1). Here, as throughout the novel, Clement departs from standard panel sequencing and constructs a tableau for the reader's contemplation. The lightbulb illuminating the scene from above is a marked stylistic contrast, drawn in the style of Pablo Picasso's *Guernica*, a work of art historical importance produced in protest of fascist violence during the Spanish Civil War. An inset panel at bottom left is twinned with a text box to describe the special problem of finger and toenails, a market for which has yet to emerge. The text box extends, shelflike, beyond the margin of the grisly tableau with a corked apothecary bottle marked "Nails," the merchandise on offer postproduction.

Local harvesting of angel parts feeds the interests and infrastructure of the emerging global order. "The eyes are sold to the Japanese," who use the corneas to develop laser technology and in "efforts to give vision to robots." The hair becomes "light cable" in the hands of "engineers at General Dynamics" (11). The local entrepreneur, embodied by the narrator, kills to survive economically, and must endure torture and evade his captors as a result of what neoliberal economists would term his "comparative advantage," his locally rooted and uniquely economically valuable resources and skills. "There was a time when angelical organs were sold to genetic research laboratories," explains the narrator. "Nobody knows what they discovered, but ever since, the CIA and NASA [National Aeronautics and Space Administration] have not stopped pursuing us" (11).

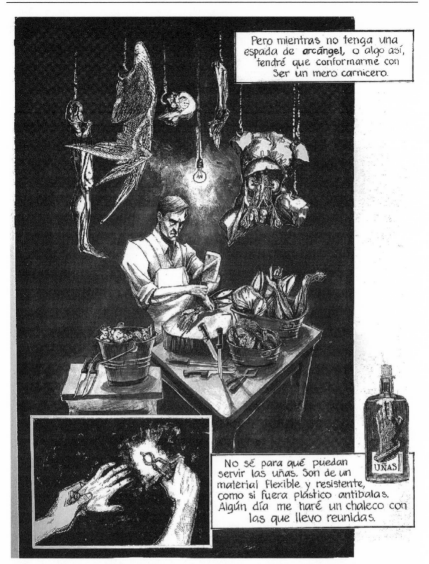

Figure 8.1. Commodification is visualized as violent and profane. The angel hunter's narrative voice at lower right: "I don't know what the fingernails could be used for. They are made of a tough and flexible material, like a bulletproof plastic. Some day I will make a vest with the ones I've collected." From *Operación Bolívar*, 15. Courtesy of Edgar Clement.

The merchandise and forces of production of capitalism, target of espionage and dispute on the global stage, carry with them a history of death, torture, and domination.

A "true history" of the commodity, supported with historically hybrid visuals, is presented to the reader in *Operación Bolívar* from a national perspective, despite the fantastical location of the plot. When the narrator evades capture by the Archangel Michael and his contingent of U.S. Special Forces, he descends through a manhole into a world of pre-Colombian ruins beneath the city, a world in fact rumored to exist by many Mexicans. The premodern substrate of the city is represented by sketching the figure of the narrator against the background of a detailed archaeological drawing of the Aztec deity Coatlicue, goddess of history, and with a stylized rendering of an *alebrije*, a dreamlike creature of fantasy typically found in the tourist markets of the indigenous-heavy southern state of Oaxaca. One of the more violent characters is Román, described as "*un policía judicial*," a police force vilified in the Mexican popular imagination for widespread allegations of human rights abuses. The torture manual Román uses in his interrogation of a captured angel is likely a reference to a manual—exposed by a 1997 investigative report by the *Baltimore Sun* newspaper—used by Latin American trainees at the U.S. military School of the Americas in Fort Benning, Georgia. Torture techniques described in Clement's photocopied image of a photocopied notebook with spiral binding are known to have been used by Mexican police on dissidents through the 1980s. In *Operación Bolívar*, the manual is published by the "Fray Tomás de Torquemada Institute of Mexican Criminology" and is adorned with an image from the colonial archives, an oval-framed portrait of Torquemada, the infamous leader of Spain's Holy Inquisition. In several frames, the front pages of the national newspapers *Reforma* and *La Jornada* are carefully positioned in the hands of characters as a narrative support, an obvious reference to the Mexican public sphere. A dialogue between the narrator and the scheming gringo capitalist is brokered by a female interpreter named Doña Marina, the name of Hernán Cortés's concubine and interpreter, also known as La Malinche, whose role in facilitating the Spaniards' vanquishing of the Aztecs (among others) earned her infamy as a namesake for treason in Mexico. The climax of the novel is reached when angels are lured to their death at Tlatelolco, site of the 1968 Mexico City massacre of student protesters by Mexican troops.

The novel's plot and hybrid visual constructions situate globalization within the national imaginary, and within the problem of national modernity. Who will control the development of the nation's resources? The reader will not find repeated here any optimistic visualizing of globalization as the royal road to modernization. On the contrary, violence and social domination, albeit hidden from everyday public view, are presented as the obscure truth behind the reigning political and economic orders. In the end, scores of angels are gunned down by an assemblage of Mexican judicial police, U.S. soldiers and mercenaries, and drug dealers, with technical support from the Pentagon and U.S. Drug Enforcement Agency. At the close of the story, the narrator has succeeded in returning the hands of Juan Grande to their rightful owner, and has managed to limit the carnage at Tlatelolco, considerable though it was. The narrator and a guardian angel, who switched sides after being betrayed by his gringo benefactor, discuss the situation in the final pages.

GUARDIAN ANGEL: And the Mexicans! You are complicit with your exploiters!

NARRATOR: Not us! The powerful! Not the people.

GUARDIAN ANGEL: And why do the people allow it?

NARRATOR: They are the Government! The owners of the country! Unmovable!

GUARDIAN ANGEL: And why don't you take up arms?

NARRATOR: And disturb the peace? Never!

GUARDIAN ANGEL: But you spend your time killing each other anyway!

NARRATOR: But we want to be modern! Civilized, you know. (158)

The Mexican national experiment with modernity—an experiment in the relationship between popular sovereignty and the development of wealth and technology—remains suspended somewhere between the Spanish conquest of the territory and NAFTA. The visual aesthetics of the novel—hybridized visual codes that range from the medieval illuminated manuscript, to high modernist painting, to nineteenth- and twentieth-century advertising copy—can be read as a graphic record of the recombinant cultural DNA of that globalized national status quo.

Mexico's national field of comic book or *historieta* production is characterized by the same predominance of humor and melodrama that marks the Mexican culture industry in general—as with the *telenovela* and the sensationalist journalism Mexicans call "*la nota roja.*" In contrast, *Operación Bolívar* directly politicizes key elements of the global order. This effect is achieved through a heightened density of meaning in the work's language and imagery (much like the symbolic "condensation" that marks the content of a dream on the Freudian view). The novel's title, for example, carries strong Pan–Latin American associations, due to the reference to nineteenth-century independence leader Simón Bolívar, at the same time that it recalls military counterinsurgency operations against radical Marxist nationalists in the region dating to the Cold War (that is, Operación Cóndor in the southern cone under the U.S.-backed dictatorships of the 1970s and 1980s, and Operación Bolívar in Colombia more recently). Similarly, the central image of the work—the figure of the angel—is fraught with discrepant semiotic accents, signifying variously and simultaneously a familiar supranational Christian spiritualism, a stupefying narcotic (that is, as "angel dust"), innocence, imperialist doctrinal propaganda (as with the Conquest), and even national democracy, as referenced in the novel by Mexico City's storied Angel de la Independencia monument, a traditional site of mass demonstrations and celebrations located on Avenida Reforma.

One can appreciate here that a politics of the image accompanies the work's stated objective of recuperating historical consciousness. Unlike the blithe consumerist realism of Dr. Simi's happy cosmopolitanism, which effaces national history in favor of a selective remembering, *Operación Bolívar* displays a dark and de-mystifying aesthetic built from the historical and contemporary imagery and visual constructs of modern globalization, which is to say from the historical period, beginning with the early modern European colonialist project and running through to the latter-day hegemony of the northern metropole (the United States in particular) and the relative dependence of the economic South. Although mythic in the way it vivifies figures from the national cultural record (angels and *nahuales* taking flight in the same airspace as Black Hawk helicopters), *Operación Bolívar* works corrosively against the globalist mythos of discovery and modernity. The optic of the graphic novel absorbs creatively some of the multiple visual languages generated not only by recent mass cultural production but also by institutional interests constitutive of European modernity (and, by extension, global capitalist expansion). Illuminated manuscripts, nineteenth- and twentieth-century advertising copy, high modernist painting, twentieth-century print media from the United States and Mexico, sixteenth-century post-Conquest pictographic codices, Hollywood film imagery, a late-twentieth-century torture manual used by the Mexican military and judicial police, weaponry blueprints from the arms industry, news photography, painstaking archaeological drawings,

Figure 8.2. U.S. hegemony is visualized as continuous with colonial empire. Above a colonial-era world map, the voice of the gringo speaks of global dominion: "Reorganize the wealth already created, already distributed, through FREE TRADE. First: AMERIKA, later: THE WORLD." From *Operación Bolívar*, 93. Courtesy of Edgar Clement.

and those objectifying target view-finders that outfit modern weapons and video games alike all converge in tracing the work's narrative arc.

The myriad visual idioms Clement employs do not simply share the page; they constitute the page. This is an assertion best illustrated graphically. Page 89 (see figure 8.2), for example, eschews the traditional comic book panel entirely, organizing the page instead as an illustrated narrative script. The narrative function of the page is to introduce a dialogue between the narrator, the angel hunter Leonides, and the gringo globalist John Smith, a U.S. capitalist who is using his influence over corrupt angels (including the Archangel Michael) and CIA agents to organize a massacre of angels. Since the dialogue entails the delivery by the evocatively named gringo (a generic Anglo-Saxon, but also Pocahontas's beloved colonial captain) Smith of an extensive discourse on free trade and his fantasy of a seamless U.S. hegemony over an hemispheric "América Unida," the standard sequencing of image panels with inset short dialogue would be inadequate to the task. But despite the fact that this and the subsequent ten pages of the novel are extraordinarily script-heavy, often including paragraph-length explanation and argument, the visual organization of the page nonetheless effectively contains the written word and maintains the predominance of the image.

The visual equilibrium in this important segment of the story arc is accomplished through a use of the image as optical architecture for the reading of the script. Page 89 constructs a tripartite arrangement of the written word. The eye is drawn first to the top half of the page, where the title page of a mock colonial-era "*relación*," or report to the royal authorities, presents in large, period-specific font information about the parties to the ensuing dialogue. The visual centrality of this text is secured with the large typeface of the key term "dialogue," with the decorative border and symmetrical cherubim, and via the superimposition of the "*relación*" on the sketched portraits of the gringo and narrator, who lock eyes with the reader. The lower third of the page is ordered by the posture of Smith, whose vertical stance and horizontally outstretched left arm repeat and reinforce from the left margin the rectangular image of a colonial-era *mapa mundi*. Directional arrows radiating outward from North America provide a center of focus and suggest paths of movement for the reader's eye that connect the image of Smith with news clippings that extend to the right margin, and upward to Smith's spoken discourse, floating across the middle of the page:

The world, my friend, has changed; more than many believe. The new inventions and new technological advances no longer increase material wealth, and the productive forces of humanity have also ceased to grow. Okay? Good! We need, therefore, to reorganize the world; reorganize the wealth already created, already distributed, through FREE TRADE. First: AMERIKA, then: THE WORLD.

Meanwhile, the visual elements that structure the page also serve as the semiotic ground for interpreting and contextualizing the dialogue presented. The horizontal balance of the character portraits and the opposing cherubim, as well as the two-headed eagle at top, offers visual substantiation of the concept of dialogue. At the same time, the "*relación*"—more precisely, the image of the "*relación*"—contextualizes the "dialogue" with a historical reminder, from the aftermath of the Conquest, of the asymmetry of power that lurks behind the apparent reciprocity of conversation. The two-headed eagle, in fact a monstrous transnational Siamese twin fusing the nationally emblematic U.S. and Mexican eagles, adds to the reader's interpretation of "dialogue" an ominous intimation of violent confrontation. The bottom third of the page operates in analogous fashion on Smith's declaration of a "New World Order." The same posture that serves as a visual framing device offers an affective and ideological lens for reading Smith's discourse: with his head bowed and arms outstretched, the gringo's neoliberalism takes on the impassioned character of a sermon, of theology. The juxtaposition of the map conjures centuries-old visions of conquest and global domination, while the newspaper headlines—like the "*relación*," text appearing as familiar image—link those visions to the historical present, to the reader's reality, and to Mexico: "The World-wide Voice of the Transnational Corporation," announces one; another cites Mexico's president Ernesto Zedillo, who presided over the implementation of NAFTA—"The Source of the World Economy Will Continue Being Trade." Taken from Mexico's *El Financiero*, the third news headline, "United and Without Obstacles the Mafia Prepares to Expand and Consolidate Its Control Over the World," injects criminality into the interpretive framework for understanding the global order of which Smith speaks.

The politics of the image in *Operación Bolívar* inheres precisely in the hybridized visuality of the page. The past and present are represented by disparate visual forms that are aesthetically conjugated—through montage, parodic imitation, and the kind of suggestive reproduction and editorializing juxtaposition that the Situationists called *detournement*—in order to reveal the past in the present, and even the present in the past, disrupting the accepted, univocal meanings of the semantic and symbolic status quo. Viewed sociologically, one can say that the aesthetic hybridization discernible in the pages of Clement's novel activates and renders critical a regional cultural repertory sedimented by historical experience into the everyday lives of Latin American elites. García Canclini has noted that modern Latin American culture is marked by a "multitemporal heterogeneity," whereby "[i]n the houses of the bourgeoisie and of middle classes with a high educational level in Santiago, Lima, Bogotá, Mexico City, and many other cities, there coexist multilingual libraries and indigenous crafts, cable TV and parabolic antennas with colonial furniture, and magazines that tell how to carry out better financial speculation this week with centuries-old family and religious rituals" (2005, 46–47). One senses in *Operación Bolívar*'s imagery and narrative an effort to organize this cultural collection as critical historical consciousness, wresting a recognition of social domination from the materials of dominant culture.

The brooding and cynical aesthetic center of gravity of the work—something like a cross between hard-boiled detective fiction and the book of Revelations—is a precipitate of its genealogical intervention in the eclectic simultaneity of the present-day elite Mexican cultural repertory. The artistic decision to publish the entire work in black and white was undoubtedly influenced by production cost concerns, but the removal of color from the work's formal syntax also afforded an easier visual integration of disparate artistic styles and media, imagery as different as television screen captures, pre-Colombian pictographic narration, modern magazine cover design, photography, the anatomical drawings of medical science, Leonardo Da Vinci's *Vitruvian Man* sketch, the cubism of Pablo Picasso's *Guernica*, World War II propaganda posters, an oil painting by Francisco Goya, and the skeletal *grabados* made famous by early-twentieth-century Mexican graphic artist José Guadalupe Posada. It is not only that the black-and-white format lends itself to the narrative's starkly oppressive sensibility; the menacing feel of *Operación Bolívar* is a direct consequence of the aesthetic hybridization it assists in performing.

It is worthwhile to explore the point of contact within the novel's imagery of art, politics, and cultural hybridization. As noted above, the collision between art and politics in *Operación Bolívar* has a communicative effect. Viewed as a matter of communication, the politics of the image in the novel is available in the volatility of the signifier: whether as word or image, the discrete units of meaning deployed in the narrative are torn open by competing historical and perspectival claims on their reception. The angel as combatant, as commodity, as victim, as figment of the religious imagination, as national symbol, all crowd into the linguistic and visual signifier presented to the reader on the page. And yet one might easily argue that some kind of disruption in the "commonsense" character of the communicative chain of speaker-message-addressee is inevitable in any genuinely political enunciation. Meaning has to be bent away from a status quo sensibility in order to turn it toward an alternative (even a reactionary alternative). In this case, however, one encounters not a subversion of an accepted meaning and its substitution by another. Rather, the cultural commonplace—of the guardian angel, for example—is not discarded or renounced so much as it is de-centered, made to stand side by side with a competitor (the angel as mercenary), and even recognize itself there. Treated semiotically, one might say that the charge of special meaning traditionally associated with all things angelic is rewired by the novel into the circuitry of meaning associated with war, vice, and profit. Tradition and modernity collide in the sign.

One might complain that such a description remains fundamentally semiotic, relating to an operation on the level of the individual sign or unit of meaning, and does not respond to the question of the aesthetics of the work. Within that very operation, however, in the encounter between Clement's graphic artistry and the cultural hybridity peculiar to Mexico's historical experience of modernization, the reader can make out the aesthetics proper to Clement's interference with the governing reception of Mexico's cultural past. If Mexican elites, and the middle-class sensibilities that sustain their rule, tend to organize the nation's cultural patrimony as a kind of storied collection of practices and artifacts subordinated to the technological knowledge, instrumental rationality, and pecuniary interests of capitalist modernization, then Clement's work can be viewed as a reorganization of that same cultural patrimony, presenting an alternative form of hybridization. In the former, official model of hybridization, the personal collection, as García Canclini has characterized the experience of hybridity, coordinates the inherited cultural record as tradition, and retains its relevance as a useful ingredient of modern life—for example, religious ritual at the service of financial advantage. In Clement's alternative, the inherited cultural record is reattached to its original instrumentality (for example, the Archangel Michael as "captain and caudillo" of the subjugation of indigenous peoples) at the same time that it is confronted with the latter-day materials of modernity, and financial advantage becomes visible as war by another means.

Stated another way, the hybrid image in *Operación Bolívar*, and therein the aesthetics of the work, is cultivated from a *re-membering* of cultural patrimony, the reversal of a mutilation of collective memory that had transpired under the weight of hegemony's official "consensus," that common sense of the reigning social order. Genealogy—and this term can be understood in the most Nietzschean sense—is implicit in the work's aesthetic hybridizations. As the severed limb of the past is reattached to the living present—Juan Grande's hands serving as metaphor—a Nietzschean transvaluation of dominant values is effected, overturning the received sense of reality and propriety that governs the present. "Free Trade" traces its roots to a Western will to power and its subjugation of others; in the corrupted, and assaulted, figure of the angel, we see that the "spirit world" does not escape from this subordination to dominant interests. A genealogical leverage against dominant cultural reception, the political energy of the work's hybrid aesthetics, can be seen also in the graphic novel's treatment of the work of art itself, that cultural object of specialized attention and suprahistorical distinction, conserved by museums and galleries and mediated for the general public by art historical experts. Here, too, conventional reception meets with interference. Museology meets the history of power at the site of the visual image.

While *Operación Bolívar* weaves a broad array of visual materials into its fabric, there are two modern art historical objects that prominently contribute to the warp and weft of the text: Francisco Goya's *The Executions of the Third of May, 1808* (1814) and Pablo Picasso's *Guernica* (1937). Clement's draftsmanship and graphic artistry are evident in his dramatic conversions of historical cultural data into comics characters and action—*nahuales* and angels battling across the page as one expects from characters in a graphic novel—and in his creativity with the narrative form of sequential art, interspersing distinct drawing styles and panel size and position in order to visualize the nonoptic senses or track the dramatic minutiae of the unfolding action. This graphics setting also serves to drag the art historical image outside the institutional frame of the museum and of traditional art criticism. There, immersed in the hybrid pictography of "the first story about the angel hunters," these rarefied images from Western art history are enlisted in a figuration of "the deeds and stories of conquests and wars" that, as the introduction reminds us, have generated the reader's present.

Goya and Picasso both are recycled and recontextualized, made to share the page with Spanish colonial visual culture and the popular visual media of nineteenth- and twentieth-century Mexico. Intermittently throughout the novel, fragments of Picasso's antifascist protest *Guernica* flash jaggedly into the visual field, as the reader views depictions of torture and physical violence. As noted above, the lightbulb shining down on the grisly scene of dismemberment in figure 8.1 is a visual synecdoche, suggestive of Picasso's large-format work. In a

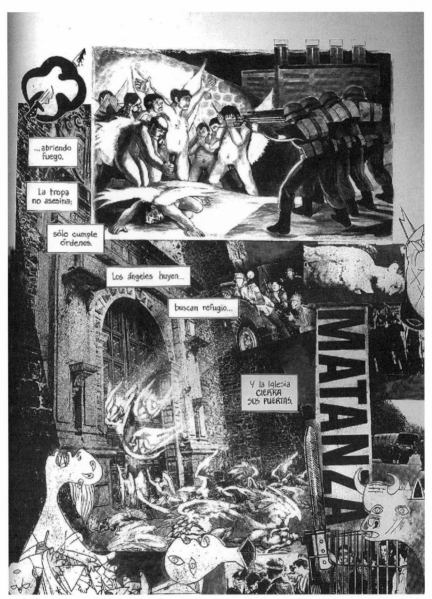

Figure 8.3. Picasso and Goya are enlisted in portraying the Tlatelolco massacre. Newspaper photographs of Mexican troops and jailed activists squeeze into the frame from the right-hand margin. From *Operación Bolívar*, 119. Courtesy of Edgar Clement.

subsequent image of Román torturing an angel, the glaring lightbulb from the Picasso work appears above the victim's head as a swinging interrogation light, while the stylized and decorated script of an illuminated manuscript explains the action below. Later, when Román himself is tortured by U.S. military personnel, the bulb appears again as a sawtoothed halo behind his terrorized visage. Goya's mournful oil painting, which documented the mass killing of Spanish patriots before a Napoleonic firing squad, is reproduced as an emotionally suggestive metaphor for the massacre of angels taking place in Angelopolis (see figure 8.3). Fragmentary motifs from Picasso's work provide visual ballast and counterpoint across the lower margin of the page, suggesting a plaintive border for an edited photograph of the ponderous church doors, against which dead angels pile up.

The siting of this fictional massacre at Tlatelolco pushes that dark, mostly forgotten moment in Spanish national history up against Mexico's more recent history of conflict, a one-sided conflict waged, as in Spain, between the official order and the nation's patriots. A descending series of text boxes narrate the horror—"opening fire. The troops do not murder; they only follow orders. The angels flee . . . seek refuge . . . and the Church closes its doors"—and visually mimic the descent of the angels to their deaths at the church doors. Here again, visual and aesthetic hybridization operates on the image, pulling apart received forms and restitching the ligatures for a recuperated history of the globalized present. The text box series connects the antiwar protest symbol at upper left (a dove adopted by the international student movement against the U.S. war in Vietnam, now skewered with a bayonet) to a vertically aligned bold newspaper headline, which drops straight down to Picasso's cubist bull at lower right. The Mexican setting for oppression is graphically secured through a montage of visual *realia*—news photo clippings that reference the massacre of student demonstrators at Tlatelolco by Mexican troops in 1968.

These aesthetic choices on the part of the artist are especially interesting because of the referential or indexical common denominator these artworks share with virtually every other visual construct in the novel: that is, violence. But the artworks do not appear in the novel solely as signs; they also carry with them a tinge of that greater cultural status and extraordinary frame of meaning that belong to the "high" aesthetic object. Unlike the Catholic visual media of evangelization, or the mass cultural visual register of print, film, television, or the commercially invested advertising image, the Picasso and Goya artworks stand out as a disinterested cultural form. According to the Western institution of aesthetics, which has traditionally viewed the work of art as the proper housing for a kind of experience that resists reduction to mere political and economic interests, advertising and political propaganda may draw on artistic technique, but they cannot generate authentic aesthetic experience. What is beautiful, like what is true, rises above sectarian, commercial, or dogmatic preoccupations.

Influential German critic Walter Benjamin, writing not too long after the fascist bombing of the Spanish town of Guernica, would choose none other than the figure of the angel to illustrate the presence of historical consciousness in aesthetic experience under the traumatic conditions of modern technological, political, and economic change. Cognizant of newly emergent mass media, the rise of fascism and war, and the absorption of ever greater social and cultural territory by the mechanics of capitalism, Benjamin termed the encounter of aesthetics and history "the angel of history," a spirited image drawn from Paul Klee's modernist painting *Angelus Novus* (1920). Benjamin transformed his viewing of Klee's painting into an allegory of contemporary historical consciousness—aesthetic sensibility amid the violence and transformation of tradition wrought by modernity:

> This is how one pictures the angel of history. His face is turned toward the past. Where we perceive a chain of events, he sees one single catastrophe which keeps piling wreckage upon wreckage and hurls it in front of his feet. The angel would like to stay, awaken the dead, and make whole what has been smashed. But a storm is blowing from Paradise. . . . This storm irresistibly propels him into the future to which his back is turned, while the pile of debris before him grows skyward. This storm is what we call progress. (Benjamin, 258)

Benjamin's angel of history is an emblem of the historical desire rendered visible in the work of art, a desire to somehow overcome or counteract the relentless maelstrom of modern history, the clash of material interests through which, as Marx famously proclaimed of capitalist development, "all that is solid melts into air." Alongside the gaze of the Western institution of art, an art historical gaze forever turned toward tradition and its own canons, the viewer feels in the individual work his or her own ache to reassemble all that has been lost, broken, mutilated. History's tradition-altering momentum shoves the work of art toward formal experimentation and novelty, as all the while the artwork attempts to "hold it together" in relation with the past. Instructively, Klee's modernist angel breaks with the recent past of European representational art, but holds close something "lost" to modern experience, displaying the "primitivist" use of color and line one associates with an ancient cave drawing or a premodern indigenous deerskin painting. As the viewer, Benjamin senses a wish is present in this artwork so visibly troubled by its moment in history; he sees in the angel an ethical impulse much like the principle of *tikkun olam*, the moral command-ment of his own Jewish tradition aimed at healing what is broken in the world.

History thrust Benjamin's angel into Goya's work, and later Picasso's, im-printing there an image of historical experience and frustrated desire. Through Benjamin's eyes one can see in each of these works not only the obvious indict-ment of an act of official violence, Franco's carpet bombing and Napoleon's im-perial firing squad in the "content" of the painting, but also a yearning to awaken these dead, to liberate them from their historically sealed fate. In Clement's graphic novel, needless to say, this angel also has been overtaken by the storm, or more appropriately for *Operación Bolívar*, the war of progress. The one-of-a-kind and irreplaceable quality of the original artworks is violated by their reproduc-tion, pressed into the service of montage, and their "high" cultural authority is dispersed in fragments, shared out among the visual detritus of the modern era. Picasso's *Guernica* is fractured into spectral shards of visual commentary, inti-mations of modern horror in the "multitemporal simultaneity" of Clement's graphic hybridizations. Goya's partisans are stripped naked, abject and broken angels lined up for execution. The angel of history finds its back to the wall.

Clement's graphic dismemberment of these artworks can be interpreted as an assault on the palace of "high" art, but there is more here than what im-mediately meets the eye. If progress is another word for war in the novel, then national liberation is the nom de guerre of Benjamin's angel as it appears in Clement's artistic appropriations. Widely recognized as harbingers of Spain's cultural modernity, and of the European nation's contributions to universal culture, both the Goya and the Picasso artworks depict episodes of oppression that were foundational to the European nation-state. Clement's mutilation of the artworks is a graphic performance, to use Benjamin's words, of the "one single catastrophe" of modern history, a catastrophe visible in the "multitempo-ral" living rooms of the Latin American elite, and in the daily lives of Mexico's indigenous peoples. Each "quotation" of the artwork carries with it traces of a social and historical moment of violence from the *longue durée* of Eurocentric modernization. Violence is spoken by each image, and in each image is concret-ized an inverted vision of official Spanish history, an image of the frustrated desires stamped out under the official seal of Spain. In each graphically compromised artwork, a recognition of historical desire—for the sovereign nation, for democracy, for liberation—flashes up and in the same instant is shown to have failed.

In this way the presence of the work of "high" art in the hybrid visual text serves as a reminder that Mexico's modernity is colored by the authoritarianism of its colonial sire, Spain, which well into the twentieth century continued to crush and forget. The registry of liberation's despair presented in Clement's selection of these particular works, and their haunting of the scene at Tlatelolco, bears the imprimatur not of the "universality" of beauty but of the particularity of the nation. The montage of images visualizes a political genealogy for the Mexican nation, a line of descent for the age of globalization: on the one hand, the lineage of official authoritarianism, from Cortés to Franco to U.S. interventionism, and from Cortés to Díaz Ordaz (the Mexican president who oversaw the Tlatelolco massacre) to the U.S.-led model of economic globalization; on the other, a close family resemblance between the native *nahuales* and *brujos*, the Spanish nationalists, the tragedy of the Spanish Republic, and the Mexican student movement of 1968. The dismembered nation, the mutilated counterofficial projects, the forgotten alternatives to the status quo, all are fallen casualties of the European war of progress, fallen angels. Importantly, what is tragic about this view of the nation is also visible in the montage: the Mexican nation that could have been is not, because globalization already happened, a long time ago, and has not stopped happening.

In *Operación Bolívar*, therefore, the nation bears a close resemblance to the "deep Mexico" identified by Guillermo Bonfil Batalla, an unofficial nation dating to the ruptures of the Conquest, a fusion of indigenous and popular cultures obscured by officialdom and preyed upon by the forces of Eurocentric modernization in Mexico. *Operación Bolívar* designs an unofficial view of the global order that foregrounds simultaneously the violence of capitalist globalization and the tendency of the institutional order (corporations and states) to obscure that violence. Notably, the critical discourse of Clement's work arises from social conditions of production more readily identifiable with Mexican civil society than with transnational corporate enterprise. When he authored *Operación Bolívar*, Clement was a member of the Taller del Perro, a visual arts collective organized around the task of renovating national traditions in the comics genre. The Taller was a latter-day representative of a phenomenon of the Mexican cultural field emergent in the 1970s, a decade known among art historians as "the decade of the groups" because of a turn toward collaborative cultural production and direct engagement with national political issues in the arts. Important segments of Mexico's current cultural production continue to be marked by this earlier political history: arts collaborations dedicated to articulating "high" artistic production with popular culture, working through a close identification with those social sectors engaged in struggle for political independence from the corruption and conservatism of the Mexican state, on the one hand, and the corporate controls instituted through privatization, on the other.

This distinctive feature of Clement's project underscores a defining feature of the globalist position articulated in some of the other comics discussed in this book (see chapters 2, 3, 4, and 7). Viewed against the contrast of *Operación Bolívar*, the strategic absences and exclusions of other graphic narratives become much more obvious. Not only are national realities and histories tendentiously glossed and de-politicized, their conflicts pointedly forgotten, but the nation itself is divested of labor and social organization. It is not simply the figure of the popular that is diminished, but that of civil society as well. Importantly, these elisions are implicated in the reshaping of Mexico's political economy under pressure from the U.S. model of globalization. In this new national scenario, what remains of the corporatist political model, the model that oversaw the Tlatelolco massacre, has been retooled in order to contain and marginalize opposition to the transferal of wealth from the public to the private sector. The result has been intensified struggle over the symbolic materials of the nation's cultural patrimony, and the emergence of social and political organizations aimed at carving out a sphere of semiautonomy from official controls.

The most famous example of this phenomenon is, of course, the neo-Zapatista movement, which, like Clement's novel, is motivated by a desire to "awaken the dead" and restore something of what has been lost in the long catastrophe of globalization. Clement's imaginative interference with the officially sanctioned hybrid cultural order occurs simultaneously and at a parallel with the neo-Zapatista refusal to forget, which also went public in 1994. Consigned to oblivion by the culturescaping of the imperial model of globalization, by the neoliberal state, and by the transnational private sector, the national desire for liberation—like the work of art, theoretically exceeding the grasping controls of the purely commercial or the strictly governmental—appears in the unofficial imagination as a fleeting, fantastical, even angelic presence that inhabits an already globalized history. In the hybrid pictography of *Operación Bolívar*, that angel of history cannot escape conscription in the ongoing war for control of the present.

EL BULBO VS. THE MACHINE

Graphic Artistry as Superpower

The superhero takes flight, launching himself in a long arc over the city with a look of determination and righteous purpose in his eyes. In his sights: a monstrous threat to the innocent citizenry looms on the horizon, a swath of crushed buildings and terrorized victims trailing behind. The superhero aims himself like a bullet, rocketing through the sky directly at his target. The self-sacrificing hero, equipped with extraordinary powers—an exceptional individual who serves as protector of the everyday, ordinary mass of society—throws himself into the path of the oncoming horror. This embodiment of the collective good slams violently into the embodiment of antisocial evil (a crazed or subhuman ferocity, hell-bent on mass destruction). As the smoke and flame of a pitched, epic battle dissipate, the battered but victorious hero stands firm, order once again successfully defended and affirmed. Individual prowess—including personal abilities that closely mimic the flight, speed, and explosive force made possible by modern technologies of energy, transportation, and war—has once again served the common good and the common man and woman.

If there is a familiar, even predictable, feel to this storyline, it is because, in generic terms, these descriptions of the comic book superhero's exploits and moral profile hew to a standard template of the superhero genre, a narrative standard generally considered to have originated in the United States with the Action Comics Superman series in 1938. The schematic narrative outline presented above is not, however, drawn from the adventures of the vaunted "Man of Steel," that globally recognizable popular cultural representative of U.S.

exceptionalism. Instead of a broad-shouldered, deep-chested Anglo male, whose red-and-blue cape and tights mirror U.S. national colors as he defends "Truth, Justice, and the American Way," in this case the hyperstrong hero hails from Mexico, speaks Spanish, and has a short, stocky body. Instead of a journalist who moonlights as a caped crusader, the Mexican hero is born from a picture bulb released from a discarded television set, brought to life by the magical incantations of an amateur television repairman in Mexico City. Behold: El Bulbo (The Bulb).

A creation of Sebastián Carrillo (alias Bachan), with significant collaboration from Bernardo Fernández (alias Bef), El Bulbo is the protagonist of a ten-issue comic book series published by Mexico City–based Shibalba Press in 2000–2001, and in book form in 2007 by Caligrama. Although dressed up in the narrative conventions of the classic U.S. superhero paradigm, El Bulbo wears his cape differently, and operates at the center of a radically different threat environment. This becomes clear when one considers the same basic narrative structure sketched out above, but now filled out with greater specificity vis-à-vis character and context: In issue #3 of Bachan's superhero series, "El Bulbo vs. Toyzilla," the animated picture tube from a junked television set faces a Godzilla-like monster who stomps madly through Mexico City, leaving terror and rubble in its wake. Unlike the Godzilla of motion picture fame, however, this monster is not an organic mutant, but a child's wind-up toy, greatly enlarged and set in motion by the evil Adolfo, another animated television picture bulb sprung magically from the same original event as El Bulbo. Adolfo is an evil doppelgänger for El Bulbo, distinguishable principally by his unmitigated evil postures and the Hitler-style mustache he sports. After having been vanquished in an earlier encounter with El Bulbo (issue #1), Adolfo has been restored to life by an equally morally compromised factory owner, who bestows upon Adolfo the visage of George Lucas's Darth Vader, the supervillain of the film-maker's *Star Wars* series. The embodiment of evil, in other words, drags along behind it an entire production chain of mass cultural authorship and antisocial malevolence.

El Bulbo's moral authority is also distinct from the U.S. superhero standard. Before engaging Toyzilla in battle, El Bulbo addresses the monster with a detailed, and somewhat lampoonish, civic discourse: "I inform you that the city has 25,000 street sweepers and cleaning services, who make their living picking up the rubble created by you and your kind, and if things continue they will soon go on strike. As a decent citizen, I exhort you to surrender, return to whatever place you have come from, and by the authority I vest in myself I exorcize you" (#3, 8). Battle is then engaged when El Bulbo's civic-minded speech draws a fiery, contemptuous snort from Toyzilla, blasting El Bulbo from the sky.

After several failed assaults, El Bulbo turns to the city's electrical power grid, availing himself of greater power for an expected final scene of combat that might finally bring the demise of the terrible plaything. No such luck, El Bulbo finds, as his newfound power is still no match for Toyzilla. Finally, enraged with frustration, El Bulbo's heroic moment is powered in the end by simple, crude anger. "If I had half a brain I would think of some ingenious strategy," El Bulbo's thought bubble informs the comic reader, "but that's not my style" (14). A furious uppercut delivered on the fly to the monster's jaw sends it skyward, and subsequently its now inert gigantic bulk plummets back to earth with an explosive "CHUNNK," leaving an enormous impact crater and smoking disaster in the center of the city, where the lifeless bodies of numerous victims can be seen strewn about. Apparently oblivious to the massive collateral damage caused by his battle with evil, El Bulbo declares triumphantly, "It's a good thing I was able to stop that monster before it destroyed the city!" (15).

What is one to make of El Bulbo's ineffectual bumbling and disproportionate destructiveness, his lack of insight and self-awareness, his ill-conceived reduction of an imminent threat to the very existence of society to mundane political preoccupations of everyday life (for example, the threat of a strike by sanitation workers)? Bachan describes *El Bulbo* as "more a humor comic than a superhero comic," and notes that none of his other works are based on the superhero figure (Carrillo 2006). But what is the Mexico-specific significance of the superhero parody? In order to understand the unconventional behaviors of this particular superhero, it is important first to acknowledge that the superhero comic book is much more than just another time-honored and market-proven package of genre-specific semiotic, aesthetic, and narrative constructs.

The history of the genre is first of all a uniquely modern one. Students of the genre note the twentieth-century origins of the superhero, with Superman, Wonder Woman, and Captain America frequently cited as foundational figures. These figures are, of course, both historically and nationally specific, concocted and entered into mass circulation in the mid-twentieth-century United States, in the context of World War II, the New Deal of the Franklin Delano Roosevelt administration, and early public morals crusades against the perceived corruptive nature of graphic narrative. In these circumstances, Superman's initial adventures have been characterized as those of a "reformist liberal," insofar as he confronted social ills such as domestic abuse, and institutional failures like police corruption, government inaction in the face of poverty, and unethical private enterprise (Gordon 1998, 2001). In addition to occasional frontal assaults on the police and business interests, the Superman of the first two years of the series also opposed U.S. involvement in European conflict, all under the moral authority special to his powers.

By 1940, U.S. involvement in World War II, the ubiquity of official patriotism, the growing commercial value of the Superman series, and morals complaints about comics in general would conspire to produce a "shift of character from iconoclast individualistic liberal reformer to mainstream liberal organizational man" (Gordon 2001, 183). The publisher of the comic even hammered out moral standards for the Superman stories, standards that "prohibited—among other things—the destruction of private property" (Gordon 2001, 181). In other words, the modern moral code inherent in the superhero profile was not built originally on philosophical universals, but on a national ethos. Thus a close relationship can be discerned between a national, status quo vision of modernity and the emergent twentieth-century cultural figure of the superhero: "the American Way" of individualism and capitalist democracy in superhuman form, dressed up in tights for good measure.

If the discursive, or propositional, features of the genre's implicit regulations comprise a recognizably national face, it is therefore necessary to interrogate the aesthetic dimension along these same lines. Geoff Klock has argued that the core aesthetic proposition of the contemporary superhero comic is its revisionary posture with respect to its own generic tradition, "because as a serial narrative that has been running for more than sixty years, reinterpretation becomes part of the survival code" (13). While this aesthetic formalism, borrowed from Harold Bloom's literary theory of poetic influence, may be useful for observing the productive relationships between generations of artists, it has little to offer with respect to the uniqueness of the superhero genre per se, and is silent on the kinds of aesthetic reenvisioning that are motivated not by the diachronic tensions between generations but by the synchronic border conflicts between national culture codes and traditions. On the first point—that is, what is unique to the genre—it is useful to recognize in both the aesthetic and the discursive dimensions of the superhero genre a distinctive interplay of individualism and collective identity, of modernity and the moral order, of power and vulnerability in the context of modern mass society. As for the second point, importantly, it is in relation to these same modern, mass societal concerns where one can begin to recognize what is distinctive, even tendentious, about El Bulbo's position in the field of comics culture in Mexico.

El Bulbo's heroism is profiled in a global battle between the recycled and reanimated television picture tube and a host of supervillains, all of whom, like El Bulbo, hail from the realm of the modern mass culture industry. The episodic conflicts of the *El Bulbo* series are as global as the mass cultural media from which El Bulbo's evil antagonists are seemingly derived—television in particular, as the principal marketing medium for children's toys; fantasy film vehicles; animated cartoons; adventure series; and related product lines. Japanese manga, Star Wars, Superman, all turn up in El Bulbo's reality, and cohabit the Mexican superhero's cultural landscape alongside other figures from transnationally syndicated television cartoon series, or who bear a striking resemblance to such characters. At the same time, the setting for the expected morally charged combat between superhero and supervillains is most frequently the Mexican metropolitan core.

These particulars of *El Bulbo* arise from the cultural preoccupations of artists (Bachan and his collaborators) who work at the urban epicenter of Mexico's own mass media market—Mexico City, the single largest urban cultural market in the Western Hemisphere, and the most important production and distribution center for the Spanish-language cultural market in the Americas. Bachan's artistic development is uniquely tied to this mass cultural arena, with all of its contradictions: his earliest interest in sequential art was as a childhood fan of Spanish translations of French and American comics series, like Alberto Uderzo's *Asterix*, Jean-Claude Mezieres's *Valerian*, the Belgian artist Morris's *Lucky Luke*, and fellow Belgian Peyo's *Smurfs*, followed by the superhero comics illustrations of John Byrne, Arthur Adams, and Alan Davis. By the late 1980s Bachan had also encountered Japanese manga in the form of Katsuhiro Otomo's *Akira* series and Masamune Shirow's sci-fi *Appleseed.* Meanwhile, he developed his drafting skills principally through six years of work for Mexican-owned Editorial Novedades, drawing for the popular *historieta* series *Hombres y Héroes, Joyas de Literatura, El Solitario,* and others, as well as for Editorial Ejea's *Sensacional de Luchas, Sensacional de Vacaciones,* and *Así Soy y Qué* (Carrillo 2007).

The artist's depiction of Mexico City and use of intertextual devices to reference visually what Arjun Appadurai has called global "mediascapes" (visual and informational environments created by transnational media conglomerates and consumer habits) draw together the national and the global into a vortex of conflict surrounding the parodic superhero. A close examination of the formal, aesthetic mechanisms through which El Bulbo is situated in his episodic confrontations with evil demonstrates that despite the idiosyncratic and playful character of the series, El Bulbo represents an important critique of the consequences for the local cultural imagination of a globalized culture industry. At the same time, many of the problems El Bulbo confronts, among them his own identity as superhero, together comprise a critical representation of free-market globalization as a corrosive force that strips traditional cultural models of their authority and relevance.

The central conflict facing El Bulbo is one that implicates his very identity as a superhero. Indeed, this conflict can be viewed as the organizing principle of the discursive and aesthetic presentation of El Bulbo to the comic book reader, wherein the heroic television picture bulb is simultaneously Olympian and plebian, high-minded and lowbrow. In important ways, El Bulbo's skewed antics and his unstable identity as the exceptional individual protector of Mexican society take on their critical, even political, meaning against the backdrop of the reader's accumulated cultural knowledge and sophistication vis-à-vis the codes of the mass cultural field. That is to say, Bachan's playful representational strategies presume a kind of double-edged cultural knowledge brought to bear by his readership. First of all, the cultural knowledge required of the El Bulbo reader includes a familiarity with generic conventions—of the superhero standard and of the related visual field of animated villains and heroes emanating from globally syndicated mass cultural programming. At the same time, the superbulb's ability to critically leverage those conventions into something new presumes on the part of the reader a nationally specific cultural competence capable of recognizing the idiosyncrasies of Mexican social realities and experience, and of acknowledging the general exclusion of these national particularities from the horizon of globally marketed mass cultural products.

It has been noted that the U.S. superhero standard has fallen on hard times in recent years. Richard Reynolds observes that by the early 1990s, it had become fashionable for graphic works to be "used as a stick to beat the superhero and other forms of genre writing," frequently deconstructing or undermining the superhero with morally ambiguous characters, fragmented narrative continuity, or even human frailty and death (as occurred famously with Superman in 1993). Interpreted symptomatically, this phenomenon of the U.S. comics market could very well indicate, as Reynolds argues, that the field of comics "is restructuring itself as a diminutive reflection of the mainstream culture which still largely rejects it" (122).

In Latin America, where Mexico has been the regional epicenter for comics distribution, the superhero has represented a vexed mass cultural figure for some time now, with a mainstream profile dominated by DC Comics and Marvel Comics imports. The graphic mugging of the superhero in Latin America could just as easily be interpreted as symptomatic of local unease with a figure representative of mainstream U.S. culture. Latin American artists and intellectuals have cast a jaundiced eye on the superhero, often perceiving in his or her individualized superpowers an implicit cultural model originating from outside Latin American national cultures. Anyone familiar with Latin America knows that this critical view predates significantly the antisuperhero trend Reynolds observes in U.S. graphic works of the 1990s.

The most emblematic work in this regard is Argentine Julio Cortázar's experimental novella *Fantomas contra los vampiros multinacionales* (Fantomas against the Multinational Vampires), published by the Russell Tribunal in 1977. The novella combined the comic book format and the popular 1960s Mexican superhero series *Fantomas, La amenaza elegante* (Fantomas, The Elegant Menace, written by Alfredo Cardona Peña for Editorial Novaro) with the avant-garde literary techniques of the celebrated Latin American novelist. In effect, Cortázar made use of the popular vehicle of the graphic story book, and the semiotic envelope of the widely read and recognizable Mexican figure Fantomas, in order to deliver for a broad regional readership a summary of the findings of the Russell Tribunal, which convened an international grouping of intellectuals and activists in Rome in April 1974 and again in Brussels in January 1975 to publicly condemn U.S. imperialism, human rights abuses, and military intervention in Latin America.

Cortázar's *Fantomas* differed from the Mexican superhero comic book in his frank recognition of the necessity of defending human rights and national sovereignty against the predations of multinational capitalist interests and U.S. superpower intervention in the third world. Whereas the *Fantomas* series published by Editorial Novaro (and later Editorial Vid) presented an appropriately muscled, macho, and masked hero who struggled against elite corruption and thievery, and occasionally against police corruption and other social ills, Cortázar's novella presented a superhero who consorted with regional intellectuals (Cortázar in Latin America, for example, and Susan Sontag in New York, among others) and showed signs of developing an awareness of real-world and world historical villainous behavior. Ultimately, in Cortázar's version of the superhero, it becomes clear that Fantomas represents an unsustainable model of

response to social problems and structural evils, such as the political manipulation and economic exploitation of third world countries by first world powers.
In the words of one of the novella's characters: "[T]he error lies in presupposing
a leader . . . , in sitting around waiting for a leader to appear and to bring us
together. . . . The error is being faced with an everyday reality like the findings of the Russell Tribunal . . . and still waiting for someone else to respond"
(Cortázar, 71). In Cortázar's variant, Fantomas is exposed as an individualistic
and even messianic cultural model, inadequate and inappropriate to real-world
problems, the solutions for which can only arise from mass organization and
democratic social movements.

A similar critique was leveled more recently against Superman and Wonder
Woman in Latin America. DC Comics had announced in 1996 a partnership
with the United Nations Children's Fund (UNICEF) and the Clinton administration in the United States, whereby Superman and Wonder Woman would
appear in popular education materials (including a comic book) explaining
about the dangers of land mines in Bosnia. A Spanish-language version of the
comic books—*Superman y la Mujer Maravilla: El Asesino Escondido* (Superman
and Wonder Woman: The Hidden Killer, 1998)—was eventually published for
distribution in Costa Rica, Honduras, and Nicaragua (U.S. Department of
State, 1998). In the Central American countries, where the U.S.-backed Contra
war had left a perilous quantity of unexploded ordnance on the ground, U.S.
popular culture enjoys a high-profile presence. Although the most obvious anti-
imperialist argument would have insisted on use of a homegrown hero or heroes
instead, the critique of the superhero comic successfully levied by Nicaraguan
anti–land mine activists held that the superhero per se was inappropriate to the
nature of the problem. "With this [comic], which was also totally inappropriate culturally given what Superman represents in the social imaginary, what
happened was that lots of kids wanted to find land mines and deliberately put
themselves in danger, so that Superman or Wonder Woman would come to
their rescue" (Powell).

Alongside this critical intellectual and activist circumspection with regard to
the cultural figure of the superhero in Latin America, one cannot ignore another
important pressure point on the genre and its received conventions: namely, the
regional commercialization of the superhero and the superhero's absorption
into advertising campaigns and market discourse at best tenuously related to the
moral discourse and aesthetics of the genre. Thus one can see Klock's revisionary pressures on the genre at work in the marketing campaign of the Mexican

company Grupo Industrial Cuadritos Biotek, which decided in 2004 to outfit its executives in black T-shirts emblazoned with the Batman symbol on the chest, and to dispatch to the schools of Mexico City, Guanajuato, and Monterrey "an army dressed up as Batman, Superman, Green Lantern and Wonder Woman, among other characters," in order to conquer the children's market for their yogurt products (de la Torre). The company's marketing strategy, coordinated with Warner Brothers in the United States, appears to be a logical extension of a previous agreement between DC Comics, Warner Brothers, and the Burger King Corporation, which resulted, as explained in the Spanish-language press, in "seven of the most popular crime-fighting Super Heroes—Superman, Batman, Wonder Woman, Green Lantern, Flash, Martian Manhunter and Hawkgirl—leaping from the pages of DC Comics and from the television screens to appear in a powerful children's promotional campaign in participating Burger King restaurants" (PR Newswire).

These are unavoidable contextual considerations for understanding El Bulbo's relationship to the aesthetic and discursive norms of the superhero genre. The parodic reworking of the superhero figure by Bachan and company, as well as their artistic revisions of the aesthetic contours of the genre, can best be understood against the backdrop of the peculiar politicization of cultural forms effected by capitalist globalization. On the one hand, nationalist cultural discourses square off; on the other, commercial processes absorb and redeploy these same discourses for transnational economic ends. The received model of the superhero, originating in the United States, weds specific discourses of economic and social modernity (individualism and technological power) with a national semiotic template (imagery signifying individual strength, collective will, moral order), and is ultimately consummated in cultural practice in the sentimental affinity between the individual reader and a collective moral order. This same affinity becomes problematic when the cultural document in question crosses national boundaries and comes in contact with other, competing configurations of individual with nation and a proposed moral order. Meanwhile, Japanese and U.S. comics enterprises and related culture industries globally diffuse images and fantasies of power, individualist agency, and moral conflict, and enter into contractual arrangements that add specific products and a consumer ethos to the mix. The resulting discrepancies with the original generic model are multiple and complex (the Turner Broadcasting Company's Cartoon Network alone reaches viewers with Justice League characters in 145 countries throughout the world).

As with any superhero, the story of El Bulbo's origins is important. The story of origins is, in fact, an emblematic moment in the construction not only of many a superhero character, but of a specific kind of narrative frame. The genesis story aids in the establishment of that character's powers and agency within a mythic time/space framework capable of standing outside the ordinary world of real historical experience, and at the same time operating within that ordinary plane of existence. One could argue that this narrative moment subtends the superhero genre's inclusion as a category of myth, especially as defined by Mircea Eliade as a story of origins that establishes a lived relationship between the quotidian and the supernatural. The tale of origin is a key moment, in other words, in the mythological nature of the superhero—providing an original guarantee for one of Richard Reynolds's definitive features of the superhero, that is, that "the extraordinary nature of the superhero will be contrasted with the ordinariness of his surroundings." Perhaps more important, the genesis narrative for the hero's superpowers allows for an ascension of the ordinary to what Umberto Eco called, with reference to the Superman stories, "a kind of oneiric climate—of which the reader is not aware at all—where what has happened before and what has happened after appears extremely hazy" ("Myth," 336).

The *El Bulbo* storyline arises from precisely this narrative structure. In issue #1 of the series, the story begins with an ordinary, urban Mexican, Eugenio, receiving an old television set from his uncle Eulalio. Eugenio, who is the narrator, explains that he had asked for the television even though it no longer worked, because "it was the television on which I watched cartoons as a kid" (1). Unable to find the parts necessary to make the television work again, the narrator takes recourse to a "repair manual" that requires less sophisticated technology. This manual turns out to be a book of black magic incantations, allowing the television to be reconstituted despite its obsolescence. The apparatus that delivered the cartoons of childhood thus becomes the supernatural source for the animated picture bulbs, which burst forth from the black magic spell with the ominous declaration, "We are going to conquer the world!" Horrified by the unintended consequence of his television fetishism, the narrator desperately tries a different spell on the one bulb remaining in the broken television set. And so El Bulbo is born ("*¡Sopas!* With a little cape and everything!" exclaims the narrator). El Bulbo's first words as a living reality are just as indicative of his moral character as the pronouncement by his evil counterparts is of theirs: "Let me at them! Where are they? How many of them are there? What have they got? How much am I getting paid?" (9).

One can hear in the newborn superhero's voice how Eco's "oneiric climate," a myth-time that allows, on Eliade's view, for the supernatural to accompany mundane experience, is penetrated by a much less dreamy plane of existence where clichéd speech, pedestrian concerns, and narrative self-consciousness crop up like day residue in an afternoon nap. Indeed, even the evil plans of the bulbs led by Adolfo have this mundane and self-referential quality. In the first episode, Adolfo gives a rallying speech to his minions in an abandoned factory ("of the sort that frequently appear in comic books," the narration observes): "The moment to awaken has arrived. The moment to rise up in arms and shout with one voice NO MORE! To say to the world: I REFUSE TO LIVE MY LIFE AS PART OF A DOMESTIC APPLIANCE THAT OFFERS VACUOUS EN-TERTAINMENT! The microchip has not made me obsolete! *Compañeros*: The world must know that it belongs to the bulbs!" (11). The evil at work here is at once megalomaniacal and ordinary; the hackneyed form of an immense and apocalyptic evil on the march is inhabited by the more routine content of personal resentment and domesticity.

On the one hand, Adolfo's plans for world domination are monumentally reactionary and deeply threatening, much like those of his namesake, Adolf Hitler, lashing out against new forms of power that have overtaken the old. On the other hand, the stakes of Adolfo's reactionary designs are the contours of the same mass cultural media environment—the television bulb and the computer microchip, the realm of personal meaning and the threat of cultural obsolescence—where the bulbs' petty self-interestedness arises and resides. The terrain of moral struggle mapped out in the tale of origin leaves no doubt as to the precise location of the hazy "oneiric climate" where supernatural beings struggle mightily amid uninspired clichés and pedestrian realities. Following El Bulbo's debut as the savior of humanity from the evil Adolfo, our superhero returns to Eugenio's apartment building to ask about his "honoraria." A knock on the door turns out to be that of the concierge, who informs "Mr. Bulbo" that several "gentlemen" are asking for him at the front door of the building. Downstairs, the superhero encounters a long, diverse line of comics characters, led by a cartoonish King Kong figure, and with a Silver Surfer–like character silhouetted in the distance against the sky, all of whom wish to "play" with El Bulbo (the concierge has helpfully provided them with numbers, in the manner of people awaiting seating at a restaurant, in order to facilitate things). A shift in frame to a full-page, single-panel final image for the issue emphatically reinforces the visual punch line: crowded with gigantic characters drawn in the

Figure 9.1. El Bulbo prepares for battle with other cartoon characters. The doorman of El Bulbo's apartment building politely requests that the cartoon antagonists not "mess up the entrance," and suggests, "Why don't you and your little friends go play in the park of the Polanco neighborhood [a wealthy enclave of Mexico City]?" From *El Bulbo* #1, 26. Reprinted by permission of Sebastián Carrillo.

style of children's cartoons, the last page suggests that the supernatural myth-time that accompanies El Bulbo in everyday life is, in fact, none other than the imagined, if somewhat predictable, cultural environment emanating from the television set and coordinated entertainment media (see figure 9.1).

As mythic discourse, the story of origin establishes the parameters of reality as occupied by the superhero. For El Bulbo, reality entails constant reminders of self-interest and economic necessity, and an awkward disjuncture between the simplistic high-stakes morality of heroes and villains and the complex needs and circumstances of a real modern society. In *El Bulbo* #2, "The Tragic Death of

Genoveva the Cow," the superhero, having been struck extra hard by "the ma-
levolent Dr. Smurf," lands in the countryside and inadvertently kills the only cow
owned by a rural Mexican couple. In consequence, El Bulbo is obliged to work off
the damage done by doing chores around the house, and taking over from the dear
departed bovine the task of plowing the couple's meager plot of land. Meanwhile,
the arch-villain Dr. Smurf has hitched a ride with a Mexican truck driver in pursuit
of his enemy. The dialogue between the supervillain and the truck driver is suggestive of the comic collision between mythos and modern reality:

> **TRUCK DRIVER**: So, what kind of work do you do?
>
> **DR. SMURF**: I'm a super villain. And I will conquer the world, imposing my
> will as Supreme Emperor of Planet Earth—a title I would already possess if
> not for the meddling of that ridiculous yellow superhero, who ruined my
> latest weapon of mass destruction and thereby required me to go hitchhik-
> ing in pursuit of him.
>
> **TRUCK DRIVER**: Hey, that whole being super evil thing, can you make
> money at that? (3)

This conversation eventually sours as the supervillain's overblown ego and threatening language result in the truck driver calmly shooting Dr. Smurf and throwing
his corpse from the cab of the truck. "That's what I get for picking up hitchhik-
ers," the truck driver says to himself. "My boss told me not to mess with *chilangos*
[a slang term for people from Mexico City], they're totally nuts" (4). Meanwhile,
El Bulbo discovers that his new employers are members of a millennial dooms-
day cult who, faced with signs of prophecy (which happen to include standard
features of the global economy—"when prices take flight, and the whole world
is connected") are preparing to be transported by aliens to a kind of Mexican nationalist consumer paradise: "a thousand years of Fun and Games with the Chi-
vas soccer team and the Zacatepec resort—with a free courtesy cocktail" (12).

El Bulbo's reality is, in effect, the point of contact between the fabricated
realm of the supernatural and the contemporary social world, between the
imagined plane of existence articulated through the products of mass entertainment culture and the lived reality of the society that consumes those products.
(It almost goes without saying that, examined objectively, the culture industry
comprises precisely such a reality: joining economic interests with the dissemination of entertaining fictions and moral fables.) From the outset, therefore, in El
Bulbo's world one encounters a corrosion of the traditional superhero mythos:

at his very birth the superhero undergoes a reduction to the status of a "professional," collapsing the important gap between the ordinariness of workaday concerns and the extraordinariness of the heroic. The hero is now an employee, hired help, who labors for a wage and kvetches about his working conditions. Bachan's comic book depicts, in this way, not only an important cultural dimension of globalization—that is, the transnational diffusion of superheroes and villains, and of the cultural model implicit to them—but also the relationship between the now globalized mass cultural field and the market forces that determine, in no small measure, its aesthetic forms and ideological values. El Bulbo's parodic embodiment of the superhero role can be viewed as a kind of critical demonstration of the revisionist pressures brought to bear by the forces of globalization on the formal contours of the superhero comic.

The reader encounters the pressures and anxieties of the global horizon repeatedly throughout the longer narrative arc of the ten-issue series. After being born from the mechanical guts of the twentieth-century's most powerful visual medium of cultural globalization, the superhero wanders through a series of adventures framed by: millennial hysteria reminiscent of the suicidal Heaven's Gate cult (issue #2); an alliance between an exploitative factory owner and a plan for world dominance (#3); the proliferation of U.S.-style Christmas decorations in commercial settings throughout Mexico City (#5); unethical genetic experimentation and murderous violence perpetrated by a Japanese transnational (#6); commercialization of the superhero and manipulation of the cultural environment for profit (#7); unemployment and wage exploitation (#8); and border-crossing and income disparities between the United States and Mexico (#10). Although at times such globalization-related concerns are indirectly present—as in issue #5, where El Bulbo is suspected by the authorities of carrying out a series of mass murders in Mexico City's business district, when the true culprits are revealed to be strings of homicidal Christmas tree lightbulbs, seasonal decorations emblematic of U.S. cultural influence—most frequently El Bulbo finds himself personally and directly entangled in the market logics of the global economic order. Even in the otherworldly issue #4, in which El Bulbo sneaks into hell to retrieve Genoveva the cow (whom he killed in issue #2) for her heartbroken owner, he must sell his soul not to the devil but to Bilal P. Gato, a coyote-like intermediary figure who facilitates El Bulbo's safe passage back across the river Styx and into Mexico. (The issue concludes with a conversation in hell between Stalin, Genghis Khan, and Carlos Salinas de Gortari—Mexico's neoliberal president from 1988 to 1994.)

Reading this illicit border crossing as a tongue-in-cheek acknowledgment of the Mexican experience of globalization might seem a stretch, except for the fact that the U.S.-Mexico border occupies such a special place in the Mexican popular imagination (from Cantinflas films to *norteña* music). And if that were not a sufficient thematic linkage, throughout Bachan's series, El Bulbo repeatedly encounters the problems of compensation, and of compromised ethical and creative autonomy faced by many a skilled laborer in globalized economic circumstances. In issue #6, the superhero is hired to solve a bloody mystery unfolding in Japan: someone is brutally assassinating manga characters, violently dismembering the lovable little animated creations before the reader's eyes. One pair of cute manga cartoon characters—stylized bunny rabbits, one pink and one blue—are hacked to pieces by an ax while discussing what love is. "A multinational corporation," says one. "A brand new BMW," says the other (2). El Bulbo discovers that the laboratory scientists of the Nasrio Corporation, corporate owner of murdered manga characters with names like Akudo the Penguin, Biyoshi the Little Pig, and the Ketsuben Bunnies, are generating the manga within a cartoon habitat "biorama," and then killing them experimentally. Corporate representatives explain to El Bulbo that no crime has been committed, since the manga are the property of Nasrio. In issue #7—written and drawn by Bef, with colors by Bachan—the superhero subsequently discovers that the entire episode was a ruse designed to trick him into signing himself over to Nasrio as yet another company employee.

What results in issue #7 is the total commodification of the Mexican superhero by a Japanese-based transnational corporation. El Bulbo awakens one morning to discover that extensive marketing agreements have turned his name and image into a brand, appearing in radio and television programming and on children's toys, T-shirts, and other merchandise, and used to promote synergistically a range of other products. A confused superhero demands answers and is informed by Ortyx Gasset, the "Latin America Regional Director" for Nasrio Corporation, that "the real motive for calling you to Japan was to analyze you, create a prototype and market it throughout the world" (6). As Gasset explains, the transnational corporation had patented El Bulbo and taken legal ownership of him and his image. Meanwhile, the evil Doctor Verboten, another of El Bulbo's several arch-nemeses, is hired by Nasrio as its new "Director of Creative Development," allowing the evil villain to work off his debts by designing monsters and machinery of mass destruction for El Bulbo to fight—with each battle serving as a new pretext for merchandizing.

Figure 9.2. The superhero is a mass-mediated commodity. "Bulbo Detergent stopped that dragon for you," declares the announcer in the top panel. Meanwhile, El Bulbo worries about his ulcer as he rides the *pesero* at the bottom of the page. "Sales keep on rising . . . but since I belong to Nasrio, I don't get a penny." From *El Bulbo* #7, 14. Reprinted by permission of Sebastián Carrillo.

The superhero now shares the workaday realities of most urban Mexicans, commuting to work on the *pesero* (private minibus that serves as a key feature of mass transit in Mexico City) and fretting about his stress level and poor compensation, despite his employer's soaring profits (see figure 9.2). The artist's use of comic book panels reminds the reader that El Bulbo is now in the grips of not only the market logic of commodification but also the reductive cultural logic of television. In figure 9.2, El Bulbo's fate is presented in three-page-width horizontal panels that read from the top down, wherein the sequentially increased size of the announcer's head in the foreground simulates a "zoom-in" camera perspective common to television news and infomercial reporting. In the same short panel sequence, Bef and Bachan alter incongruously several contextual details (the announcer's suit color, the Bulbo product being hawked, the monster battled by the superhero in the background), intimating visually and satirically the sameness-despite-differences of much televisual discourse. The panels in this case, as elsewhere in the *El Bulbo* series, serve as semiotic elements that reference other visual cultural forms (here signifying televisual discourse at work) in addition to their function as framing and sequencing devices.

Although El Bulbo eventually escapes from his contractual obligations with Nasrio (the corporation is bankrupted by the astronomical collateral liabilities resulting from one of El Bulbo's battles), in the concluding issue the reader finds El Bulbo consulting with a more financially successful superhero about how to improve his earning power. "How do you do it to be such a successful hero? I've been in the biz for a good while and I just can't seem to get ahead" (7). Here, the narrative reaches, in an important sense, its logical conclusion in the final episode. Underemployed, and having discovered that his Mexican government paycheck cannot be cashed due to lack of sufficient funds, El Bulbo turns to the private sector model represented by La Cucaracha (The Cockroach), a masked superhero who lives in a mansion with a butler and conducts his work with the aid of numerous advanced technological gadgets and rigorous physical training, rather than an innate superpower. The parallels with Batman, who also takes his name from a creature of the night, are unavoidable, and Bachan's freelance hero appears to exploit the homologies in order to draw out the private sector cultural model implicit in Batman: the public sector is incapable of adequately fighting crime and requires the assistance of the private entrepreneur. Whereas Batman presents the secret life (and greater crime-fighting efficacy) of the U.S. metropolitan bourgeois Bruce Wayne, La Cucaracha is his peripheral counterpart, a Mexican superhero who has been able to amass his personal wealth and status by seeking more lucrative work on the northern side of the U.S.-Mexico border. In "Gringolandia," La Cucaracha observes, "they pay in dollars, you know." Neoliberal economics have produced a counterpart to the Justice League: "All of us members of the NAFTA League work [in the United States] and live here [in Mexico]" (7).

The message vis-à-vis the superhero is clear: one must be employable, no matter what one does. Regardless of the moral commitments or claims of a social project or ethical program, a position in the marketplace must be staked out like any street vendor or craftsperson, like any product or service. Despite his dramatically and obviously exceptional individual nature, El Bulbo finds himself in a world where, in the final analysis, he is no different than the vast majority of the other 100 million inhabitants of Mexico. The superhero is threatened with unemployment or declining wages, like most any other wageworker in the globalized economy. At the end of the series, El Bulbo is arrested by "La Migra" (U.S. Immigration authorities) and deported to Mexico. La Cucaracha, it turns out, has a green card.

While the mythic standing of the superhero is undermined repeatedly by the greater power of real-world exigencies, the resultant unstable identity of the hero (Is he myth, or is he cliché? Is he grand, or just pathetic?) draws attention to his status as artifice, as the deliberate construction of an author who has recourse to an extensive menu of aesthetic options. The aesthetic dimension, the manner in which the visual "feel" of the narrative is organized for the reader, takes on its special importance in *El Bulbo* as a corollary of Bachan's consistent transgressions against the well-worn conventions of the superhero genre. In addition to contributing to the lampooning of the superhero's mythic status, the shifting formal elements of El Bulbo's presentation serve to elaborate a kind of real-world cultural agency—a manipulation and display of aesthetic differences that operate against the predictable standards and homogeneity of the mass-mediated cultural environment.

This aesthetic effect is nowhere more in evidence than with the dual identity trope—another staple of the superhero comic, which operates in the *El Bulbo* series against the grain of its typical function in the genre. Conventionally, superheroes often appear outwardly normal and average, despite the superhuman powers bestowed upon them by strange fate or otherworldly intervention. Rather than wearing a disguise in their everyday lives, the superheroes don a costume precisely in order to reveal their hidden, exceptional nature. This inner/outer binary structure is, in a sense, the ideological DNA of a mass cultural figure that celebrates individualism as a foundational principle of modern mass society: that is, outward appearances of "sameness" are deceptive; the individual secretly harbors unique abilities and moral commitments fundamental to the survival of mass society. The cape and tights allow for a dramatic performance of a collective fantasy with regard to the irreducibility of the individual. (One might note that this superhero fantasy flies in the face of overwhelming evidence to the contrary, given contemporary institutional practices in mass marketing, surveillance, and social control.)

In contrast, El Bulbo is fundamentally, and obviously, superhuman (or sub-human), since his squat, round, bright yellow body and alien features are unmistakably not standard issue Homo sapiens. Instead of passing as a fellow citizen, the animated television picture bulb wanders the city with all the subtlety of a walking, talking television bulb in a red cape. His occasional attempts to disguise himself entail absurdist gestures, such as wearing a Halloween-style fake nose, glasses, and mustache. His superhero getup is impossible to hide because it is not a costume but his very nature, available for all to see. Instead of emerging as the superhero figure from out the undifferentiated masses, this superhero figure attempts in vain to dissolve into anonymous humanity. The relative realism with which human figures are sometimes drawn in the comic further exacerbates El Bulbo's dilemma. Eventually, he disguises himself under a ridiculously oversized trench coat and fedora, consequently making him look very much like another recognizable mass cultural figure: peering out from under the ridiculous camouflage appear the bulging white eyes and inscrutable black-hole face of Warner Brothers' Marvin the Martian (issue #5).

Here and elsewhere in the series, Bachan's narrative is driven by an appropriation of received mass cultural forms. The superhero does not "pass" as an average citizen, but instead blends into or is profiled against the visual idioms of contemporary mediascapes. An alien form in human society, El Bulbo is at home in the scenery generated by the culture industry. Bachan's masterfully cartoonish El Bulbo is produced through simple, bold line drawings and a bright color palette more typical of children's cartoons than of superhero comics. This deceptively simple representational style, with its playfully distorted scenery and minimal use of shading to suggest volume, plays out against a serial background that is stylistically amended and reworked from one issue to the next, bringing the continuity of Bachan's rendering of the central figure El Bulbo into contact with a mutable array of distinct representational styles drawn from modern visual culture. Representational realism blinks on and off, as El Bulbo's appearance is sketched with greater or lesser economy, borrowing variously from one set of representational codes or another. The trained eye of the comic book reader is actively engaged in the discernment of the symbolic and aesthetic features of a cultural environment that readers can see themselves cohabiting with the absurdist superhero.

In issue #2, the evil Adolfo shape-shifts into a Darth Vader miniature ("I hope Lucas [that is, George Lucas, creator of the *Star Wars* film series] doesn't sue me," says the narrative voice). During his adventures in the Japanese cartoon "biorama," El Bulbo's stylistic representation changes to that of the Japanese manga style popularized by the multibillion dollar Pokémon enterprise

Figure 9.3. El Bulbo as private eye, through the lens of silent film noir. From *El Bulbo* #7, 29. Reprinted by permission of Sebastián Carrillo.

controlled by Nintendo: more simplified lines, geometrical shapes, and bright, single color contrasts give El Bulbo an aesthetic kinship with the doe-eyed innocence of the manga figures and their dreamy manga environment. In issue #5, El Bulbo appears in his own nightmare amid a swirling U.S.-style commercialized Christmas aesthetic—shiny bells, candy canes, and jolly Santa worthy of a shop-window display (20). In issue #9, El Bulbo—in a reprise of his Marvin the Martian impersonation—is presented to the reader within the double aesthetic composition of hard-boiled detective fiction and silent film, complete with sepiatoned film noir lighting contrasts and story board–style decorated narrative panels instead of the usual dialogue balloons (see figure 9.3). (Here again, as shown in figure 9.2, the comic book panel does double duty as a visual sign, indicating that the superhero is now appearing within the cultural frame of the movie projector.) Matt Groening's Marge Simpson character makes a cameo appearance in issue #8, "another gringo tourist assaulted in the city" (5). Similarly, Gabriel Vargas's La Borola shows up as an office cleaner in issue #6. The videogame staple Pac Man turns up as El Bulbo's primitively rendered nemesis in issue #7. In issue #10, La Cucaracha is drawn, in strong contrast to El Bulbo, with the pronounced musculature and more anatomically detailed line drawing of a Batman comic.

Throughout the series, the artist's borrowings from the mass cultural field have a distinctively contrapuntal flair, each mass cultural "quotation" or intertext constituting either an irreverent retort to the dominance of these forms in the cultural environment or a pointed recycling of their symbolic cachet for the purpose of satirically positioning El Bulbo's shenanigans within the now globalized symbolic and cultural market. As a consequence, the buffoonish superhero operates as a pretext for a public performance of the Mexican graphic artist's artistic prowess: multiple aesthetic styles mingle and clash across the narrative arc of the *El Bulbo* series. Indeed, nearly every one of the ten issues of the *El Bulbo* series offers a gallery of other artists' portraits of El Bulbo, visual interpretations of the superhero that, in the stark aesthetic contrasts they strike with Bachan's original, remind the reader that the hero is a cultural artifact, and one with infinite possible aesthetic guises.

In the "Galería" section of each issue, the differential effects of the aesthetic dimension are pressed upon Bachan's superhero character, with consequences ranging from the light-hearted to the sinister. Edgar Clement's interpretation of El Bulbo in issue #1 is as a postapocalyptic assassin portrayed through the hyperrealist, posthumanist machine aesthetic made famous by *Heavy Metal* magazine in the 1980s. In issue #3, Ricardo Pelaez's El Bulbo is a gritty, tarnished antihero. In issue #4, Tony Sandoval presents El Bulbo in an angry, three-color pastel doodle of a desert landscape. Patricio Betteo's variation on the theme in issue #5 is a glistening, metallic caricature. In effect, the Bulbo galleries open a space for artistic performance, and for differential aesthetic experience, a space largely excluded from the industrial mode of cultural production for which superheroes, supervillains, and comic book and cartoon characters are a standardized efflux. In *El Bulbo*, the auteur comic strikes back. Even the writing is shared out to multiple artists, as with Bef, who wrote the storylines for issues #4, #6, and #7, and other guest writers who contributed ministories in the back pages of each episode.

The arch-nemesis against which the author's comic exacts its comedic revenge in this case is the graphic image as industry, beholden to advertising interests and production cost considerations (of the sort that make the Editorial Novedades series a commercial success and an aesthetic failure). Thus Bachan's misappropriation and mimicry target not only the commercial monolith of the superhero genre but also the semiotics of advertising discourse and the mechanics of the market. Alongside the gallery images and the main story of each issue, the reader encounters deliberate signs of economic failure and shameless self-promotion: the "Galería" section is presented to the reader as needed filler due to the absence of advertisers; an insert in issue #2 contains a publicity photograph showing two Mexican professional wrestlers (El Santo and Tinieblas) reading *El Bulbo*; the cover of issue #3 playfully interpellates the newsstand vendor—with instructions for how to display the comic—and the potential buyer—with an exhortation to disregard the magazine displayed adjacently. In an apparent reference to marketing data that has suggested the semiliterate character of Mexican reading habits, the cover of the series bears the subtitle "The magazine for us functional illiterates." "I am not a condom," declares the condomlike El Bulbo from the back cover of issue #6 in a simulated public service announcement. In issue #7, the "Reader's Gallery" of artist renderings of El Bulbo is joined by a full-page promotion of a pseudo-product, "Bulbo-Cola" (figure 9.4), which reproduces with precision the semiotics of Coca-Cola discourse, from the exact tone of red to the flowing cursive font, to the vacuous consumerist command: "Turn It On!" (*Préndela*) (29).

In these parodic gestures, the graphic dexterity of the artist displays itself as the critical agency or power that proposes a saboteur's battle with what cultural theorist Fredric Jameson has called "the supersession of everything outside of commercial culture, its absorption of all art high and low, along with image production itself" (135). Parody is the aesthetic center of gravity in this comic; the artist's ability to reproduce at will and whimsy from the mass cultural canon affords the pushing together of unlike visual discourses in an effort to disrupt the flattening of aesthetic experience by generic standards. The superhero in Pokémon manga guise, as hard-bitten noir detective, as corporate brand, generates revealing juxtapositions of otherwise familiar visual tropes. As parody, these variants of the superhero allow, à la Mikhail Bakhtin, a "dialogue" between distinct discourses (for example, the superhero and other elements of commodity culture) and hence a critically altered vantage on each (Bakhtin 1986). (In figure 9.4, Coca-Cola advertising is revealed as mythic supernaturalism, and the superhero is exposed as a commodity.) If there is a superpower equal to the task of confronting the effects on the visual image of media conglomeration, in the

Figure 9.4. El Bulbo inhabits commercial semiotics: Bulbo-Cola is "The Spark that Turns You On." From *El Bulbo* #9, 12. Reprinted by permission of Sebastián Carrillo.

El Bulbo series it can be found in the plasticity of the series' visual artistry. The artist's agency is greatly diminished in the context of industrialized cultural production and its tendencies toward homogenization, but the artist's motility and labile negotiation of visual forms nonetheless demonstrate the power to bend the gaze through recourse to the reproductive schemata of parody instead of the reproductive logic of the culture industry.

Although, as noted above, Bachan views the series as belonging more to the genre of humor than that of the superhero comic, the comedic thrust of *El Bulbo* relies consistently on the author's methodically corrosive manipulation of superhero conventions. Bachan has noted the relationship between regional reality and the artful overturning of the superhero mythos, even among his diverse collaborators:

Provided that the author that helped me on this was either Mexican or Latin American, they usually understood or came up with story ideas for Bulbo amazingly fast and well. I suppose Bulbo connected with our normal Latin American reality. Actually, a few of them actually WANTED to do a normal superhero story, and came up with a good Bulbo comedy. It turns out that Bulbo is surprisingly easy for Mexican artists to understand and handle. I never had to explain him, or even make corrections whenever somebody came to me with a new story for him. (Carrillo 2007)

The deliberateness of the artist's maneuvering of generic form is clear in the thematizing of the superhero as ideologeme, as a building block for ideological positions: in one of several mininarratives in the series (written by Lucas Marangón), El Bulbo attends a meeting of the Mexican Society of Superheroes dedicated to "setting aside our differences and taking effective action to rescue the reputation of Mexican superheroism" (24). The high-minded meeting, which takes place against the backdrop of a superhero convention prominently featuring Superman, quickly devolves into mutual recriminations between radical nationalist superheroes and more commercially successful, and clearly U.S.-derivative, members of the "NAFTA League." "What's happening here is that you are jealous of us because you're all a bunch of LOSERS," charges La Cucaracha. To which the response is: "Don't be cheap, speak Spanish," and "Yeah, you NAFTA League superheroes shouldn't even be here, middle class *malinches* [traitors to the nation]!" (25). Characteristically, El Bulbo invites the wrath of both factions by brutalizing a vengeful comic book fan, who represents the shared economic interest and hence the only common ground for all present.

The corrosion of the superhero mythos—pointedly undermining a cultural figure of great familiarity to the contemporary cultural consumer—operates simultaneously to throw into relief the economic realities ushered in through free-market policies and discourses. In the final analysis, this is El Bulbo's true fight: a struggle for survival not against an easily identifiable, external threat to the national society that gave birth to him, but rather against the threat of irrelevance and dispensability that overshadows the local imagination, a local imagination that resides within a cultural landscape being mapped out elsewhere. In short, El Bulbo's reality, and his struggles there, is the same reality faced by the graphic artist.

The humor of Bachan's comic draws upon the cultural knowledge of the Mexican mass media consumer in order to reconstruct the superhero as an agent of anagnorisis, what aesthetic theory since Aristotle has described as a consciousness of not-not-knowing, a becoming aware of the unwitting character of one's prior state of awareness. Stated differently, El Bulbo serves as the trigger for a kind of critical awareness already present as potential in the mass cultural literacy of the comic book reader. With El Bulbo, the reader is invited to cast a sly, sidelong look at the fading horizon of everything classically embodied in the superhero figure—the collective will, individual exceptionalism, and moral clarity. The reader sees in the figure of El Bulbo a sign of the graphic artist watching the near eclipse of idiosyncratic or differential forms of power and agency (art and nation in particular) by the inexorably global orbit of mass commercial culture and the pressures of the transnational capitalist market. Bulbo's antics—the parodic edge of which operates through the double cultural knowledge of the Mexican reader, who is cognizant of both the global cultural horizon and the nation's social realities—leverage an X-ray view of mass cultural reality into that pessimistic gaze.

CONCLUSION

Ariel Dorfman and Armand Mattelart read Donald Duck in order to expose the imperial cultural model at work. Their critical reading operated at a parallel to a productive project aimed at launching a nationally oriented cultural model, grounded in the authentic needs and sensibilities of popular sectors, and subtending a "true" national sovereignty. Their reading was a critical market intervention—a guide for consumption, and an opening of cultural space for imagining an alternative symbology and discourse in the cultural market. Their argument also presented the rationale for a state policy that would favor Chilean production. Such a policy is rejected today—hence the common rejection of the Dorfman and Mattelart mode of critique—because of the dominance of neoliberalism in policy circles, but also because of the highly variegated, multimedia, and multidirectional transnational diet of symbolic goods that comprises popular culture, almost anywhere on the planet. An "authentic" national identity becomes difficult to construct or defend when the component parts are manufactured in, or recycled from, elsewhere. The Virgin of Guadalupe—the emotionally and spiritually charged standard of mobilization for conquistadors, national liberation fighters, Zapatista revolutionaries, Chicano activists in the United States, and neo-Zapatista rebels, spanning five centuries of colonial and postcolonial history in Mexico—is an image now mainly reproduced for Mexican consumption by the People's Republic of China, as Thomas Friedman merrily observes in his *The Earth Is Flat.*

In this "global era," critical reading of the cultural field requires greater attention to the intertextuality and dialogism of contemporary cultural production, to local uses of cultural materials made elsewhere. Most everyone is familiar with Donald Duck, and while we might agree with Dorfman and Mattelart's 1971 diagnosis of the ill-effects of too much Duck in a nation's cultural diet, we can also recognize that to an important degree, Donald has already been digested and redigested, integrated to innumerable globalized local cultural environments. One of the ways in which Donald Duck has been culturally metabolized, thanks in part to Dorfman and Mattelart's reading, is as synecdoche for empire, the part taken for the whole. But Donald, and other elements and symbolic representatives of the U.S. cultural model, are also metabolized in other ways. The radical nationalist premise of Dorfman and Mattelart's work was a binary proposition—it's the Duck or us, the empire or the nation. Without the nationalist critique, in other words, the Duck's consumption would irreparably poison national identity with imperialist false consciousness. While any reader of Antonio Gramsci's writings about hegemony will recognize here the cultural activist's engagement with the politics of culture, a good Gramscian will also recognize that Dorfman and Mattelart's critique of the imperial duck is only one of numerous existing and possible positions staked out around the affable feathered adventurer from the metropole. There is more than one optic with which to consume the comic book, and, in fact, more than one possible national lens for interpretation. There is more than one way to eat the Duck.

Importantly, part of the cultural work of consumption occurs in the process of production of other artifacts of the cultural field, other comics, for example. One can best grasp the politics of comic book culture not by pitting nation versus empire in a bipolar battle to the death, but by mapping out the multiple claims on the nation, and the competing construals of its relationship to the U.S. model, as they appear in the images and narratives of present-day comic book production. There is an intriguing constellation of ideological positions discernible in the Mexican comics under discussion in the preceding chapters. The domestic comic book is uniquely positioned within Mexican society to provide a map of many of the ideological fault lines that underlie the political dominance of neoliberalism. As a well-established, if declining, national culture industry, Mexican comics cannot be simply dismissed as imperialist imports. As a popular cultural medium, they cannot solely reflect the doctrinal consensus of elites or the individual sensibilities of the graphic artist. Visualizing the globalization problematic in comic book form, even in the case of neoliberal propaganda vehicles like the Vicente Fox administration's "A mitad del camino," requires mediation through appeals to popular sentiment, desire, and aesthetic taste.

It is tempting to assume for comic books in Mexico a special kind of cultural agency, and thereby either blame them for the propagation of ruling-class interests or, alternatively, celebrate them for enabling a critical social consciousness. Nonetheless, the question of how effective the comic book is at promulgating strategic ideological values or critique remains open to debate, and to further investigation. (Although the fact that government agencies, nongovernmental organizations, and commercial enterprises alike frequently turn to the comic book format as a propaganda tool suggests that many believe the medium to be a powerful one and are willing to make budgetary decisions based on that belief.) The objective of the preceding chapters is to demonstrate that the field of domestic comic books in Mexico is marked by a range of identifiable ideological positions and perspectives on the globalization problematic, served up for popular consumption in a specific national context.

What becomes of those ideological positions at the point of consumption is a notoriously complex question. Regardless of how or whether that question is settled, analysis of a representative cross section of Mexican comics demonstrates that specific, competing perspectives on the experience of globalization in Mexico, including variants of neoliberal ideology and its critique, are available to Mexican comic book readers. In addition, the discrepancies among those ideological positions, and the tensions between those ideological positions and the neoliberal model proffered by the United States through both its official policy discourse and the mass diffusion of the U.S. cultural model through entertainment media, are evidence that there is significant daylight between Mexican popular culture and the culture of empire. Mexican comic books reveal several lines of fracture within the governing consensus in Mexico, as well as between the governing and the governed.

These fractures are especially clear with regard to representations of the United States. To take an example from chapter 9: if the superhero is an ideologeme of empire, a strategic unit for ideological construction in the relationship between U.S. power and the global cultural consumer, then the scene at the Mexican Society of Superheroes in *El Bulbo* #4 is a kind of narrative sabotage. The Mexican comic book artists' depiction of an important segment of the global mediascape—cartoons engaged in a battle for control of society—is carried off with such a heightened degree of self-conscious appropriation and metacommentary that one can hardly ignore the retaliatory "culturescaping" function of the comic book vis-à-vis U.S. mass cultural exports. The imagined deliberation among Mexican superheroes about the problem posed by Superman shapes the reader's view, from a Mexican vantage, onto the global mediascape. This view contrasts sharply not only with U.S. globalism but also with Dr. Simi's celebration of Zorro and Tarzan as cinematic agents for assertion of the proper moral order, discussed in chapter 7.

Meanwhile, Bachan's satirical de-centering of the U.S.-derived superhero paradigm draws attention to the social and cultural effects of capitalist globalization—to the reduction of individual agency and of aesthetic agency, in particular. It also beckons the reader to notice the extent to which the parameters of cultural and social life in Mexico are already globalized. On this view, resistance is not futile so much as it is consigned to operate within well-established parameters, and it matters little whether one views these parameters in terms of the symbolic content of the comic book or in the operations of the culture industry that produces it, whether in terms of the heroic supremacy of the individual, embodied in the superhuman savior and the individualist habitus that awaits the reader in periodic installments, or in the regional supremacy of the U.S. comics industry. The superhero has been universalized—or globalized—and Superman is hegemon. Opposition to his rule seeks to recruit a Mexican, or Pan–Latin American superhero, but a superhero nonetheless. Only a viable commercial vehicle will have the power to challenge the U.S. Man of Steel. And yet Superman has been corroded by the narrative, exposed as a competitor, a construct, and an enterprise in the global market.

One confirms while reading Mexican comic books that the superhero is not the only ideologeme of empire that circulates in Mexico's graphic narrative. Race, social class, technology, mobility, upper-middle-class luxuries, even gender, also operate in the cultural switchboard of the post-NAFTA imagination as dominant signs in the construction of local (nation-specific) views on globalization. The Fox administration's visual emphasis on modernization was constructed with an emphatic semiotics of technology and mobility. This is mirrored in the images of mobility associated with upper-middle-class luxury in *El Libro Semanal*, and again in *Dr. Simi*'s narratives of social liberation through transportation and information infrastructure. In contrast, technology takes on a sinister profile in *El Bulbo* (Nasrio corporation's murderous manga laboratory, for example) and in *Operación Bolívar* (where cutting-edge technologies are derived from the body parts of assassinated angels). Upward mobility is a moral reward in *El Libro Semanal*, but Borola's desire for upward mobility borders on diagnosable mental illness in *La Familia Burrón*. Manrique's critique of empire lampoons racial self-loathing in Mexicans' inferiority complex relative to the United States. In *El Libro Vaquero*, racial discernment is the basis for identifying both the dangers of the migrant's passage into the United States and the moral promise of the northern neighbor.

Dissection of the ideological "content" of post-NAFTA Mexican comics hinges on careful attention to aesthetic forms and discursive patterns, on fore-grounding visual rhetoric, semiotics, and narrative structures in order to reveal coherence in the text's perspective. And just as this kind of critical reading identi-fies multiple signs of empire, it also identifies multiple valences for those signs, as they are positioned distinctly within the visual and narrative elements of the texts. That alone makes this a political reading—that is, because it exposes ideo-logical differences across the cultural field, and thereby reveals a particular claim to represent shared values and reality as a tendentious claim, disputed by other, competing claims.

Superficially, one can divide the cross section of comics analyzed here into two groups. Among the proglobalization narratives: the Fox administration's "A mitad del camino," *El Libro Vaquero, El Libro Semanal,* and *Las aventuras del Dr. Simi.* Among the antiglobalization narratives: the López Obrador administra-tion's *Historias de la ciudad,* Daniel Manrique's "La discriminación en México," the Mexican Electrical Workers Union's "Que no nos roben la luz," Gabriel Vargas's *La Familia Burrón,* Edgar Clement's *Operación Bolívar,* and Bachan's *El Bulbo.* But this simplistic taxonomy obscures numerous important differences. This is not a two-camp cultural field.

Within the antiglobalization category, one can identify several distinct posi-tions. López Obrador's propaganda vehicle occupies a weak nationalist position, evading direct confrontation with globalization as a phenomenon of empire, and surreptitiously supplanting popular sovereignty with a central authority. *La Familia Burrón* projects an antiglobal "feel" by enshrining the space of the local working class at its center, but its narrative resolution consistently supports a conservative populist position—popular cultural tradition tends to trump other values, even when its characters resign themselves to market-driven social and cultural change. This contrasts sharply with Manrique's radical embrace of pop-ular cultural sovereignty, despite the fact that his *historieta* occupies itself with the same local working-class sociality as Vargas does. And the Electrical Workers Union's comic book is marked by a strong nationalism, but one centered on the use of state power. Clement's *Operación Bolívar* is unique in staking out a discernibly anticapitalist position, while Bachan's *El Bulbo* represents a post-global position, for which irony and parody are the only critical leverage available against globalization represented as a fundamentally settled question.

Within the proglobalization category, the field is no less varied. Both the Fox administration and Farmacias de Similares project in their comic book narratives a transnational corporation-friendly vision of globalization, but the *Dr. Simi* comic makes private initiative the exclusive moral agent of globalism's promise, while the Fox comic presents a technocratic globalism. *El Libro Vaquero* offers, in its Manichaean good versus evil plots, a pro-U.S. take on U.S.-Mexico relations, but with pointed criticisms of the history of U.S. racism and a heroic role for the "outsider." *El Libro Semanal* is a consistently globalist narrative, but hedged with a conservative morality that uses gender and social class to give the free market a national "feel." Both of the NIESA *historietas* stake out globalist positions, but both are characterized by a degree of circumspection, either about the United States or about the cultural situations of economic wealth and modernity associated with globalization. The Fox administration's comic combines technocracy with nationalism, while *Dr. Simi* eschews nationalism almost entirely. At the same time, although the Team Simi variant of globalism makes the private corporation the story's moral protagonist, the series still builds in the corporatist imaginary left over from decades of one-party, statist rule. In other words, instead of easy identification with U.S. globalism, one finds in these proglobal Mexican comics technocratic, corporate, and conservative nationalist variations of neoliberalism, with each colored by elements of Mexico's modern political history and national popular culture.

The ideological field legible across the range of comics examined here evokes a relationship—in some cases direct and in others indirect—between Mexican comic books and the social forces at work in Mexican society and politics. Based on available data or distribution method, the Mexican working class is the primary readership for *El Libro Vaquero*, "Que no nos roben la luz," and "La discriminación en México," but each text corresponds to a distinct class condition: unionized labor engaged in a battle with state economic planners, in the case of "Que no nos roben"; Manrique's "La discriminación" operates within the self-concept and sociality of a working-class barrio community formed initially by rural-to-urban internal migration; *El Libro Vaquero* appeals in special ways to the Mexican migrant to the United States, a transnationalized segment of the Mexican working class. Although clearest among the antiglobalization comics, all of the comics respond in some way to the preoccupations about globalization articulated by Mexico's social movements, including the anticapitalist neo-Zapatismo of the Chiapas rebellion, the antiofficial urban social movements that emerged in Mexico City's barrios under the Partido Revolucionario Institucional (PRI), the proponents of migrants' rights, and efforts to protect the nation's cultural patrimony from privatization. As for the country's governing interests, the comic books reveal notable ideological divisions, or at the very least divergent ideological strategies for legitimating their rule. López Obrador's populist corporatism harkens back to the PRI's political model; Fox's technocratic neoliberalism maintains continuity with the PRI's modernizationist economic model. NIESA's comics evince ambivalence about the national (by way of moral) implications of an unconditional embrace of the United States and free-market purism. Dr. Simi is as proglobal as they come, but even he tends to confront and criticize pure market motives.

These social relations at work in Mexico's national reality are so marginal for neoliberal discourse and economic policy that the U.S. *Country Commercial Guide* for Mexico mentions under the heading "Civil Society" only national business associations. And yet national civil societal networks also trace the possibility of rescuing cultural politics from the commercial U.S. cultural model dominant in the Americas. This feature of the U.S. cultural model—the attenuation to near invisibility of noncommercial interests and agency—is the core discrepancy in the competing representations of globalization legible in these Mexican comics. In this sense, perhaps the most glaring sign of empire in Mexican comics is an absence: the glossing over or complete eviction of organized civil society from those graphic narratives that most closely replicate the U.S. model. Labor unions, block clubs, community organizations, nongovernmental organizations, social movements of any kind, are conspicuously absent from the Fox administration's visual representation of the Mexican republic, obscured by the private lives of individuals in *El Libro Semanal* and *El Libro Vaquero*, and replaced by the corporate Team Simi in *Las aventuras del Dr. Simi.*

Elements of a semiautonomous civil society have grown both more combative and increasingly marginal to the institutional and cultural instruments of official representation in post-NAFTA Mexico. Institutional assaults on activist networks opposing neoliberal policy have included efforts at probusiness labor law "reform," continued isolation of the neo-Zapatista movement, the closing of bank accounts channeling international solidarity monies to Chiapas, the undermining of proposed indigenous autonomy, and legalistic maneuvers to foreclose on the presidential candidacy of Mexico City mayor López Obrador.

At the same time, unionists have increasingly rejected official control of organized labor amid declining union density and privatization of key sectors such as the railway system, telecommunications, and mining. Ongoing privatization has fractured official unionism, and resulted in the formation in 2002 of the Union, Campesino, Social, Indigenous and Popular Front, a promising alliance against neoliberal policy representing labor, campesino, indigenous, and middle-class organizations. The Mexican Network of Action Against Neo-Liberalism, formed initially in 1991, includes a broad spectrum of labor, environmental, and nongovernmental groups and remains active nearly twenty years later. The Ejército Zapatista de Liberación Nacional's "Other Campaign" haunted the 2006 presidential campaigns with a national tour reminding Mexicans of the unresolved social injustice, corruption, and weakening of national sovereignty that have accompanied the status quo. In this context, the politics of the critical reading of Mexican comic books can be found in a strong affinity for what is currently the subordinate, anti-imperial position. Critique of the dominant sign levels the playing field, as it were, making space for making meaning of a different kind.

WORKS CITED

Aguayo Quezada, Sergio. "Defender migrantes." *El Norte*, January 19, 2005.

Alatriste, Sealtiel, "Elevar el índice de lectura en México significaría emprender estrategias de capacitación efectivas." *Líderes Mexicanos*, December 1, 1995.

Anderson, Benedict. *Imagined Communities*. New York: Verso, 1991.

Appadurai, Arjun. *Modernity at Large*. Minneapolis: University of Minnesota Press, 1996.

Authers, John. "Migrants Send 3.34 Billion Dollars to Mexico." *Financial Times* (USA Edition), May 27, 2004, 5.

Ávilez, Raúl, and Armando Ávilez. *PGMan, El indestructible*, nos. 1–3. Andrés Manuel López Obrador presidential campaign, June and July 2006.

Bachan. *El Bulbo*. Episodes #1–10. Mexico City: Shibalba Press, 2000–2001.

Bakhtin, Mikhail. *Rabelais and His World*. Trans. Helene Iswolsky. Bloomington: Indiana University Press, 1984.

———. *Speech Genres and Other Essays*. Ed. Caryl Emerson and Michael Holquist; trans. Vern W. McGee. Austin: University of Texas Press, 1986.

Barajas, Rafael. *Cómo sobrevivir al neoliberalismo sin dejar de ser mexicano*. Mexico City: Grijalbo, 1996.

———. *La historia de un país en caricatura: Caricatura mexicana de combate (1826–1872)*. Mexico City: Consejo Nacional para la Cultura y las Artes, 2000.

Barajas, Rafael, José Hernández, and Antonio Helguera. "Que no nos roben la luz: Por qué oponerse a la privatización eléctrica." Mexico City: Sindicato Mexicano de Electricistas, 2004.

Barker, Martin. *Comics: Ideology, Power and the Critics*. Manchester: University of Manchester, 1989.

Barthes, Roland. *S/Z*. New York: Hill and Wang, 1974.

Bartra, Armando, and Juan Manuel Aurrecoechea. *Puros Cuentos: La historia de la historieta en México*. Vols. 1–3. Mexico: Grijalbo, 1988, 1992, and 1994.

———. "Fin de fiesta: Gloria y declive de una historieta tumulturaria." *Curare. Espacio crítico para las artes*, no. 16. Mexico City: July–December 2000.

Benavente, Fray Toribio de. *Historia de los indios de la Nueva España*. Madrid: Alianza Editorial, 1988.

Benjamin, Walter. "Theses on the Philosophy of History." In *Illuminations*, 253–64. New York: Schocken Books, 1969.

Bolaños Cadena, Laura. Letter to the editor. *La Jornada*, February 6, 2003.

Bonfil Batalla, Guillermo. *Mexico profundo: Una civilización negada*. Mexico City: Grijalbo, 1990.

Brecher, Jeremy, and Tim Costello. *Global Village or Global Pillage*. Boston: South End Press, 1994.

Brennan, Timothy. "The Empire's New Clothes." *Critical Inquiry* (Winter 2003): 337–67.

Burgess, Katrina. "Mexican Labor at a Crossroads." In *Mexico's Politics and Society in Transition*, ed. Joseph S. Tulchin and Andrew D. Selee, 73–107. Boulder, Colo.: Lynne Rienner, 2003.

Cancino, Fabiola. "Critica Monsiváis comics; prepara GDF uno más." *El Universal*, July 3, 2004.

Carrillo, J. Manuel. "Promoverán la candidatura de Fox con la figura de Kalimán." *La Jornada*, April 12, 1999.

Carrillo, Sebastián. Personal correspondence with the author, November 6, 2006.

———. Personal correspondence with the author, January 22, 2007.

Casas, Bartolomé de las. *Brevísima relación de la destrucción de las Indias*. Madrid: Ediciones Cátedra, 1999.

Castillo, Bernal Díaz del. *Historia general de la conquista de la Nueva España*. Mexico City: Editorial Porrúa, 1967.

Cavanagh, John, and Sarah Anderson. "Happy Ever NAFTA?" *Foreign Policy* (October–September 2002): 58–65.

Clement, Edgar. *Operación Bolívar*. Mexico City: Ediciones del Castor, 1999.

Collier, George A., with Elizabeth Lowery Quaratiello. *Basta!: Land and the Zapatista Rebellion in Chiapas*. Oakland, Calif.: Institute for Food and Development Policy, 1994.

Comité Editorial del Gobierno del Distrito Federal. *Sensacional de chilangos: Breve antología de narrativa gráfica contemporánea mexicana*. Mexico City: Gobierno del Distrito Federal, 2000.

Consejo Nacional para la Cultura y las Artes. *Encuesta Nacional de Lectura*. Mexico City: CONCA, 2006.

Cortázar, Julio. *Fantomas contra los vampiros multinacionales*. Barcelona: Ediciones Destino, 2002.

Davis, Mike. *Magical Urbanism: Latinos Reinvent the U.S. Big City*. New York: Verso, 2000.

de la Torre, Hugo. "Salen 'superhéroes' a vender: Viste Grupo Industrial Cuadritos Biotek como personajes de comic desde ejecutivos hasta distribuidores de yogurtinfantil." *Reforma*, September 8, 2004.

Derrida, Jacques. "Plato's Pharmacy." In *Dissemination*, 61–171. Trans. Barbara Johnson. Chicago: University of Chicago Press, 1983.

Dorfman, Ariel. *The Empire's Old Clothes*. New York: Pantheon Books, 1983.

Dorfman, Ariel, and Armand Mattelart. *How to Read Donald Duck: Imperialist Ideology in the Disney Comic*. New York: International General, 1984.

Eco, Umberto. "The Myth of Superman." In *Contemporary Literary Criticism: Modernism through Poststructuralism*, ed. Robert Con Davis, 330–44. New York: Longman, 1986.

———. *Travels in Hyperreality*. New York: Harcourt Brace Jovanovich, 1986.

Eliade, Mircea. *Myth and Reality*. Trans. Willard R. Trask. New York: Harper and Row, 1963.

Estill, Adriana. "The Mexican Telenovela and Its Foundational Fictions." In *Latin American Literature and Mass Media*, ed. Edmundo Paz-Soldán and Debra A. Castillo, 169–89. Hispanic Issues, Vol. 22. New York: Garland, 2001.

Farmacias de Similares. *Las aventuras del Dr. Simi*. Selected editions, 2004–7.

Flores, Juan Luis. "Proyectan otro cómic contra GDF." *El Universal*, October 23, 2004.

Foucault, Michel. *Discipline and Punish*. Trans. Alan Sheridan. New York: Vintage Books, 1979.

Friedman, Thomas L. *The World Is Flat: A Brief History of the Twenty-first Century*. New York: Farrar, Straus and Giroux, 2007.

Gans, Herbert. *Popular Culture and High Culture: An Analysis and Evaluation of Taste*. New York: Basic Books, 1999.

García Canclini, Néstor. *Consumidores y ciudadanos: Conflictos multiculturales de la globalización*. Mexico City: Grijalbo, 1997.

————. *Hybrid Cultures*. 2nd ed. Minneapolis: University of Minnesota Press, 2005.

García Hernández, Arturo. "Desata comic el inicio de una gran cruzada por el salario mínimo justo." *La Jornada*, December 2, 2006, http://www.jornada.unam.mx/2006/12/02/index.php?section=cultura&article=a02n1cul.

García-Tort, Carlos, and Miguel Cervantes. "Los Burrón: Dramatis personae o un elenco cachetón." *La Jornada Semanal*, May 10, 1998, http://www.jornada.unam.mx/1998/05/10/sem-garcia.html.

Gilbert, Alan. *The Latin American City*. London: Latin American Bureau, 1994.

Gómez-Peña, Guillermo. *The New World Border*. San Francisco: City Lights, 1996.

Gordon, Ian. *Comic Strips and Consumer Culture, 1890–1945*. Washington, D.C.: Smithsonian Institution Press, 1998.

————. "Nostalgia, Myth, Ideology: Visions of Superman at the End of the 'American Century.'" In *Comics and Ideology*, ed. Matthew McAllister, Edward H. Sewell Jr., and Ian Gordon, 151–76. New York: Peter Lang, 2001.

Grajeda, Ella. "Gasta GDF 2 mdp en comic." *El Universal*, June 8 2002.

Gruzinski, Serge. *La guerra de las imágenes: De Cristóbal Colón a "Blade Runner" (1492–2019)*. Mexico City: Fondo de Cultura Económica, 1994.

Guerrero, Maurizio. "Detrás del Dr. Simi." *Poder y Negocios*, April 10, 2007, 24–29.

Gutiérrez Rentería, and María Elena. "La comunicación en América Latina: Informe de México." *Chasqui: Revista Latinoamericana de Comunicación*, no. 74, 2001, www.comunica.org/chasqui/gutierrez74/htm.

Halbwachs, Maurice. *On Collective Memory*. Ed. and trans. Lewis A. Coser. Chicago: University of Chicago Press, 1992.

Hall, Stuart. "The Work of Representation." In *Representation: Cultural Representations and Signifying Practices*, ed. Stuart Hall, 13–64. London: SAGE, 1997.

Hardt, Michael, and Antonio Negri. *Empire*. Cambridge, Mass.: Harvard University Press, 2000.

————. *Multitude: War and Democracy in the Age of Empire*. London: Penguin Books, 2005.

Hernández Arana, Alma. "Sindicato del Seguro Social confirma paro nacional: Caos en la ciudad; inician hoy marchas de la UNT." *El Economista*, August 31, 2004.

Herner, Irene, et al. *Mitos y monitos: Historietas y fotonovelas en México*. Mexico City: Universidad Nacional Autonoma de Mexico, 1979.

Hinds, Harold E., and Charles Tatum. *Not Just for Children: The Mexican Comic Book in the Late 1960s and 1970s*. Westport, Conn.: Greenwood Press, 1992.

Historias de la ciudad, nos. 1–5 (2001–6). Mexico City: Gobierno del Distrito Federal.

Hodge, Robert, and Gunther Kress. *Social Semiotics*. Ithaca, N.Y.: Cornell University Press, 1988.

Huntington, Samuel P. "The Clash of Civilizations?" *Foreign Affairs* (Summer 1993): 22–49.

Instituto Nacional de Estadística, Geografía e Informática. *Encuesta industrial mensual*. www.inegi.gob.mx.

Jameson, Fredric. *The Cultural Turn: Selected Writings on the Postmodern, 1983–1998*. New York: Verso, 1998.

Jiménez, Gabriela. "Legado cultural en caricatura sobre las raíces indígenas en México." *Noticias del día*. Consejo Nacional para la Cultura y las Artes, June 12, 2001, http://www.cnca.gob.mx/cnca/nuevo/2001/diarias/jun/120601/ladiscri.html.

Klock, Geoff. *How to Read Superhero Comics and Why*. New York: Continuum, 2003.

Knight, Christopher. "Visions of Imperial Power." *Los Angeles Times*, October 29, 2006.

Kraidy, Marwan M., *Hybridity: Or the Cultural Logic of Globalization*. Philadelphia: Temple University Press, 2005.

Kunzle, David. "Dispossession by Ducks: The Imperialist Treasure Hunt in Southeast Asia." *Art Journal* (Summer 1990): 159–66.

La Botz, Dan. *Democracy in Mexico: Peasant Rebellion and Political Reform*. Boston: South End Press, 1995.

————. "Labor After the PRI." *Multinational Monitor* 22, no. 3 (March 2001): 14.

————. "Mexico's Labor Movement in Transition." *Monthly Review* (June 2005), www.monthlyreview .org/0605laabotz.htm.

López Parra, Raúl. "De la historieta rosa al pornocómic." *Revista Mexicana de Comunicación* (May–June 2003): 43–46.

Luhnow, David. "In Mexico, Maker of Generics Adds Spice to Drug Business." *Wall Street Journal*, February 14, 2005.

Manrique, Daniel. *La discriminación en México*. Mexico City: Centro de Artes y Oficios, 1999.

Martín-Barbero, Jesús. "Memory and Form in the Latin American Soap Opera." In *To be Continued . . . Soap Operas Around the World*, ed. Robert C. Allen, 276–84. New York: Routledge, 1995.

Martínez, Fabiola. "El SME incorpora la historieta a su lucha contra la privatización del sector eléctrico." *La Jornada*, July 10, 2004.

Matelski, Marilyn J. *Soap Operas Worldwide*. London: McFarland, 1999.

Mato, Daniel. "Telenovelas: Transnacionalización de la industria y transformaciones del género." In *Las industrias culturales en la integración latinoamericana*, ed. Néstor García Canclini and Carlos Moneta, 229–57. Buenos Aires: Editorial Universitaria de Buenos Aires, 1999.

Medios Publicitarios Mexicanos. *Tarifas y Datos de Medios Impresos*, no. 169 (February 2001).

"A mitad del camino." *Tercer informe de gobierno del Presidente Vicente Fox Quesada*, September 2003, http://tercer.informe.presidencia.gob.mx/.

Monsiváis, Carlos. "Los ochenta años de Gabriel Vargas." *La Jornada Semanal*, May 10, 1998, http:// www.jornada.unam.mx/1998/05/10/sem-monsi.html.

Morgan, Fiona. "A Wrench in the 'Ruling Party Machine.'" June 28, 2000, Salon.com.

Nederveen Pieterse, Jan. *Globalization and Culture: Global Mélange*. Oxford: Rowman and Littlefield 2004.

Negt, Oskar, and Alexander Kluge. *Public Sphere and Experience: Toward an Analysis of the Bourgeois and Proletarian Public Sphere*. Trans. Peter Labanyi et al. Minneapolis: University of Minnesota Press, 1993.

NIESA Editores. *El Libro Semanal*. Selected editions, 1994–2007.

————. *El Libro Vaquero*. Selected editions, 1994–2007.

————. http://www.niesa.com.mx/niesa:web/revistas.html.

O'Donnell, Guillermo. "Tensions in the Bureaucratic-Authoritarian State and the Question of Democracy." In *Promise of Development: Theories of Change in Latin America*, ed. Peter F. Klarén and Thomas J. Bossert, 276–99. Boulder, Colo.: Westview Press, 1986.

Olvera, José Antonio, and Humberto Tapia. "La historieta del recuerdo." Etcéter@, July 2007, http:// www.etcetera.com.mx/pag54ne33.asp.

Paredes, Americo. *"With His Pistol in His Hand": A Border Ballad and Its Hero*. Austin: University of Texas Press, 1971.

Paz, Octavio. *Labyrinth of Solitude*. Trans. Lysander Kemp. New York: Grove Press, 1985.

Pitol, Sergio. "Borola contra el mundo." *La Jornada Semanal*, May 10, 1998, http://www.jornada.unam .mx/1998/05/10/sem-pitol.html.

Powell, Carlos. "Desminar campos y conciencias: Las huellas de la Guerra." *Envío Digital*, no. 250 (January 2003), http://www.envio.org.ni/articulo/1199.

Presidency of the Republic of Mexico. "Vicente Fox entregó el Premio Nacional de Ciencias y Artes 2003." Press release, December 11, 2003, http://fox.presidencia.gob.mx/actividades/?contenido=7042.

Priego, Ernesto. "A History of Mankind for Beginners." *Críticas*, April 1, 2002, http://www.criticasmagazine.com/article/CA201136.html.

PR Newswire. "Los personajes de la Justice League de DC Comics Ingresan con Toda la Fuerza en los Restaurantes Burger King de Toda la Nación." April 15, 2003.

Ramírez Tamayo, Zacarías. "Aplican el comic a la comunicación interna." *El Universal*, November 25, 2003, http://www2.eluniversal.com.mx/pls/impreso/noticia.html?id_nota=37110&tabla=finanzas.

Reyes, Jaime. "La historieta nacional en 10 cuadros." El Ángel section, *Reforma*, May 21, 2006.

Reynolds, Richard. *Super Heroes: A Modern Mythology*. Jackson: University Press of Mississippi, 1992.

Rosales Ayala, Hector. *Cultura, Sociedad Civil y Proyectos Culturales en México*. Mexico City: Consejo Nacional para la Cultura y las Artes, 1994.

Rowe, William, and Vivian Schelling. *Memory and Modernity: Popular Culture in Latin America*. New York: Verso, 1991.

Rubenstein, Anne. *Bad Language and Naked Ladies, and Other Threats to the Nation*. Durham, N.C.: Duke University Press, 1998.

Ruiz, José Luis. "Divulgan logros vía cómic." *El Universal*, September 2, 2003.

Sahagún, Fray Bernardino de. *Historia general de las cosas de Nueva España*. Mexico City: Editorial Porrúa, 1985.

Sánchez, José Alejandro. "López, como Hugo Chávez, lanza campaña anticomplot." *Crónica de Hoy*, July 5, 2004.

Schwarz Huerta, Mauricio-José. *Todos somos Superbarrio*. Mexico City: Planeta, 1994.

Secretaría de Relaciones Exteriores. *Guía del migrante mexicano*. Government of the Republic of Mexico, November 2004.

Silvert, Kalman H. "The Politics of Social and Economic Change in Latin America." In *Promise of Development: Theories of Change in Latin America*, ed. Peter F. Klarén and Thomas J. Bossert, 76–103. Boulder, Colo.: Westview Press, 1986.

Smith, Geri. "Drugmakers Feel the Heat in Mexico." *Business Week*, August 11, 2003, 28.

Soong, Roland. "Action Comics in Latin America." Zona Latina, 2001, http://www.zonalatina.com/Zldata192.htm.

Stavans, Ilan. *Latino USA: A Cartoon History*. New York: Basic Books, 2000.

Touraine, Alain. *The Post-Industrial Society*. Trans. Leonard X. Mayhew. New York: Random House, 1971.

"Unions Call for National Resistance to Neoliberalism." *Mexican Labor News and Analysis*, 12, no. 1 (January 2007), www.ueinternational.org/Mexico_info/.

U.S. Department of State. "U.S. Government and United Nations Enlist Superman and Wonder Woman in Landmine Awareness Campaign." Press release, June 11, 1998.

———. *Country Commercial Guide: Mexico*. Fiscal year 2001.

———. *Doing Business in Mexico: A Country Commercial Guide for U.S. Investors*. Fiscal year 2004.

———. *Country Commercial Guide: Mexico*. Fiscal year 2007.

Vargas, Gabriel. *La familia Burrón*. Vols. 1–10. Mexico City: Editorial Porrúa, 2005.

———. *La familia Burrón*. Selected episodes. Mexico City: Editor G y G, 1994–2007.

Vila, Pablo. *Crossing Borders/Reinforcing Borders: Social Categories, Metaphors, and Narrative Identities on the U.S.-Mexico Frontier*. Austin: University of Texas Press, 2000.

Volosinov, V. N. *Marxism and the Philosophy of Language*. Cambridge, Mass.: Harvard University Press, 2006.

Waisbord, Silvio R. "The Ties that Still Bind: Media and National Cultures in Latin America." *Canadian Journal of Communication* 23 (1998): 381–401.

Ward, Peter. *Mexico City.* Boston: G. K. Hall, 1990.

Warnock, John. *The Other Mexico: The North American Triangle Completed.* Montreal: Black Rose Books, 1995.

Washington Times. "Illegals and the State Department." Editorial, January 13, 2005.

Wiarda, Howard. *Latin America: The Cultural and Political Tradition.* New Haven, Conn.: Yale University Press, 2001.

Wittebols, James H. *The Soap Opera Paradigm.* New York: Rowan and Littlefield, 2004.

INDEX

Page numbers in *italics* indicate illustrations.

Action Comics, 18

Adams, Arthur, 191

Allende, Salvador, 6

Almazán, José Antonio, 99–100

American Idol, 75, 76

"A mitad del camino" (Half Way There), 28–36, *32*; aesthetics of, 20, 29, 31; civil society and, 36; compared to Historias de la Cuidad, 40, 42; distribution of, 28; globalization and, 27–28, 31, 33–34, 46, 216, 217; imagery in, 30–31, 33, 35–36; mass appeal of, 47; NAFTA and, 34; narrative of, 29–30, 33; neoliberalism and, 34–35, 213–14; race in, 33; social forces and, 218; themes of, 4; U.S. culture and, 33, 34; U.S.-Mexico border in, 34

Andean Free Trade Agreement (AFTA), 2

Anderson, Benedict, 42

Appadurai, Arjun, 7–8, 10, 191

Argentina, 2

Aristotle, 211

Asamblea de Barrios, 46

Así Soy y Qué, 191

Aurrecoechea, Juan Manuel, 3

Bachan, 5, 188, 189, 191, 192, 208, 209. *See also* Carrillo, Sebastián; *El Bulbo*

Bakhtin, Mikhail, 111, 113, 160, 208

Baltimore Sun, 172

Barajas, Rafael, 20, 93, 94, 96; and the *La Familia Burrón* exhibit, 120

Works: *Como sobrevivir al neoliberalismo sin dejar de ser mexicano* (How to Survive Neoliberalism and Still Be Mexican), 94, 101; *Como triunfar en la globalización*, 94; *Historia de un país en cariacatura*, 100; *How to Succeed at Globalization: a Primer for Roadside Venders*, 94; *Me lleva el TLC: El tratado retratado* (Carried Away with NAFTA: A Portrait of the Treaty), 94; "Que no nos roben la luz" (Don't Let Them Steal Our Light), 99, 102, 104. *See also* El Fisgón

Bartra, Armando, 3

Batman, 6, 195, 203

Bef, 188, 207. See also *El Bulbo*

Benavente, Toribio de (Motolinía), *Historia de los indios de Nueva España*, 166, 167

Benjamin, Walter, 183–84

Betteo, Patricio, 21, 207

Bloom, Harold, 190

Bolaños Cadena, Laura, 85

Boliva, 2

Bonfil Batalla, Guillermo, 185

Bosnia, 194

Bribiesca Azuara, Guadalupe, 28

Burger King, 195

Bush, George W., administration, 2, 11
Byrne, John, 191

Calderón, Felipe, 106–7
Calderón, Rafael, 27
Caligrama, 164, 188
Cantinflas, 201
Captain America, 189
Cárdenas, Cuauhtémoc, 23, 40
Cárdenas, Lázaro, 26, 40, 137
Cardona Peña, Alfredo, *Fantomas, La amenaza elegante* (Fantomas, The Elegant Menace), 193
Carrillo, Sebastián, 17, 19, 20, 188; *Vinny, El Perro de la Balbuena*, 21. See also Bachan, *El Bulbo*
Carter, Jimmy, administration, 8
Casas, Bartolomé de las, *Brevísima relación de la destrucción de las indias*, 169
Casino de la Selva, 29
Castillo, Bernal Díaz del, 166
Central American Free Trade Agreement (CAFTA), 2
Cervantes, Miguel, "Los Burrón: Dramatis personae o un elenco cacherón" (The Burróns: Dramatis Personae or a Chubby-Cheeked Cast of Characters), 121–22
Chávez, Hugo, 41
Chiapas uprising, 3, 15
Clement, Edgar, 5, 15, 17, 19, 20, 164, 185, 207. See also *Operación Bolívar*
Clinton, William, administration, 2, 194
Colombia, 2
Congreso de Trabajo (Congress of Labor), 16
Consejo Nacional para la Cultura y las Artes (National Council for Culture and the Arts), 5, 73, 108
Cortázar, Julio, *Fantomas contra los vampiros multinacionales* (Fantomas against the Multinational Vampires), 193
Cortés, Hernán, 109, 166, 172, 185
Costa Rica, 194
Costco, 29
Country Commercial Guide for Mexico, 8–9, 13, 74, 88, 152, 170, 218
Country Commercial Guides, 8, 11, 75
Country Human Rights Reports, 8

cultural hybridization, 11–12
cultural models, 13, 75

Da Vinci, Leonardo, *Vitruvian Man*, 178
Davis, Alan, 191
DC Comics, 12, 193, 194, 195
Derrida, Jacques, "Plato's Pharmacy," 145–46
Díaz Enciso, Fernando, 108
Díaz Ordaz, Gustavo, 185
Díaz Ordaz administration, 138
Disney, 28
Doña Maria (La Malinche), 172
Dorfman, Ariel: *The Empire's Old Clothes*, 7; *How to Read Donald Duck*, 7, 11–12, 212, 213

Ebrard, Marcelo, 25
Eco, Umberto, 156, 196
Ecuador, 2, 11
Ediciones del Castor, 164
Editorial Caligrama, 21
Editorial Ejea, 191
Editorial Meridiano, 94
Editorial Novaro, 193
Editorial Novedades, 191, 208
Editorial Panamericana, 119
Editorial Porrúa, 119, 120
Editorial Vid, 21, 193
Ejército Zapatista de Liberación Nacional (EZLN), 219
ejido, 14
El Barzón, 15
El Bulbo, 5, 21, 187–89, 191–92, 195–211; aesthetics of, 204–7; commodification and, 201–4; corrosion of superhero myth in, 199–200, 209–11, 215; Galería section of, 207, 208; and globalization, 19, 192, 195, 200, 201, 211, 214–15, 216, 217; imagery in, 202–3; Japanese manga style in, 201, 205; mass culture and, 191, 192, 205–7, 210; modernization in, 215; NAFTA League in, 203, 210; story of origin, 196; summary of, 187; themes of, 200, 210; U.S. cultural model and, 200
Issues: #1, 196–98, *198*; #2-"The Tragic Death of Genoveva the Cow," 198–99, 208; #3-"El Bulbo vs. Toyzilla," 188–89, 200, 207, 208; #4, 200, 207, 214–15; #5, 200, 205, 206, 207;

#6, 200, 201, 207, 208; #7, 200, 201–3, *202*, *206*, 207, 208; #8, 200, 207; #9, 206, *209*; #10, 200

El Financiero, 177

El Fisgón, "Que no nos roben la luz" (Don't Let Them Steal Our Light), 96, 103–4, 106, 107

Eliade, Mircea, 196

El Libro Mensual, 72, 77. See also *El Libro Semanal*

El Libro Semanal, 5, 17, 20, 70–75, 76–91, 135; aesthetics of, 70, 73, 79, 85; "Aves sin nido" (Birds without a Nest/Personal ads), 90; distribution of, 48, 72–73; female characters in, 85, 89; Fox administration and, 48; and globalization, 73, 74, 75, 76–77, 84, 85, 86, 88, 216; *Guía del migrante mexicano* (Guide for the Mexican Migrant) and, 48; imagery in, 79, 81, 86–87, 89; Mexican culture and, 76, 77; Mexico City in, 82–83, 84; modernization in, 88, 215; morality in, 81–82, 84–85, 88, 89, 89–90; and neoliberalism, 74–75, 86, 88–89; political and, 83; readership, 73; social class in, 74, 75, 77–78, 215–16; social forces and, 218; telenovela form and, 77, 90; themes of, 71–72, 73, 75, 80–81, 83, 84–85; U.S. cultural model and, 19, 76–77 84

Issues: "Con la Cruz a Cuestas" (With the Cross on Her Back), 81–82; "El Interesado" (The Interested One), 70–71, 76–77, 84–85; "Insatisfechos" (Unsatisfied), 78–81, *80*, 83, 85; "Maldita Ambición" (Damned Ambition), 85–88, *87*, 89, 90; "Un Ayer Escabroso" (A Rough Yesterday), 81, 83

El Libro Vaquero, 5, 17, 19, 20, 47–48, 52–53, 54–69; aesthetics of, 54, 55, 63–64; distribution of, 48, 72–73; female characters in, 58, 59–60, 63; Fox administration and, 48; and globalization, 48, 52, 73, 216, 217; *Guía del migrante mexicano* (Guide for the Mexican Migrant) and, 48; historical setting for, 57–58; imagery in, 55–56, 58–60; morality in, 62–63, 65; narrative of, 47; politics and, 49, 50, 53; race in, 59–60, 62, 64–65, 216; readership of, 73, 217; social class in, 62,

65–67, 75; themes of, 52, 54, 66–67, 68, 73; transformative message of, 67–68; U.S.-Mexico border in, 54, 68–69

Issues: "Como buitres hambrientos" (Like Hungry Vultures), 55, 67; "El Color de Mal" (the Color of Evil), 66, 67–68; "Extraños Enemigos" (Strnge Enemies), 66; "Hermandad Sagrada" (Sacred Brotherhood), 66; "La Mano de la venganza" (The Hand of Vengeance), 66; "La Mujer del Bandido" (The Bandit's Woman), 66; "Sobre cadáveres" (Over Dead Bodies), 55, 68; "Venganza Natural" (Natural Vengeance), 66; "Viejos rencores" (Old Grudges), *56*, 61–66, 67

El Premio Mayor" (The Big Prize), 77

El Proceso, 72

"El salario actual, una infamia para el trabajador" (Current Wages, a Disgrace to the Worker), 96

El Santo, 77, 208

El Solitario, 191

El Universal, 41

Excélsior, 119

Fantastic Four, 6

Fantomas, La amenaza elegante (Fantomas, The Elegant Menace), 118, 193

Farmacias de Similares, S.A., 19, 93, 143–44, 148, 155, 159. See also *Las aventuras del Dr. Simi*

Farmacias El Fénix, 144

Fernández, Bernardo, 188. *See also* Bef; *El Bulbo*

Flash, 195

fotonovela, 77

Foucault, Michel, 92, 93

Fox administration: "Acciones" (Actions), 25; "Construyendo un México fuerte" (Building a Strong Mexico), 25; "El cambio en México ya nadie lo para" (Change in mexico Can No Longer Be Stopped), 25; *El Libro Vaquero* and, 48; *Guia del migrante mexicano* (Guide for the Mexican Migrant), 17; and historietas, 14, 18, 26, 45–46, 93; labor movement and, 95; neoliberalism and, 27; privatization and, 101. *See also* "A mitad del camino"

Fox, Vicente: caricatures of, 103, 104; and historietas, 4, 22–23; and *La Familia Burrón*, 119; and the *News*, 72

Franco, Francisco, 185

Free Trade Association of the Americas (FTAA), 2, 8

Frente Auténtico de Trabajo (Authentic Labor Front), 16

Frente Sindical Mexicano (Mexican Labor Front), 16

Friedmand, Thomas, *The Earth Is Flat*, 212

Frontera Violenta (Violent Border), 21

Gallitos Comics, 164

Gans, Herbert, 67

García Canclini, Néstor, 10, 11–12, 17, 168, 178, 179

García Fuentes, Ricardo, 21

García-Tort, Carlos, "Los Burrón: Dramatis personae o un elenco cacherón" (The Burróns: Dramatis Personae or a Chubby-Cheeked Cast of Characters), 121–22

Gates, Bill, 144–45

General Electric, 99

General Office of Public Opinion and Image, 28

globalization: analysis of, 6–10, 12–13, 27, 138; effects of, 27; and Mexico, 1, 2–3; nationalism and, 2, 10–12, 17–18; opposition to, 11, 14–17; U.S. Policy and, 1, 2, 8–10. *See also* "A mitad del camino"; *El Bulbo*; *El Libro Semanal*; *El Libro Vaquero*; *Guía del migrante mexicano*; historietas; "La discriminatión en México"; *La Familia Burrón*; *Las aventuras del Dr. Simi*; NAFTA; *Operación Bolívar*

Gómez-Peña, Guillermo, 17–18

González, Luz Elena, 152

González Loyo, Oscar, 28; *Karmatron*, 21

González Torres, Javier, 143

González Torres, Victor, 142, 143, 145, 147, 148–49, 155, 160. See also *Las aventuras del Dr. Simi*

Goya, Francisco, *The Executions of the Third of May*, 178, 180–82, 184

Gramsci, Antonio, 69, 213

Green Lantern, 195

Groening, Matt, *The Simpsons*, 28

Grupo Industrial Cuadritos Biotek, 195

Grupo Industrial Durango, S.A., 18

Grupo Por Un País Mejor (Group for a Better Country), 143

Guadalupe Posada, José, 93, 178

Guía del migrante mexicano (Guide for the Mexican Migrant), 51; distribution of, 48–49; *El Libro Vaquero* and, 49, 50; globalization and, 49–50, 51–52; imagery in, 50–51; national identity and, 51; neoliberalism and, 51–52; racial characteristics in, 50–51; U.S.-Mexico border in, 69

Gutiérrez, Lucio, 2

Gutiérrez Vega, Hugo, 121

Halbwachs, Maurice, 118, 137, 141

Hardt, Michael, 10

Hawk Girl, 195

Heavy Metal (magazine), 207

Helguera, Antonio, 20, 99, 102, 106

Hernández, José, 20; "Que no nos roben las luz" (Don't Let Them Steal Our Light), 99, 104–5, 106, 107

Hidalgo, Miguel, 25

Historias de la ciudad (Stories of the City), 36–46, 43; aesthetics of, 37, 42; civil society and, 40–42, 46; distribution of, 36; globalization and, 44–45, 46, 216; imagery in, 37, 42–45; mass appeal of, 47; narrative of, 36–39; neoliberalism and, 27; politics and, 4, 20, 23; telenovela form and, 78; themes of, 40

Issues: #1, 37–38, 39; #2, 38–39, 43; #3-"Las fuerzas oscuras contra Andrés Manuel López Obrador (The Dark Forces against AMLO), 4, 25, 41; #4, 40, 43; #5, 44

historietas: aesthetics of, 20; corporate uses of, 96–99; culture and, 5, 26; gender roles in, 215; globalization and, 4, 5–6, 12, 100–1, 215–17; history of, 3–5; mass appeal of, 47; multiple ideological positions of, 214; neoliberalism and, 27, 213–14; organized labor and, 93, 97; politics and, 4, 18–19, 22–28, 41, 45–46, 99–100, 216, 219; popular culture and, 18, 19; post-NAFTA, 215–16; privatization in, 101; race in, 215; readership of, 73; social class in, 215; as social critique, 93–95;

social forces and, 217–18; transnational market for, 48; U.S. culture in, 214–15
Hodge, Robert, 53–54
Hombres y Héroes, 191
Honduras, 194
Humala, Ollanta, 2
Huntington doctrine, 9

Instituto Mexicano de Seguro Social (IMSS) (Mexican Social Security Institute), 26, 28, 96, 143

Jameson, Fredric, 208
Joyas de Literatura, 191

¡Ka-Boom! Estudio, 21, 28, 92
Kalimán, El Hombre Increible (Kaliman, The Incredible Man), 4, 21, 22–23, 118
Kladt Sobrino, 3
Klee, Paul, *Angelus Novus*, 183–84
Klock, Geoff, 190, 194
Kluge, Alexander, 97
Kress, Gunther, 53–54

Labastida, Francisco, "Una vida ejemplar," 23
"La Bola del padre Hidalgo" (Father Hildalgo's Rabble), 25, 26
Laboratorios Best, 144
"La discriminación en México," 108–11, *112*, 113–15; aesthetics of, 109; and globalization, 109, 113, 117; imagery in, 109–11, 113–15; politics and, 116, 117; pop culture and, 116–17; readership of, 217; themes of, 108–9, 110, 115; U.S. in, 109, 113–14, 115
La Familia Burrón, 118–41; aesthetics of, 19, 21, 124, 125, 128, 129; collective memory and, 118–19, 121, 137, 140–41; conflict in, 125–27; distribution of, 119–20; exhibition of, 120–21; gender roles in, 132; and globalization, 119, 134–37, 138–41, 216; history of, 119; imagery in, 125–26, 131, 132; and Mexican culture, 5; neoliberalism and, 129–30, 140; nostalgia and, 122–23; politics and, 16, 137–41; race and, 216; social class in, 216–27, 128, 129–30, 216; themes of, 124, 133–34; tradition vs. modernity in, 130–33, 135;

vecindad in, 120–21, 122, 123, 126, 127, 128, 129, 138, 140
Issues: #1376, 125, 130; #1484, 124–25, 135–36, *136*; #1488, 126, *127*, 134; #1490, 131–33; #1491, 133, 134; #1496, 134–35; volume #8, 124

Lagrimas y Risas (Tears and Laughter), 21
La Jornada, 21, 85, 93, 96, 172
La Jornada Semanal, 121, 122
land mines 194
Las aventuras del Dr. Simi, 20–21, 142–43, 144, 145–63; aesthetics of, 143, 146–47, 148, 154–56; audience for, 144; and branding, 19, 147, 155; character summary, 142, 145; compared to *Historias de la ciudad*, 147; gender roles in 154–55, 162; and globalization, 152–54, 155, 158, 161, 216, 217; González Torres and, 145, 146, 147, 156, 161, 162; hyper-reality in, 155–56; imagery in, 149; marketing and, 19; modernization in, 160–61, 215; morality in, 145, 146, 159–60, 161–62; neoliberalism and, 144–45; photographs in, 155–56; politics and, 148–49, 151–52, 156–59; profit motive and, 158–59; Simidog in, 154, 157; social class in, 154, 158, 159; social forces and, 218; themes of, 147; U.S. in, 144–45, 154, 159, 215
Issues: #33-"Carrera por la vida" (Race for Life), 152, *153*, 155; #39-"Peces" (Fish), 149; #46-"Un mundo de libros" (A World of Books), 162; #52-"Motivos para luchar" (Reasons for Fighting), 149–50, *150*; #53-"Magia" (Magic), 162; #58-"Dragones y Princesas" (Dragons and Princesses), 162; #59-"Vidas Sencillas" (Simple Lives), 154, 160–62; #60-"¡Cacería!" (Hunting!), 154; #61-"Salvar el Paraíso," 157, *157*; #62-"El día que me quieras . . ." (The Day That You Love Me . . .), 154, 162
Lewis, Oscar, *Los hijos de Sánchez* (The Children of Sánchez), 138
Liconsa stores, 28
López Obrador, Andrés Manuel: "Fuerzas oscuras," 26; and historietas, 4; policies of, 38, 39; *PGMan*, 25, 46; presidential candidacy, 25, 143, 149, 218. See also *Historias de la ciudad*; López Obrador administration

López Obrador administration, 4, 14, 18, 45–46. See also *Historias de la ciudad*; López Obrador, Andrés Manuel

Los ricos también lloran (The Rich Also Cry), 77

Lucas, George, 205

Luz y Fuerza (Light and Power), 100

Madrid, Miguel de la, 26

Manrique, Daniel, 15, 20, 95. See also "La discriminación en México"

Mansalvo Carreola, Rubén, 71–72

March of Silence, 41–42, 43

Marcos, Subcomandante, 151–52

María la del barrio (María from the Barrio), 77–78

Martian Manhunter, 195

Martín-Barbero, Jesús, 91

Martínez, Arturo, 143

Marvel Comics, 12, 193

Marvin the Martian, 205, 206

Marx, Karl, 170, 183

Mattelart, Armand, *How to Read Donald Duck*, 7, 11–12, 212, 213

Memín Pinguín, 21

Menchú, Rigoberta, 155

Mexican comics. *See* historietas

Mexican cultural model, 76

Mexican Network of Action Against Neo-Liberalism, 219

Mexico: border with U.S., 29, 34, 49–50, 54, 68–69, 201, 214–15; economic development of, 27; globalization and, 1, 2–3, 12–13, 27, 138; insurgencies and, 14; mural arts in 3, 14; neoliberalism and, 1, 2–3, 27, 137; organized labor and, 16–17; political history of, 137–38, 139; popular culture in, 1; privatization in, 100; religion in, 146; U.S. culture and, 1, 6–7, 13; U.S. policy and, 1, 8–10. See also NAFTA

Mexico City, earthquake, 16, 46, 95; in *El Libro Semanal*, 82–83, 84; in *La Familia Burrón*, 120, 128; March of Silence in, 41; politics in, 16, 23, 46, 83, 218; vecindades in, 120, 128

Mezieres, Jean-Claude, *Valerian*, 191

modality of message, 53–54

Monsiváis, Carlos, 41, 120–21, 122, 138

Morales, Evo, 2

Morris, *Lucky Luke*, 191

Murillo, Marifer, 152, 155, 157–59, 160

NAFTA (North American Free Trade Agreement): consequences of, 12–13, 17–18, 49, 88, 136, 138, 152, 218–19; and cultural convergence, 9; indigenous movements and, 2–3, 14–15; organized labor and, 16–17; privatization and, 24; responses to, 1; U.S. cultural model and, 13. See also "A mitad del camino"

nationalism vs. globalization, 2

Negri, Antonio, 10

Negt, Oscar, 97

neoliberalism: declining wages and, 27; and Mexico, 1, 2–3, 27, 137; opposition to, 2–3, 11; promises of, 91; and religion, 146; social forces and, 8–10; and U.S. policy, 1. See also "A mitad del camino"; *Guía del migrante mexicano*; *Historias de la ciudad*; historietas; *La Familia Burrón*; *Las aventuras del Dr. Simi*; *Operación Bolívar*

neo-Zapatistas, 3, 27, 83, 151–52, 186, 218

News (Mexico City), 72

Nicaragua, 194

NIESA Editores, 5, 17, 19, 21, 47, 48, 71, 72, 73. See also Novedades Editores

Nintendo, 206

¡No compres problemas! (Don't Buy Trouble), 25

North American Free Trade Agreement. *See* NAFTA

Novedades Editores, 5, 47, 72. See also NIESA Editores

Novib, 108

Nueva Impresora y Editora. *See* NIESA Editores

O'Donnell, Guillermo, 28

O'Farrill family, 72, 76, 77, 83

Omnibus Trade and Competitiveness Act, 8

Operación Bolívar, 164–82, *171*, *175*, *181*, 184–85; aesthetics of and, 167–68, 170, 172, 173, 177–78, 179–80, 182, 185; artistic value of, 5; capitalism in, 169–70; compared to other comics, 186; as cultural critique, 19; cultural hybridization and, 168, 179; cultural perspective of, 179–80; distrubition of, 164; and globalization, 165–66, 167, 169–74, 185, 216–17; high art and, 182–83, 184–85; historical background for, 165–66, 174, 184–85; imagery in, 168, 172, 174–77, 178–79, 180–82; Japanese in, 170; modernization in, 215; neoliberalism in, 177; plot summary, 165, 168–69, 170, 172, 173, 176–77; politics and, 174, 177, 178–79, 184–85; U.S. cultural model and, 170

organized labor, 95–96

Otomo, Katsuhiro, *Akira*, 191

Pac Man, 207

"Pan-Latin American Kids Survey", 6

Partido de Acción Nacional (PAN) (National Action Party), 22–23, 25, 28, 45, 95, 100, 103–4, 147

Partido de la Revolución Democrática (PRD) (Party of the Democratic Revolution), 16, 23, 78, 83, 147; *Super Marcelo*, 25

Partido Revolucionario Institucional (PRI) (Institutional Revolutionary Party), 3, 13–14, 17, 18, 22, 23–24, 25, 26, 27, 40, 45, 46, 51, 72, 84, 95, 104, 118, 137, 139, 144, 218

Paulat, Jorge, *La discriminación del indio* (Discrimination against the Indian), 108, 114

Paz, Octavio, The Labyrinth of Solitude, 114

Pelaez, Ricardo, 207

Peña Cabrena, Nicanor, 28

Peña Cabrera, José Luis, 28

Peru, 2

Petróleos de México, 100, 104

Peyo, *Smurfs*, 191

Picasso, Pablo, *Guernica*, 170, 178, 180–82, 184

Pitol, Sergio, 121, 122, 138

Pokémon, 205

popular culture and nationalism, 212–13

Popular Unity Government (Chile), 6

privatization, 24, 45, 101

Productora e Importadora de Papel, S.A. (PIPSA) (Producer and Importer of Paper), 18, 24, 45

Promotora K, 21

"Que no nos roben la luz" (Don't Let Them Steal Our Light), 101–7, *105*; aesthetics of, 101–2; distribution of, 99; and globalization, 107, 117, 216; imagery in, 98, 101–2, 103–7; neoliberalism and, 106–7; politics and, 116, 117; pop culture and, 116–17; privatization and, 101, 102; readership of, 217; text of, 102; U.S. in, 115

Quintero, José, *Buba*, 21; on Operación Bolívar, 165

Quirino Salas, José, 15

Ramírez Codex, 166–67

Rassini, *Contacto Comix*, 92–93, 96–97, 109

Red Mexicana de Acción Frente al Neoliberalismo (Mexican Network of Action Against Neoliberalism), 16

Reforma, 172

Republican Party (U.S.), 29

Reyes Hernández, Francisco, 143

Reynolds, Richard, 192, 196

Río, Ricardo del. *See* Rius

Rius: *La Vida de cuadritos* (The Life of comics), 93–94; *Los Agachados* (The Hunched Over), 94; *Los Supermachos* (The Supermachos), 94

Rivera, Diego, 14

Rowe, William, 123

Rubenstein, Anne, 23

Russell Tribunal, 193, 194

Sahagún, Bernardino de, *Historia General de las cosas de Nueva España*, 166

Salinas de Gortari, Carlos, 15, 23, 26, 49

Sam the Sham and the Pharaohs, "Wooly Bully," 115

Sandoval, Tony, 21, 207

Schelling, Vivian, 123

Secretaría de Relaciones Exteriores (Ministry of Foreign Relations), 48

Sensacional de Chilangos, 23

Sensacional de Luchas, 191

Sensacional de Vacaciones, 191

Shibalba Press, 188

Shirow, Masamune, *Appleseed*, 191

Sindacato de Seguro Social (Social Security Workers Union), "Alicia en el pais de la inseguridad social," 26, 96

Sindicato Mexicano de Electricias (SME) (Mexican Electrical Workers Union), 16–17, 99–100. *See also* "Que no nos roben las luz"

Sontag, Susan, 193

Spiderman, 6

Stavans, Ilan, *Latino USA: A Cartoon History*, 7

Summit of the Americas, 2

Super Barrio Gómez, 46

superhero genre, 6, 187, 189–90, 192–95

Superman, 6, 187, 189–90, 194, 195

Superman y la Mujer Maravilla: El Asesino Escondido (Superman and Wonder Woman: The Hidden Killer), 194

Taibo, Benito, 143

Taller de Gráfica (TGP), 93

Taller de Perro (Dog's Workshop), 164, 185

Tarzan, 159, 215

Teléfonos de México, 28

telenovela genre, 37, 39, 73, 77, 91, 173

Telesistema Mexicano, 77

Televisa, 72, 77

Tinieblas, 208

Torquemada, 172

Touraine, Alain, 13, 75–76

"Tratado de Libre Comercio." *See* NAFTA

Trump, Donald, 144

Tuynman, Josh, 72

TV Guide, 73

Uderzo, Alberto, *Asterix*, 191

Union, Campesino, Social, Indigenous and Popular Front, 219

Unión de Colonos de Santo Domingo (Union of Residents of Santo Domingo), 95

Unión Nacional de Trabajadores (National Union of Workers), 16

United Nations Children's Fund (UNICEF), 194

United States: border with Mexico, 29, 34, 49–50, 54, 68–69, 201; 214–15; culture, 1, 6–7, 11–12, 13, 19, 75–77, 84, 170, 200; military, 172; policy, 1, 8–10, reality television, 75; soap operas, 90; War on Terror, 10–11

Universidad Nacional Autónoma de México (National Autonomous University) 3, 16

urbanization of Latin America, 83

Uruguay, 2

Valencia, Sixto: *Las aventuras del Dr. Simi*, 143, *Memín Pinguín*, 148

Vargas, Gabriel, 16, 17, 19, 21, 118, 119, 124, 207. See also *La Familia Burrón*

Vásquez, Modesto, 22

Venezuela, 2

Vila, Pablo, 60

Villa, Pancho, 151

Ward, Peter, 84

Warner Brothers, 28, 195, 205

Wayas, Elizabeth, 152, 153

Wonder Woman, 189, 194, 195

X-Men Adventures, 6

Zapata, Emiliano, 3, 151

Zapatista Nation Liberation Army, 3, 29

Zedillo, Ernesto, 16, 177

Zorro, 159, 215